Dance Integration

36 DANCE LESSON PLANS FOR SCIENCE AND MATHEMATICS

Karen A. Kaufmann, MA
University of Montana

Jordan Dehline, BFA
University of Montana

Human Kinetics

Library of Congress Cataloging-in-Publication Data

Kaufmann, Karen A.
  Dance integration: 36 dance lesson plans for science and mathematics / Karen A. Kaufmann, MA, University of Montana, Jordan Erin Dehline, BFA University of Montana.
    pages cm.
  Includes bibliographical references.
  1. Dance--Study and teaching. 2. Dance--Curricula. 3. Movement education. 4. Mathematics--Study and teaching--Activity programs. 5. Science--Study and teaching--Activity programs. I. Title.
  GV1589.K379 2014
  793.307--dc23

                    2013038986

ISBN-10: 1-4504-4133-5 (print)
ISBN-13: 978-1-4504-4133-9 (print)

The web addresses cited in this text were current as of April 2014, unless otherwise noted.

Acquisitions Editor: Gayle Kassing, PhD
Developmental Editor: Jacqueline Eaton Blakley
Assistant Editors: Rachel Fowler, Anne Rumery, Elizabeth Evans, and B. Rego
Copyeditor: Alisha Jeddeloh
Permissions Manager: Dalene Reeder
Graphic Designer: Keri Evans
Cover Designer: Keith Blomberg
Photograph (cover): © William Munoz
Photographs (interior): © William Munoz, unless otherwise noted
Photo Production Manager: Jason Allen
Art Manager: Kelly Hendren
Associate Art Manager: Alan L. Wilborn
Illustrations: © Human Kinetics, unless otherwise noted
Printer: The P.A. Hutchison Company

Printed in the United States of America   10 9 8 7 6 5 4 3 2 1

The paper in this book is certified under a sustainable forestry program.

Human Kinetics
Website: www.HumanKinetics.com

United States: Human Kinetics
P.O. Box 5076
Champaign, IL 61825-5076
800-747-4457
e-mail: humank@hkusa.com

Canada: Human Kinetics
475 Devonshire Road Unit 100
Windsor, ON N8Y 2L5
800-465-7301 (in Canada only)
e-mail: info@hkcanada.com

Europe: Human Kinetics
107 Bradford Road
Stanningley
Leeds LS28 6AT, United Kingdom
+44 (0) 113 255 5665
e-mail: hk@hkeurope.com

Australia: Human Kinetics
57A Price Avenue
Lower Mitcham, South Australia 5062
08 8372 0999
e-mail: info@hkaustralia.com

New Zealand: Human Kinetics
P.O. Box 80
Torrens Park, South Australia 5062
0800 222 062
e-mail: info@hknewzealand.com

E5815

With the hope that more children
will be dancing in schools to learn.

CONTENTS

Part III Dance and Science Learning Activities

PREFACE

Arts educators in the United States celebrated when the arts were named as a core academic subject in 2001 with the passage of No Child Left Behind legislation. The designation named 10 core subjects in all, qualifying the arts for federal grants and other support. Yet since then, many school districts have reduced arts instruction to allow for more instructional time in math and reading. Many children have little to no opportunity for formal arts instruction. At the same time, and deepening the paradox of mixed messages, a set of skills were identified as extremely important for schools to develop: imagination, innovation, and creativity. These are all essential elements of arts education, thus making the arts a logical and essential part of children's education.

As part of finding our way through these contradictions, we have been sharing our art form of dance with schoolchildren over many years. As we collaborated with classroom teachers, our dance classes became more and more connected to the curriculum. We took requests from teachers: "My first-graders are learning about poetry. Can you find a way to dance with poetry?" "Um . . . sure!" "Can you develop a lesson plan on dinosaurs?" "Well . . . yes!" "Any chance you could create dance classes about the Lewis and Clark excursion?" "Absolutely!" That was always the correct answer, but the truth is, in the beginning we struggled to link the art form of dance to other disciplines.

These initial curricular dance classes were a challenge. After much envisioning and scheming, we set up a pilot program that lasted 1 1/2 years. Math Movers provided after-school classes twice a week, using dance to reinforce math learning in grades 3 through 6. The teachers reported that students were making great gains in their math comprehension and their test scores were going up. Using children's inherent love for moving and creating, we brought the math curriculum to life for them in new ways. Building on this, we soon developed long-term artist residencies in multiple schools, pairing highly trained dance-teaching artists with the classroom teachers in their own classrooms during the regular school day, integrating creative dance with the curriculum.

We've had great success connecting dance to the elementary curriculum, and we've also known some miserable failures! As we envisioned, designed, and taught brand-new lessons using dance to reinforce the curriculum, many questions and challenges arose: How can we use dance most effectively to contribute to student learning? Where does the main focus of the lesson lie—with the content area or dance? How much lesson emphasis should be given to dance? How much emphasis should be placed on the content area? What aspects, exactly, should be assessed? What exactly is the role of the dance specialist in the classroom? How much assistance should the generalist teacher offer the dance specialist before, during, and after teaching?

Over the years a new field has emerged called *arts integration*. Featuring innovative approaches to teaching and learning, these questions have received further scrutiny and exploration. Students are guided through creative practices that integrate the skills in an art form, such as creative dance, with a content area such as math or science. As arts-integrated practices have evolved, so have the assessment practices. Today's best practices contain dual objectives and assess learning in both areas.

This book contains the combined wisdom of the two authors, along with that of Eric Johnson, a master dance educator in Seattle who gave freely of his time while we developed this manuscript. We are indebted to Eric for his expertise in the field and his willingness to delve into the nitty-gritty to help us develop ideas that meet current educational strategies, remain true to the art form of dance, and assess learning equally in both the art form and the content area.

The dance integration lesson plans in this book enable teachers to deliver information using bodily-kinesthetic approaches that actively engage students in learning. Students construct meaning for themselves and demonstrate their understanding using dance performance and choreography. This approach enlivens classrooms and motivates students in new ways. It also revitalizes teachers, who gain access to new learning modalities that inspire and excite children.

This book is intended for classroom teachers, physical education teachers, dance educators, and certified dance specialists. Anyone with a passion for moving and an interest in teaching dance and the curriculum will find this book helpful. The classroom teacher can readily use these lesson plans despite not being a trained dancer; however, we recommend that teachers engage physically with their bodies, moving with their students throughout the lesson. Strong connections are made when a dance educator or dance specialist partners with a classroom teacher. The most important qualifications are for teachers to be willing to explore dance themselves, create a safe atmosphere for experimenting with movement, and delight in the kinesthetic discoveries of the students as they make connections to the curriculum. This can all be great fun!

Teachers will discover a wealth of material in this book, with 36 field-tested lesson plans that span the K-5 mathematics and science curriculum. Each lesson walks the teacher through a warm-up followed by a developmental progression of activities that lead to formative and summative assessments and reflections in both dance learning and the content area. Each lesson integrates one or more area of dance with the selected mathematics or science learning topic. The progression of the lesson enables students to explore, experiment, create, and perform their understanding. Written in a conversational narrative with additional notes for teachers, the format enables teachers to comfortably and successfully use dance to enhance knowledge of another content area. Each lesson explores an essential question relevant to the discipline and connects to an enduring understanding that goes

well beyond the scope of the lesson into students' lives outside of the classroom. Although the lessons may be taught in sequence, they also stand alone as single lessons.

This book is organized in three parts. Part I introduces the role of dance in education, defines dance integration, and describes the uses, benefits, and impacts of dance when used in tandem with another content area.

Part II details 17 dance and math lesson plans divided between five chapters. Organized to parallel the *Common Core State Standards for Mathematics*, the lessons were selected to address the math domains: counting and cardinality, operations and algebraic thinking, numbers and operations, measurement and data, and geometry.

Part III details 19 dance and science learning activities. It consists of four chapters organized by science topics as outlined in *A Framework for K-12 Science Education*: physical science, life science, earth and space sciences, and investigation, experimentation, and technology and the *Next Generation Science Standards*.

Parts II and III are grounded in the elements of dance, and throughout the scope of lessons teachers will gain well-rounded understanding of the basic vocabulary of dance along with the math or science content. The dance learning activities arise from the *Standards for Learning and Teaching Dance in the Arts*, which outline what children should know and be able to do in dance. The appendixes provide a selection of simple warm-up activities, music resources suitable for dance integration, assessment examples, and additional resources.

Unique to this book is the wealth of useful information rigorously connecting the art of dance learning directly to the K-5 mathematics and science curriculum. We hope that teachers will use and adapt these lessons both to enliven their students' learning and to expand their own teaching strategies.

ACKNOWLEDGMENTS

Many people contributed to the formation of this book. Eric Johnson worked tirelessly with us to hammer out language and a format that would be most useful to teachers new to dance. We are most grateful for his time and expertise.

Over the years many classroom teachers partnered with us as these lessons were developed. Special thanks to Maribeth Rothwell, Claudia LaRance, Christy Meurer, Dorothy Morrison, Maureen Loewenwarter, Sue Dickey, Karen Lessnau, Carrie Sweatland, Julie Line, Britt Sonsalla, Mary Manning, Heather Roos, Whitney Maddox, Peggy Manning, Sherrie Harris, and Wendy Lofthouse. Your classrooms have served as a laboratory for dance integration.

Sixteen master teachers in the Creative Pulse graduate program for teachers read and responded to these lesson plans in their early stages, giving comments and suggestions that deepened the work. Thanks go to Lindsey Schwickert for serving as a sounding board.

Catherine Schuck, Heather Roos, and Maribeth Rothwell invited us into their classrooms to photograph their students for this book. Special thanks go to Alanna Vaneps, curriculum coordinator for Missoula County Public Schools, for ideas and research. School principals Jerry Seidensticker and Kelly Chumrau, regional director Karen Allen, Dr. Tammy Elser, and Jackie Boshka have consistently supported dance integration behind the scenes, and we are grateful for their belief in our work. Thanks to Beck McLaughlin and the Montana Arts Council for the ongoing grants that funded these dance integration residencies. Warmest appreciation goes to Dr. Stephen Kalm, Nicole Bradley Browning, Michele Antonioli, Heidi Jones Eggert, Teresa Clark, Desiree Stanley, and Erin McDaniel along with faculty and staff at the University of Montana School of Theatre and Dance.

ACTIVITY FINDER

The 36 lesson plans in this book are designed at either a basic or intermediate level or to be adaptable to both levels. Each lesson plan contains a primary dance focus selected because of its relevance to the math or science content. Each lesson should take approximately 45 to 60 minutes, except where otherwise noted. The same dance concepts are repeated in multiple lessons, connecting in new ways with diverse math and science themes. The lessons are designed for ages 5 to 11, based on when the content is generally taught in schools. Teachers are encouraged to adapt and expand the lessons as needed to fit district curriculums.

Mathematics concept	Dance concept	Age range	Level
Chapter 4 Counting and Cardinality			
Counting	Locomotor and axial actions	5-6	Basic
Comparing Whole Numbers	Levels	5-7	Basic
Ordinal Numbers	Choreographic sequence	5-6	Basic
Chapter 5 Operations and Algebraic Thinking			
Addition	Axial actions	5-7	Basic
Subtraction	Locomotor actions	6-8	Basic
Multiplication and Division	Timing relationships	8-11	Intermediate
Chapter 6 Numbers and Operations			
Place Value	Levels	6-8	Basic
Fractions	Reach	8-11	Basic
Chapter 7 Measurement and Data			
Pennies, Nickels, and Dimes	Levels	6-8	Basic
Time	Levels, shape	7-9	Basic
Measurement	Locomotor actions	5-7	Basic
Perimeter and Area	Locomotor actions	7-10	Basic
Bar Graphs	Tempo, levels	7-9	Intermediate
Chapter 8 Geometry			
Two-Dimensional Shapes	Shape, pathways	5-7	Basic
Three-Dimensional Shapes	Shape, relationships, touch	5-7	Basic
Symmetry and Asymmetry	Shape	7-11	Basic
Angles and Lines	Shape	9-11	Basic

Science concept	Dance concept	Age range	Level
Chapter 9 Physical Science			
Magnets	Body parts, touch, group shape	6-8	Basic
Balance and Force	Counterbalance, balance	9-11	Intermediate
Atoms and Molecules	Energy qualities, spatial relationships	8-11	Intermediate
States of Water	Energy qualities, tempo, spatial relationships	6-11	Intermediate
Chapter 10 Life Science			
Vertebrate Classification	Locomotor actions	7-11	Basic
Butterfly Life Cycle	Choreographic sequence	5-8	Basic
Frog Life Cycle	Counts	6-8	Intermediate
Plant Life Cycle	Levels, size	5-8	Intermediate
Five Senses	Abstraction, choreography	5-11	Basic-intermediate
Bones	Body parts, choreography	5-11	Basic-intermediate
Chapter 11 Earth and Space Sciences			
Weather	Energy qualities	5-7	Basic
Constellations	Props, shape	5-11	Basic
Moon Phases	Reach	6-9	Basic
Water Cycle	Energy qualities, tempo, relationships, levels	6-9	Intermediate
Erosion and Weathering	Energy qualities	8-11	Basic
Igneous, Sedimentary, and Metamorphic Rocks	Stillness	8-11	Basic
Chapter 12 Investigation, Experimentation, and Technology			
Investigation, Experimentation, and Problem Solving	Choreography, problem solving	5-11	Basic-intermediate
Dance Viewing Through Technology	Observing, responding	5-11	Basic-intermediate
Dance and Photography	Shapes, choreography	5-11	Basic

THE ROLE OF DANCE IN EDUCATION

1

INTRODUCTION TO DANCE INTEGRATION

A group of nine-year-olds carefully observe one another, waiting for their cue. At just the right moment they all jump to a high level and finish their dance with 8 counts of leaping, stretching, and reaching. Suddenly they freeze in identical shapes for an unexpected ending. The students grin and bow as their classmates clap with appreciation. The students share high fives as they return to their place in the audience.

Classrooms come alive with joy when children push the desks aside and dance the math or science curriculum. The quality of learning improves and students across the learning spectrum become engaged and connected. The integration of dance with the curriculum provides an exciting solution for improving education.

This chapter describes the excitement and value of learning mathematics and science through dance. Dance integration is defined, the transformational uses of dance for academic achievement are highlighted, and the multiple benefits of dance integration are celebrated. Classrooms are transformed when dance is synthesized with other content areas.

Rethinking Education

Dance is one of the most powerful yet undervalued solutions for school reform. Children aged 5 to 11 are natural movers and are uncomfortable sitting at desks for long periods of time. Luckily, education doesn't have to repress children's desire to move! Learning and retaining information is most effective when children are active, listening, and expressing ideas physically in the space. The elementary curriculum lends itself to a natural synthesis with dance.

Leading educators and researchers in the United States agree. For instance, the President's Committee on the Arts and the Humanities describes numerous studies that have "documented significant links between arts integration models and academic and social outcomes for students, efficacy for teachers, and school-wide improvements in culture and climate" (President's Committee on the Arts and the Humanities, Reinvesting in Arts Education: Winning America's Future Through Creative Schools, Washington, DC, May 2011, p. 19). Dance is no longer an extracurricular activity, reserved for after-school study in private studios; it is relevant during the school day because the body is one of the primary ways children learn! Requiring students to sit still at their desks is unnecessary and doesn't correspond to children's natural inclinations.

Research indicates that 85 percent of school-aged learners are predominately kinesthetic learners (http://abllab.com/about-us/), making dance a natural fit in the elementary classroom. The lesson plans in this book provide field-tested dance integration activities in mathematics and science designed for both the classroom teacher as well as the dance specialist. The goal is enlivened classrooms that promote academic success and lifelong understanding for all students.

For more than a century, schools have been organized around distinct subject areas. During the typical school day a student will spend time studying various subjects, including math, science, social studies, communication arts, health, and physical education. The disciplines are distinct with little carryover between them. This structure of education isolates learning areas, consequently defining them as unrelated. What is the result of creating distinct lines between areas of study? Music scholar Janet Barrett (2001) writes, "Although educational institutions segment knowledge into separate packages called 'subjects,' deep understanding often depends on the intersections and interactions of the disciplines" (p. 27).

Art and music, and occasionally drama and dance, are also taught as separate subjects. As a result of these divisions, school arts specialists frequently report feeling isolated from the rest of the curriculum. Arts curriculum expert Madeleine Grumet writes (2004), "Integrated arts programs have rescued the arts from educational cul-de-sacs where they have been sequestered . . . and they have rescued the academic curriculums from their dead ends in the flat, dull routines of schooling that leave students intellectually unchallenged and emotionally disengaged" (pp. 49-50).

Although the arts (visual art, dance, drama, music, and media arts) are legally defined as a core content area in U.S. education, they are commonly considered a special subject and are usually the first area to be cut to make room for something new. However, educators must never underestimate the power of the arts to inspire and delight children. Dance promotes endless pathways for children to create meaning and find fulfillment in learning.

What Is Dance Integration?

Large geometric shapes are taped to the floor. The students stand barefoot on one side of the classroom. The teacher says, "Tiptoe over to the parallelogram and make a shape in the area. Gallop over to the rhombus and make a balancing shape on its perimeter." Geometry comes alive for students when they experience it firsthand with their bodies.

Arts integration has evolved since the early 1990s as school districts and artists have experimented with various models of implementation. The term *dance integration* is often described through a variety of words, including *interdisciplinary*, *multidisciplinary*, *arts-infused*, and *cross-disciplinary learning*. Books, journal articles, and dissertations refer to a wide range of approaches and philosophies within these terms. Often, the primary emphasis is on math or science and the art form of dance is given minimal attention. When dance is used casually to enhance an activity without regard to the art form itself, it is not true integration.

The word *integration* comes from the Latin word *integrare*, which means to make something whole. Richard Deasy (2003), director of the Arts Education Partnership, defines *arts integration* as "the effort to build a set of relationships between learning in the arts and learning in the other skills and subjects of the curriculum" (p. 2).

We define *dance integration* as meaningful instruction that combines the art form of dance with one or more content areas based on mutual concepts and authentic connections shared by both disciplines. In our definition, the integrity of each discipline is maintained while improving academic understanding and focusing on student achievement. Our approach to dance integration places the learning of dance knowledge and skills directly alongside math or science learning, with the two areas having equal emphasis.

Rather than teaching particular dance steps, we use creative movement in the dance integration class. *Creative movement* involves movements that are spontaneously created in order to express an idea or experience. Creative movement grows directly out of the elements of dance, using the same vocabulary used by dancers and choreographers. When creative movement is used intentionally to increase learning targets in mathematics and science, it is known as *dance integration*.

Geometry comes alive for students when they experience it firsthand with their bodies.

The content areas of dance, mathematics, and science all retain their depth and integrity. Each area contains learning objectives and embedded assessments and meets educational standards. Most importantly, throughout the dance integration experience students are involved in artistic processes that are authentic to dance: exploring and experimenting, creating, performing, and responding.

Arguments for Arts Integration

In the last decade arts integration has quickly caught on in arts education discussions, yet a few still argue against integrating the arts with other disciplines, fearing the loss of integrity of the art form as a specific discipline. They argue for arts for arts' sake and advocate for the pure teaching of arts-specific skills and knowledge. A response to this is articulated in this Northern Illinois website on Arts Integration Theory, "Arts Education is not a substitute for teaching the arts for their own sake" (http://www.neiu.edu/~middle/Modules/science%20mods/amazon%20components/AmazonComponents3.html).

The authors of this book are committed to the development of both dance integration programs and stand-alone dance classes, with the belief that one need not cancel out the other. Our varied roles as dancers, choreographers, teachers, and concert producers provide us with a stake in

dance integration and preserving the art form and building audiences through training in technique, performance, and choreography. The heart and soul of dance as an art form are well preserved in our approach to dance integration.

Characteristics of Dance Integration Programs

What exactly makes a dance integration class? Dance integration programs reflect a wide variety of depth and meaning. Just because a class incorporates the body does not mean it is dance integration! Arts education expert Liora Bresler (1995) describes the less effective subservient integration style, which has garnered intense criticism from the arts community. Examples of subservient integration might be students doing the hand movements in the "Eensy Weensy Spider" or waving their arms back and forth every time the wind blows in a story. In these examples the body is used, but students are not learning specific dance or movement skills or increasing their knowledge about the art form of dance. Grant Wiggins, president of Authentic Education, finds Bresler's notion of subservient integration to be prevalent in schools and cautions arts specialists to be "aware and knowledgeable of the types of integration and their outcomes and to be strong educators in their own field" (Burnaford, 2007, p. 22).

In a successful dance integration program, a student will synthesize knowledge in two disciplines simultaneously. For example, a science lesson on the bones teaches about the skeletal system and students identify various bones in the body such as the femur, tibia, humerus, and phalanges. They learn about the human skeleton and how it supports other structures of the body. In the integrated dance lesson on bones, the teacher encourages the students to move using various body parts while naming the bone, such as "Point to your humerus. Can you lift and drop the humerus? Can the humerus initiate your movement with the rest of your body following?" Movement explorations continue, incorporating each vocabulary word in the science curriculum. The bones are reviewed; for example, the teacher says, "Wiggle your phalanges . . . make a big circle with your femur . . . lift and drop your tibia."

Next, students form small groups and select a card with three bones written on it. Together they create and rehearse simple dances that clearly show the three bones moving. Each group performs the dance for the rest of the class. Students self-assess their own dance and peer assess classmates, asking, "What bones did the dance use?" The performance is assessed using a rubric: Was it clear which bones the performers were using, and did they continue to use those bones throughout the dance? At the end of class for review and summative assessment, the teacher points to bones and asks students to name them. The lesson concludes with a discussion connecting the bones to daily life, such as, "I use my pelvis to close the door when my hands are full. I use my phalanges to write a text message." As a result of the integrated bones lesson, students have had a personal experience with the vocabulary, applying it to their own lives. As opposed to studying bones from a textbook, dancing the bones brings the material alive for students and makes it personal, engaging them in the learning.

Metaphors for Integration

Many symbols have been used to describe the process of integrated learning. Four metaphors are relevant to the synthesis of dance with mathematics and science.

Spiraling

Highly effective teaching continually spirals back to themes already introduced, offering students immersion and reimmersion in doing, making, and sharing. This leads to students expressing their personal understandings through movement studies. Educational theorist Jerome Bruner's (1960) theory of discovery learning recognizes that learners actively construct their own knowledge based on the things they know now and have known in the past. In Bruner's spiral curriculum, basic ideas and concepts are repeatedly revisited and built upon until the learner understands them fully. The same dance themes resurface frequently throughout these lesson plans. For example, students may experience high, middle, and low levels as the primary dance concept in one class, and then they are asked to consider the levels in their choreography in future classes. Revisiting ideas helps students integrate knowledge.

Webbing

Dance integration can also be perceived as a complex web consisting of many individual threads connected to make a strong whole. Arts education professor Julia Marshall (2006) argues for substantive arts integration that connects to state standards when she argues for "lessons that go deep: mining the concepts behind images, ideas and processes—and broad: making a web of connections between art content, art making and other domains and ideas. Therefore they do not isolate art as a hermetic field but call for an integrated arts education that connects to all areas of inquiry" (p. 19). Each activity in this book forms a web of connections, threading together content, vocabulary, and dance-making processes.

Weaving

A weaving contains numerous individual strands interlaced to form a whole. Author Susanna Brown (2007) uses a weaving metaphor to describe arts integration: "Arts integration is like a weaving wherein the design may repeat a pattern or be variable. Just as the warp and weft strings are integral parts of a woven whole, the arts are an integral part of the curriculum and are valuable in all aspects of teaching and learning" (p. 72). The template for dance integration lesson plans weaves together the learning targets, knowledge, vocabulary, standards, and assessment processes from both disciplines.

Scaffolding

Originally coined by Jerome Bruner, educational theorist Lev Vygotsky (1962) elaborates on a model of teaching that encompasses *scaffolding*, where learning is conducted from the ground up, building on the foundation of the known. At the beginning of a new task, the learning is concrete, external, and visible. In Vygotskian theory, learning proceeds from the concrete to the abstract (Wilhelm, Baker, & Dube, 2001). In this book, creative dance provides an immediate and highly personal starting point from which to experience the known and move into the new. When used along with traditional teaching approaches, the dance integration class provides yet another level of scaffolding for the learner to construct meaning.

Dance and Academic Achievement

It's 10:45 on Monday morning and time for dance. Students put their papers and books away and push the desks aside to create a wide-open space in the center of the classroom. Erasers and pencils are picked up and the floor is cleared of papers and wrappers. The students take off their shoes and sit in a circle in the movement space. The warm-up begins. Students take a deep cleansing breath, filling their bodies with fresh air, and then exhale the air out. They follow the teacher, bending and crossing the midline, stretching high and sinking low, twisting from side to side. The music plays softly and the students move silently and intently. The students are now ready to learn.

Ideally, during the school week students experience dance integration as well as traditional methods of math and science instruction. They may experience mathematics through movement one day and with a textbook and worksheets the next. The diverse modes of instruction provide a lifeline for students to connect to the curriculum. Students transition easily between teaching methodologies when their learning style is acknowledged. As described in a 2010 article in *Education Week*, studying the arts provides a variety of academic and social benefits to young people and can enhance students' ability to learn skills in reading, language development, and math. The arts in education are a powerful way to promote creativity and critical thinking, among other skills (Robelen, 2010).

Transforming the Classroom

Encouraging students to think with their bodies readies them for learning. If the space and time allow, creative movement is best experienced with bare feet. With shoes off, students feel the earth under their feet, providing a more sensitive movement experience. When the floor is not conducive to bare feet or there are safety concerns, shoes may be worn. As the classroom is transformed into a movement space, students naturally transition into kinesthetic learning.

No matter where your dance space is, you will divide it into an audience area and a stage (performance area).

Teachers report that students interact with the open classroom space differently than they do during the regular school day. The large open space mimics a dance studio—a large room with a big floor and mirrors, although mirrors are unnecessary in the school dance class. The movement space is often divided into the audience area (where students sit quietly to watch each other perform) and the stage (where the dance sharing takes place).

Dance and Learning

Teachers who use dance integration will observe the "Aha!" experience among students when concepts that seemed abstract in the textbook are made concrete and understandable in the movement space. Likewise, the experience enlivens teachers who are seeking to improve their teaching. Students find integrated arts lessons to be rich and deeply layered experiences. Teachers report that arts integration classes provide moments of exhilaration, personal transformation, and academic or life-choice changes. Teachers and artists often experience profound changes in their approach to individual students, to learning, and to the classroom in general. "The arts provide a window to understand the connections among all subject areas" (Burnaford, 2007, p. 19).

Recent advances in education have addressed the need to revitalize education in STEM fields (science, technology, engineering, and math). But there are many who believe that *STEM* is missing one important component, the arts, which turns the acronym to *STEAM*. As described in a *Scientific American* blog by Stephen Ross Pomeroy (2012), "Though many see art and science as somewhat at odds, the fact is that they have long existed and developed collaboratively. . . . At TED 2002, Mae Jemison, a doctor, dancer, and the first African American woman in space, said, 'The difference between science and the arts is not that they are different sides of the same coin . . . or even different parts of the same continuum, but rather, they are manifestations of the same thing. The arts and sciences are avatars of human creativity.'"

Dance integration promotes a comprehensive dance education. The four-part process of exploring and experimenting, creating, performing, and responding leads to multilayered experiences resulting in dance literacy (figure 1.1). Students learn the basic practices of dancers and choreographers, such as movement invention, revision, memorization, and rehearsal. They become comfortable sharing their movement ideas with others, and they learn to watch others attentively. They

Figure 1.1 Artistic processes lead to dance literacy.

become comfortable talking about dance and critiquing others skillfully; for example, "I appreciate the way the dancers changed their relationship to one another. They started far apart, next they were close together in a clump, and they ended in a long line touching finger to finger." Deeply embedded knowledge is transmitted over time, with the students becoming fluent creators, practitioners, and viewers.

The integrated dance class inspires curiosity and transforms the learning experience from compliance to one of intrinsic motivation and joy. When students break free of the textbook environment and draw upon their own ideas and strengths, their experience is deeply enriched. Silk Road Connects, an arts-integrated program for middle school students in New York, refers to *passion-driven learning* that is sustainable and transferable. In the words of Yo-Yo Ma, "Passion-driven education liberates students and gives them the self-confidence to discover who they are as individuals and how they fit in the world" (www.silkroadproject.org/Education/EducationOverview/tabid/170/Default.aspx). Students with a passion for learning are prepared to thrive in the diverse situations they will encounter throughout their lives.

Integrated Brain

The brain is divided into two hemispheres, and people feel most whole and connected when the two sides of the brain are engaged. Critical thinking is often thought of as a left-brain function and creative thinking as a right-brain function, yet humans need both sides for optimal function. Fortunately, "Research shows that both hemispheres of the brain are actively engaged when learning through dance" (Brown & Parsons, 2008). "We call on the left side for logical speech, hearing, reading, writing, math, analyzing, verbal memory, reasoning, judgment, using symbols, and managing time. The right side provides us with spatial perception, visualizing, synthesizing, visual memory, insight, intuition, seeing whole things at once, understanding analogies and metaphors, and gut-level feelings. Both sides are important" (Gelineau, 2012, p. 21). Dance integration builds a better brain.

When children are raised in active, stimulating environments, they produce more and denser neural connections (Bruer, 1991; Nash, 1997). When the body is inactive for 20 minutes or longer, the ability of the neurons to communicate with each other declines (Kinoshita, 1997). The cerebellum plays a role in memory, emotion, language, decision making, spatial perception, and nonverbal cueing (Wolfe, 2001), and "exercising the actions of the cerebellum through movement strengthens neural pathways leading to cognitive areas of the brain" (Clancy, 2006, p. 5). Human movement develops neural networks and memory. When teachers provide brain-compatible movement experiences for students, it supports higher-order thinking skills, reduces tension, and enables the brain to shift from thinking with the dominant hemisphere to using both halves of the brain together.

The link between movement and learning is supported by brain science. "The brain and body's movement and learning systems are interdependent and interactive. For example, motor development provides the framework that the brain uses to sequence the patterns needed for academic concepts. The body's vestibular system controls balance and spatial awareness and facilitates the students' ability to place words and letters on a page. The four visual fields needed for eye tracking is strengthened. Proper development and remediation of these systems are critical to a child's ability to learn" (http://abllab.com/about-us/).

Movement is known to organize the central nervous system, laying the foundation for sensory-motor development. Researchers have identified eight developmental movement patterns that humans progress through in the first year of life. Movements such as the patterns found in the BrainDance (appendix A) repeat these patterns and improve proprioception, memory, attention and eye tracking, balance, behavior, and motor skills (Gilbert, 1992). Movement and deep, full breaths allow blood and oxygen to flow to the respiratory system and brain, all of which supports learning.

Bodily-Kinesthetic Intelligence

Teaching is most effective when it is oriented directly to a child's learning style and intelligence. Howard Gardner's (1983) multiple intelligence theory has changed the way educators view intelligence. Traditional teaching approaches primarily emphasize the mathematical-analytical and verbal-linguistic intelligences. Bodily-kinesthetic learners think via movement. To teach to this intelligence, a teacher takes a hands-on approach, moving to illustrate concepts and using movement examples in explanations. Kinesthetic imagery is drawn upon and students learn by touching manipulatives. Students are asked to use the body to communicate ideas and are encouraged to practice fine and gross motor activities (Clancy, 2006, p. 16).

In the dance integration class, students learn processes from the mathematical and verbal-linguistic intelligences by consulting the bodily-kinesthetic intelligence in concert with other intelligences. The kinesthetic learner develops connections in math and science that lead to enduring understanding.

Integrated Thinking Skills

Thanks to the Partnership for 21st Century Skills, a national group of business and education leaders came together as a catalyst to position 21st-century skills at the center of U.S. education. The group determined that "every child in the U.S. needs 21st century knowledge and skills to succeed as effective citizens, workers and leaders. This can be accomplished by fusing the 3Rs and 4Cs." The term *three Rs* traditionally refers to the basic subject areas taught in schools: reading, writing, and arithmetic. Today, however, the three Rs are listed as "English, reading or language arts; mathematics; science; foreign languages; civics; government; economics; arts; history; and geography" (www.p21.org/about-us/our-mission). Fusing these subjects with the four Cs (critical thinking and problem solving, communication, collaboration, and creativity and innovation) represents an appreciation of the integrated thinking skills needed for a complete education. The three Rs serve as the umbrella for core content, and the four Cs are the skills needed for success in college, life, and career.

Students who possess curiosity, imagination, creativity, and evaluation skills are better able to tolerate ambiguity. These skills help people explore new realms of possibility, be more understanding of the perspectives of others, and express their own thoughts and feelings more readily, producing "globally aware, collaborative, and responsible citizens" (www.p21.org/storage/documents/P21_arts_map_final.pdf).

Developing integrated thinkers leads to informed citizens who are able to negotiate and interface with the complex world they are facing. These skills are important parts of the artistic processes of exploring and experimenting, creating, performing, and responding, and they are used to evaluate learning in the arts. The four integrated thinking skills (creative thinking, critical thinking, communication, and collaboration) are part of every school dance experience.

Creative Thinking and Dance

Creativity can and should be taught in school. The creative dance class is centered on creative thinking, as students are continually creating something new. Students are instructed to access their own movement response as opposed to copying the teacher's movement. Because students spend a lot of time finding the right answer in school, an approach that stifles creativity, at first they can hardly believe what they're being asked to do! With a little encouragement, students tap into their own creative ideas, and with practice, their creative thinking expands.

Creative students brainstorm fluently and remain curious and open to new ideas. They are flexible, resilient, and comfortable with ambiguity, and they learn to view failure as an opportunity to learn, understanding that mistakes are an important part of the process. The climate is fertile for creative thinking when children feel that their contributions are welcome and worthy (Gelineau, 2012).

With a little encouragement, students tap into their own creative ideas.

The success of any creative experience partly depends on the atmosphere the teacher has created in the classroom. The teacher sets up a structure for creative thinking to take place by prompting students to find individual solutions, such as "How many different ways can you find to leap and jump lightly like the molecules in gasses?" The open-ended prompt is worded to encourage the learner to invent many ideas. For a dancer, creative thinking means experimenting with novel solutions to a movement problem or discovering new ways to express oneself. Creativity usually occurs thru *improvisation*, the process of spontaneously inventing movement in the moment. "Improvising puts the mover in touch with the creative flow of the present" (McCutchen, 2006, p. 175).

Critical Thinking and Dance

> "Critical thinking is that mode of thinking—about any subject, content, or problem—in which the thinker improves the quality of his or her thinking by skillfully analyzing, assessing, and reconstructing it. Critical thinking is self-directed, self-disciplined, self-monitored, and self-corrective thinking" (www.criticalthinking.org/pages/our-concept-of-critical-thinking/411).

Through dance, students learn that solutions to problems can take many forms. The kinds of critical-thinking skills students use in dance include mental alertness, attention to sequence and detail, and memorization. Students observe, listen to directions, and follow complicated instructions. The dance class involves reasoning, understanding symbols, analyzing images, and knowing how to organize knowledge. Dance making involves composing, evaluating, changing, reevaluating, deleting, and adding (Hanna, 2008).

When students create a dance, they make judgments by selecting one movement over another. Students of all ages who are new to dance usually select the first thing they think of. Through experience, students learn to analyze their decisions and look critically at all the possible choices, weighing the differences and making revisions and alterations. The teacher sets up the experiences that develop critical-thinking skills in dance, such as, "Go back and repeat what you just danced, but this time decide how tightly or loosely to make the movement," or, "Can you make your amoeba movement travel slowly throughout the room? Remember our three directions: forward, backward, and sideways." Critical thinking is related to creative thinking, and these processes are referred to as *higher-order thinking and processing skills*.

Clear Communication Through Dance

The art of dance is all about communication. Dance can communicate ideas, processes, feelings, experiences, memories, dreams, and hopes. Dance can tell a story and be used for entertainment. Many cultures use it for healing or to communicate directly to the gods.

Dance is abstract, yet it is highly personal to the mover. Whenever we move, we communicate things about ourselves. The movements we select and the myriad ways they are intentionally put together are perceived and interpreted by others. Humans are hardwired to interpret the movements of others. The smallest gesture of the hand or face reveals volumes to the beholder. Every dance integration class enables the movers to communicate their ideas, and the teacher encourages students to communicate their intentions clearly and invites viewers to think critically about what they see.

How Dancers Collaborate

At first, most students prefer to work closely with their friends and with students of the same gender. Collaboration requires working effectively with lots of people, including people who think differently than we do. Working with others in small groups develops respect for a variety of ideas and requires compromise in order to accomplish a common goal. The groups constantly change in the dance class, with new collaborations of boys and girls formed each day. A good collaborator listens well, is open to new ideas, and values the individual contributions made by others. Students learn to share responsibility for collaborative work and make their own contributions to the whole.

Other Benefits of Dance Integration

A large yellow sun sits in the center of the room. The students are highly animated and engaged as they dance the solar system. The 10-year-olds wear signs identifying their planet and together they determine where their planet needs to be in proximity to the sun. There's a lot of spirited conversation as the students place themselves in the correct order, with Mercury the closest and Pluto the farthest from the sun. The students orbit the sun by tiptoeing, gliding, and skipping, demonstrating the length of a complete orbit for each planet. Next the planets demonstrate rotation as they orbit—a challenging movement because it makes them dizzy. The teacher encourages them to explore orbiting and rotating while still maintaining their equilibrium. Before long they all switch planets and begin the solar system dance again.

In addition to improving academic learning in math and science and developing integrated thinking skills, students benefit from dance integration in many other important ways. These include physical outcomes, positive messages about the body, improved school climate, and inclusive practices.

Physical Outcomes

Deepened self-awareness of the body in space provides a physical consciousness that lasts a lifetime. Students learn healthy practices and improve coordination, balance, flexibility, and motor control. Stress is released and stamina and physical strength increase. Knowledge of where one's weight is centered and how to alter the muscular tension in a movement develops subtlety and artistry in a pleasurable physical activity. Students learn the importance of personal space and develop knowledge about others' boundaries and physical preferences.

Positive Messages About the Body

The first 5 years of life involve extraordinary learning through crawling, reaching, handling, tasting, and touching. A child arrives at school as an expert of learning through the body. When we tell students to sit still and keep their hands to themselves and their feet on the floor, we give them the message that their natural movement responses are bad. Negative messages about the body are internalized, often leading to guilt about the need to move. It's unfortunate that many children learn in school that their body's natural responses are wrong or bad.

Humans need to move, and our schools can easily reinforce a healthy body image. When the teacher watches students moving and comments favorably about their body shapes or movement qualities, it reinforces that the students' movement, and consequently their relationship with their body, is on a positive and healthy track. Messages about our bodies—whether positive or negative—often stay with us throughout our lives.

Improved School Climate

With the overwhelming pressures and expectations facing schools today, why should principals consider offering dance integration at their school? One of the main advantages noted by parents and educators is the positive change in school climate that occurs. *School climate* refers to the character and quality of school life. Through dance integration a sense of community forms that builds unity and an identity within a school.

Parents want their child challenged, stimulated, and engaged. Nothing is more frustrating than hearing that their son or daughter is bored at school. Parents appreciate their children's inherent joy in moving. Parent groups are strong advocates for school arts programs and parent-teacher organizations often fund arts programs. Hearing their children describe their excitement about the dance and math or science class over dinner reassures parents that their children are learning.

Teachers are refreshed by the welcome change in routine and the individuality and excitement the dance class promotes. They see students who were struggling academically now raising their hands and taking leadership positions in dance. Teachers also report that physically moving with their students enhances their relationships with them and brings joy into learning.

Children often describe dance as the most fun part of the day. Integrating dance with the curriculum breaks up the monotony of the school day and breathes life into learning. Students relish opportunities to create their own movement responses and express themselves at school. Our backdoor approach begins with engagement in movement and leads gradually to a kinesthetic relationship with a math or science topic in a way that feels organic to the learner. This engagement and interest in dance carries naturally into expressing their understanding of the mathematics or science area.

Inclusive Practices

The use of dance to teach mathematics and science is highly effective with students who are at risk of educational failure, many of whom feel alienated from the traditional curriculum. Students who have disabilities or who learn with diverse learning styles often excel when kinesthetic processes are used (Kaufmann, 2006). Learning through dance and movement is valuable to students who have difficulty learning through traditional approaches, including students who are at risk of educational failure or who are identified as having special needs. Often these students cannot find a home at school. Luckily they can find a lifeline in the dance class, delighting teachers who thought these students were lost.

Summary

Classrooms are transformed and students tune in when learning is active and personal. Dance integration involves meaningful instruction that combines the art form of dance with one or more content areas based on mutual concepts and authentic connections shared by both disciplines.

The learning of dance knowledge and skills sits directly alongside math or science learning, with the two areas having equal emphasis. Thanks to the many benefits of dance integration, teachers can enliven their classrooms with dance activities that are designed to improve academic achievement and reinforce integrated thinking skills.

References

Barrett, J. (2001). Interdisciplinary work and musical integrity. *Music Educators Journal, 87*(5), 27-31.

Bresler, L. (1995). The subservient, co-equal, affective, and social integration styles and their implications for the arts. *Arts Education Policy Review, 96*(5), 31-37.

Brown, S. & Parsons, L.M. The Neuroscience of Dance. Scientific American, June 2008. http://www. neuroarts.org/pdf/SciAm_Dance.pdf

Brown, S.L. (2007). An arts-integrated approach for elementary-level students. *Childhood Education, 83*(3), 172-173.

Bruer, J.T. (1991). The brain and child development: Time for some critical thinking. *Public Health Reports*, 113(5), 388-397.

Bruner, J. (1960). *The process of education.* Cambridge, MA: Harvard University Press.

Burnaford, G., Brown, S., Doherty J., & McLaughlin, H.J. (2007). Arts integration frameworks, research and practice: A literature review. Arts Education Partnership. www.eugenefieldaplus.com/academics/A+%20research/artsintegration.pdf.

Clancy, M.E. (2006). *Active bodies, active brains: Building thinking skills through physical activity.* Champaign, IL: Human Kinetics.

Deasy, R.J. (Ed.). (2003). *Creating quality integrated and interdisciplinary arts programs: A report of the Arts Education National Forum.* Washington, DC: Arts Education Partnership.

Gardner, H. (1983). *Frames of mind: A theory of multiple intelligences.* New York: Basic Books.

Gelineau, R.P. (2012). *Integrating the arts across the elementary curriculum.* Belmont, CA: Wadsworth.

Gilbert, A.G. (1992). *Creative dance for all ages.* Reston, VA: AAHPERD.

Grumet, M. (2004). No one learns alone. In N. Rabkin & R. Redmond (Eds.), *Putting the arts in the picture: Reframing education in the 21st century* (pp. 49-80). Chicago: Center for Arts Policy at Columbia College.

Hanna, J.L. (2001). Beyond the soundbite: What the research actually shows about arts education and academic outcome. *Journal of Dance Education, 1*(2), 81-85.

Hanna, J.L. (2008). A nonverbal language for imagining and learning: Dance education in K-12 curriculum. *Educational Researcher, 37*(8), 491-506.

Kaufmann, K.A. (2006). *Inclusive creative movement and dance.* Champaign, IL: Human Kinetics.

Marshall, J. (2006). Substantive art integration = exemplary art education. *Art Education, 59*(6), 17-24.

Nash, M.J. (1997). Fertile minds. *Time, 149*(5), 48-56.

Northern Illinois University. "Arts Integration". http://www.neiu.edu/~middle/Modules/science%20mods/amazon%20components/AmazonComponents3.html

Pomeroy, S.R. (2012). From STEM to STEAM: Science and art go hand-in-hand. *Scientific American*, guest blog, August 22, 2012. http://blogs.scientificamerican.com/guest-blog/2012/08/22/from-stem-to-steam-science-and-the-arts-go-hand-in-hand/.

Robelen, E. (2010, November 16). Schools integrate dance into core academics. *Education Week.* www.edweek.org/ew/articles/2010/11/17/12dance_ep.h30.html.

Vygotsky, L.S. (1962). *Thought and language.* Cambridge, MA: MIT Press.

Wilhelm, J., Baker, T., & Dube, J. (2001). *Strategic reading: Guiding students to lifelong literacy.* New Hampshire: Heinemann.

Wolfe, P. (2001). *Brain matters: Translating research into classroom practice.* Alexandria, VA: Association for Supervision, and Curriculum Development.

2

TEACHING DANCE INTEGRATION: FINDING RELATIONSHIPS

Ms. Anderson, a second-grade teacher, addresses her students. "Pennies are the lowest value of coins, worth 1 cent. We'll dance at a low level for our penny dance, so slowly sink down to the floor. Begin to stretch out long and bend up tight at a low level. Now find ways to twist and untwist on a low level. Now can you travel through the room at a low level by creeping . . . slithering . . . sliding? Let's freeze and count how many dancers are on a low level. Each is worth 1 cent. We have 18 dancers! How many cents is this? Yes, 18 cents!"

Approaches to teaching and learning in dance, mathematics, and science continue to evolve with the release of new educational standards and teaching methodologies. This chapter describes the enduring understandings and essential questions in dance, mathematics, and science. The elements of dance are introduced with a discussion of the movement vocabulary used in an integrated dance class. The thinking skills and learning processes used in mathematics and science underscore educational standards. A step-by-step description of each facet of the integrated dance lesson plan is provided to help teachers understand the structure of the lesson plans in this book and be able to develop original ones. Finally, sample teacher and student assessments serve as exemplars for the evidence of learning.

Foundations: Dance, Mathematics, and Science

Content standards in dance, mathematics, and science continue to evolve with a vision of educational excellence for all students. Each educational discipline contains its own values, approaches, and systems for acquiring knowledge. Rigorous standards outline the essential skills and knowledge students need to be literate in the disciplines. Standards determine what must be taught, not how to teach it.

Dance integration is about forming relationships among disciplines, concepts, ideas, and the human body. Teachers new to dance integration are likely to ask the following questions: How will the science or mathematics teacher collaborate with a dance specialist? How will the dance specialist bring his art form to the math or science classroom? How will the cognitive content in mathematics and science connect to dance making and creativity? How will students understand the relationship between the two areas? How can the heart and soul of both disciplines be celebrated through this new experience?

The National Coalition for Core Arts Standards (NCCAS) identifies enduring understandings and essential questions to help organize the information within an art form. Often called *big ideas*, this information helps students understand why the topic is worth studying (http://nccas.wikispaces.com).

Essential Questions and Enduring Understandings in Dance

Essential questions promote deeper meaning and go to the heart of the discipline. They promote inquiry within a discipline and spark our curiosity and sense of wonder. They have no single right answer. Students make meaning for themselves throughout their lives. The lesson plans in this book encourage further understanding of these essential questions about dance:

- Why do we dance?
- How is dance a universal form of human expression?
- How can other disciplines influence our understanding of dance?
- How do artists use choreography to express their ideas?
- Why do we use dance terminology when responding to dances?
- How can reflecting on our own and others' work help us improve as creative artists?

Enduring understandings are statements that summarize the overarching ideas and processes that are central to a discipline and have lasting value outside the classroom. They form the heart of the curricular standards. Wiggins and McTighe (2005) suggest that the enduring understanding goes beyond the material being covered to include its value beyond the classroom or the ideas and processes that reside at the heart of the discipline. They synthesize the areas that students can revisit throughout their lives and provide a conceptual framework for study in the content area. This book encourages further comprehension of these enduring understandings about dance:

- Dance fosters artistic appreciation, imagination, and significance, and it provides deeper understandings. It is personally satisfying to express oneself with artistic body movement.
- There are many ways to express an idea and each person has a unique form of expression.
- Dancers rely on tools, techniques, and discipline to create a work of art.

- Performing dance fosters meaning making, deeper emotional responses, and more inventive decision making. Viewing a dance helps us gain new insights and awareness.
- Underlying structures in dance can be understood by analysis and inference.
- Dancers often work collaboratively, sharing ideas to develop a dance performance.

Basics of Creative Dance

Dance education involves a depth and scope of learning that is equal to the disciplines of mathematics and science. In creative movement, students learn through engagement with their whole self. They use movement as a means of communication and self-expression and as a way of responding to others. Dance education begins with awareness of the movement of the body and its creative potential. Students learn skills and knowledge that expand their movement vocabulary, enhance their listening and viewing skills, and help them begin thinking critically about dance.

The elements of dance help to organize the movement material for the teacher. The lesson plans in this book are developed from a worksheet from the Perpich Center for Arts Education (figure 2.1), which provides a concise overview of the content, vocabulary, and skills used in dance. Although the Perpich chart does not provide an exhaustive list of every movement used in dance, it is a highly useful tool to organize movement activities. Teachers may find the acronym *BASTE* to be helpful when recalling the five dance elements:

- Body (*who?*)
- Action (*what?*)
- Space (*where?*)
- Time (*when?*)
- Energy (*how?*)

The first step in teaching dance integration involves fluency using the elements of dance. Within each element are movement concepts, as described next. The specific dance terminology for the elements of dance is italicized.

Body

A dancer moves many *parts of the body* individually, in combination, or as the *whole body*. Arms, head, back, hips, shoulders, elbows, legs, feet,

Figure 2.1 The elements of dance.

The Elements of Dance

Ask:	WHO?	DOES WHAT?	WHERE?	WHEN?	HOW?
Answer:	A dancer	moves	through space	and time	with energy
B.A.S.T.E.	**BODY**	**ACTION**	**SPACE**	**TIME**	**ENERGY**
Concepts (in **bold** font) with some suggestions for word lists and descriptors under each concept.	**Parts of the Body** Head, eyes, torso, shoulders, fingers, legs, feet, etc.	**Axial** *(in place)* Open - - - - - - - - - - - Close Rise - - - - - - - Sink or Fall Stretch - - - - - - - - - Bend Twist - - - - - - - - - Turn	**Place** In Place - - - - - - Traveling	**Duration** Brief - - - - - - - - - - Long	**Attack** Sharp - - - - - Smooth Sudden - - - - - Sustained
	Whole Body Design and use of the entire body	**Laban Effort Actions** Press Flick Wring Dab Slash Glide Punch Float	**Size** Small - - - - - - - Large	**Speed** Fast - - - - - - - - - Slow	**Tension** Tight - - - - - - - Loose
	Initiation Core Distal Mid-limb Body Parts	**Traveling** *(locomotor)* Crawl, creep, roll. scoot, walk. run, leap, jump, gallop. slide. hop, skip, do-si-do, chainé turns ....and many more!	**Level** High - - - - - - - - - - Low	**Beat** Steady - - - - - - Uneven	**Force** Strong - - - - - - Gentle
	Patterns Upper/lower body, homologous, contralateral, midline, etc.	*This is just a starting list of movements. Many techniques have specific names for similar actions. "Sauté" is a ballet term for "jump."*	**Direction** Forward - - - - Backward Upward - - - - Downward Sideward - - - - Diagonally Liner - - - - - - - Rotating	**Tempo** Quick - - - - - - - Slow	**Weight** Heavy - - - - - - Light **Strength:** push, horizontal, impacted **Lightness:** resist the down, initiate up **Resiliency:** rebound, even up and down
	Body Shapes Symmetrical/Asymmetrical Rounded Twisted Angular Arabesque		**Pathway** Traveling, traced in air curved, straight,angular, zig-zag, etc.	**Accent** Single - - - - - - Multiple On Beat - - - - Syncopated Predictable- -Unpredictable	**Flow** Bound (Controlled) - - -Free
	Body Systems Muscles Bones Organs Breath Balance Reflexes		**Plane** Sagittal (Wheel) Vertical (Door) Horizontal (Table)	**Rhythmic Pattern** Patterned - - - - - -Free Metric Breath, 2/4, 6/8, etc waves, Polyrhythms word cues, Cross-rhythm event cues, Tāla felt time	**Energy Qualities** Vigorous, languid, furious, melting, droopy, wild, lightly, jerkily, sneakily, timidly, proudly, sharp, smooth, sudden, sustained etc.
	Inner Self Senses Perceptions Emotions Thoughts Intention Imagination		**Focus** Inward - - - - - Outward Direct - - - - - - Indirect **Relationships** In Front - - -Behind/Beside Over - - - - - - - - Under Alone- - - - - -Connected Near - - - - - - - - - Far Individual & group proximity to object	**Timing Relationships** Before After Unison Sooner Than Faster Than	

© 2011 Perpich Center for Arts Education. May be reproduced for professional development and classroom use by teachers.

toes, and fingers extend, bend, and twist in various ways. Movement can be *initiated* from the core or center of the body (near the navel), distal reaches (head, fingertips, and toes), midlimb (elbows, knees), or an individual body part. People naturally move their bodies in *patterns* that use the upper and lower body, right and left sides, or cross-lateral movements. Moving body parts form *body shapes* that are symmetrical, asymmetrical, rounded, twisted, angular, straight, wide, or narrow.

All movement arises from our *body systems*, which include the remarkable coordination and functioning of our muscles, bones, and organs and the use of our breath. Inhalation and exhalation of the breath helps the student experience a movement more fully, such as rising on the inhalation and sinking on the exhalation. Every person responds to her senses, perceptions, and emotions. The body serves as the conduit between the *inner self* and the outer world, communicating thoughts, intentions, and imagination.

Action

Dancers move by traveling through the space or moving body parts while staying in one place. A movement anchored to one spot is called *axial movement*. Examples of axial movements include the following: bend, stretch, twist, open, close, rise, sink, shiver, shake, twist, swing, tilt, float, rise, fall, and suspend. *Traveling movements* locomote us through the room and include the following examples: walk, run, leap, hop, jump, gallop, tiptoe, skip, slide, roll, slither, gallop, and creep.

Space

As dancers move, they interact with and define the space in many ways. Some actions travel through the room while others stay in one *place*. Some movements use a space that is small in *size* and others fill up the larger space. Dancers use the space intentionally; whenever they move or are still, they take up space.

Three vertical *levels* (high, middle, low) and movement that travels in many *directions* (forward, backward, sideways, upward, downward, diagonally) also help define space. These experiences help us view the space around us in new ways. We design various floor and air *pathways* (straight, curving, zigzag, circular, random) that enable us to share the space with others in artistic ways while avoiding collisions.

As we experience spatial activities, we begin to see the space around us as a three-dimensional stage. All human movement exists on three *planes*: the sagittal (wheel), vertical (door), and horizontal (table). We define space with our eyes as well. Dancers' eye *focus* helps define the space (if they keep their eyes on one spot they define space directly; if their focus meanders around the space, their view is indirect). When a performer maintains an inner or outward focus, it helps define the space symbolically, informing the audience of the performer's intention. Spatial *relationships* form when two or more dancers interact in front of or behind one another, over or under one another, alone or connected, or close together or far apart.

Students who are learning dance are asked to use space intentionally and with clarity, demonstrating spatial principles. They also discuss the specific spatial principles they observe in their own and their classmates' dances.

Time

Dance exists within the framework of time. Sometimes the timing of a movement is instinctive and connects to the movement itself. For example, most people skip in a rhythm that feels natural to them. Other times music defines the timing through rhythms and musical textures that inform the movement. For instance, a dance performed to classical music is often very different from one performed to a hip-hop song!

All movement exists within a *duration* of time, which can range from brief to long. The *speed* or *tempo* may be fast or slow and may be performed to a steady or uneven *beat*. When a dancer accentuates a movement, it is called an *accent*. When performing a series of movements, *rhythmic patterns* develop that use either metric patterns or free patterns experienced by breath, felt time, or word cues. Students who are learning dance are asked to respond in movement to beats, accents, tempos, and rhythms and to discuss the timing and patterning of a dance.

Energy

Dancers have many choices available to convey a specific emotion, theme, or idea. Energy involves the detailed nuance of how the movement is performed. A dancer may *attack* the movement sharply and suddenly or smoothly and sustainedly. The dancer consciously uses muscular *tension*, making the muscles tight or loose. The *force* ranges from strong and powerful to light and gentle. Dancers learn to use their *weight* to convey strength, lightness, and resiliency. The *flow* of the movement may be highly controlled and bound or free flowing. Dancers use many descriptive words to describe the way the movement is felt and expressed. These *movement qualities* convey the intention of the dance and may be sharp, smooth, floaty, jerky, wild, droopy, soft, percussive, or explosive. Students intentionally use energy concepts to convey a specific idea. They are also expected to discuss the energy concepts they view in others' dances.

The elements of dance are inherent in every dance experience. Teachers can emphasize one or two areas to harmonize with the science or mathematics content area.

Basics of Learning Mathematics

In math education, students are expected to learn skills and knowledge, as well as habits of mind, to foster mathematical understanding and expertise. Standards define what children should know and be able to do. Math learning is organized using *domains*—larger groups of related standards that form overarching ideas that connect topics across grade levels. Mathematical literacy allows students to master topics by developing procedural fluency as well as conceptual understanding.

The dance and mathematics learning activities in this book are organized around the following domains identified in the common core standards:

- Counting and cardinality
- Operations and algebraic thinking
- Number and operations in base 10 and fractions
- Measurement and data
- Geometry

Each of the five areas contains two to five detailed dance integration lesson plans that use dance to increase understanding of the math theme. Students work independently and collaboratively to solve problems, thinking critically in a mathematical way with the understanding that there are many approaches to a solution. Students learn skills to carry out procedures flexibly, accurately, efficiently, and appropriately. They learn to see mathematics as sensible, useful, and worthwhile. A belief in diligence and one's own efficacy develops.

According to the Georgia Department of Education (July, 2011, p.1), "Mathematics is the economy of information. The central idea of all mathematics is to discover how knowing some things well, via reasoning, permit students to know much else—without having to commit the information to memory as a separate fact. It is the connections, the reasoned, logical connections that make mathematics manageable." Dancing the math curriculum increases its relevance to students' lives.

Cornerstones of Learning Science

In science education, students learn scientific concepts and develop scientific thinking skills through the investigation of authentic problems in real-world settings. Students develop a basic understanding of their environment and enrich their inquisitiveness by learning new things about their world through investigation and inquiry. As they become skilled observers of their world, students generate new questions for investigation, predict outcomes, and test the results with competence. Peter Dow (1999) of the National Science Foundation writes, "Scientific inquiry has its roots in the inherent restlessness of the human mind. . . . The skills of skeptical questioning and independent thinking may be essential goals of schooling."

The building blocks for learning science are in place before children enter school (National Academy of Sciences, 2007). Despite the commonly held opinion that children are concrete and simplistic thinkers, young children's thinking is surprisingly sophisticated. When children enter school, they already have substantial knowledge of the natural world, which provides a building point for developing scientific concepts. As children grow up, they develop commonsense views of the world that help them make sense of what they see and experience. These ideas are practical, but they aren't necessarily connected to scientific thought. For example, the earth looks flat, but we know through science that the earth is round. Science enables children to learn deeper meanings about the world and to become critical thinkers. The skills developed in learning science parallel the thinking skills used in dance: multiple ways of finding solutions, gathering and weighing evidence, and applying and testing ideas. These processes encourage curiosity, inventiveness, perseverance, and risk taking—skills of inquiry that are crucial for lifelong learning.

Inquiry involves the active exploration of a question or idea. Driven by curiosity and wonder, we use creative- and critical-thinking skills to engage in questions of personal interest. Through inquiry-based learning, children confront their preconceptions of how the universe works, compare these ideas to what they read in books or learn in an experiment, and then discuss their findings. "Inquiry is central to science learning. When engaging in inquiry, students describe objects and events, ask questions, construct explanations, test those explanations against current scientific knowledge, and communicate their ideas to others. They identify their assumptions, use critical and logical thinking, and consider alternative explanations. In this way, students actively develop their understanding of science by combining scientific knowledge with reasoning and thinking skills" (National Science Education Standards, 1996, p. 2).

The integrated dance and science lessons in this book are organized around the following major areas:

- Physical science
- Life science
- Earth and space science
- Engineering and technology

Each of the four areas contains examples with three to seven detailed dance integration lesson plans that use dance to increase understanding of the science theme. The dance and science learning activities help build enthusiasm and skills for science by personalizing the topic.

Organization of Dance Integration Activities

The integrated lesson plans in this book share a common structure that has been found to be highly effective for lesson development and implementation. The structure is useful to understand before adapting the lessons found in this book, and it is an excellent starting point for developing original lessons. The template begins with the lesson title, the age range the lesson is geared toward, a list of materials needed, and music suggestions.

Essential Question and Enduring Understanding

Each lesson plan poses an essential question that forms the heart of the lesson and an enduring understanding that summarizes the core processes, significant facts, or information that is central to the lesson and has lasting value to the student. These statements frame the big ideas and lasting importance of the lesson plan.

Learning Targets

Once the foundation of the lesson is known, the teacher identifies the learning targets for dance and science or mathematics. Drawn from local curriculums and national standards, the learning target must be clear and attainable.

Here are some examples of dance learning targets:

- Students perform movement at high, middle, and low levels.
- Students learn, identify, and practice various energy qualities.
- Students use locomotor and axial actions to abstractly represent ideas.

Here are some examples of math learning targets:

- Students understand the monetary value of pennies, nickels, and dimes, and they calculate the value of a set amount of coins.
- Students identify two-dimensional shapes.
- Students learn ordinal numbers and connect them to cardinal numbers.

Here are some examples of science learning targets:

- Students recognize that forces act on objects, influencing motion or balance.
- Students learn about magnets, magnetic poles, and the two forces (attract and repel) that magnets can have.
- Students understand the general structure of an atom and a molecule.

Standards

Each integrated lesson plan meets educational standards in both dance and science or dance and mathematics. These standards are listed side by side to illustrate the integration of the content areas, drawing from *Standards for Learning and Teaching Dance in the Arts* (National Dance Education Organization, 2009), *Common Core State Standards for Mathematics* (National Governors Association Center for Best Practices, 2010), and *A Framework for K-12 Science Education* (National Research Council, 2012) which led to the *Next Generation Science Standards* (NGGS Lead States, 2013). As new standards are released, direct connections may be made with these learning activities.

Warm-Up

The lesson always begins with a warm-up that is intended to transition students into learning kinesthetically. Children interact with the space as they stretch and bend and twist their bodies, shaking out the kinks after sitting at desks. Sometimes the lesson plan suggests a specific warm-up that is connected to the theme; other times a general warm-up is suggested. Appendix A provides a selection of warm-up activities suitable for the dance integration class and is referenced within individual lessons.

Build Knowledge

Following the warm-up, the teacher begins building knowledge in dance. The teacher introduces the dance target. A verbal explanation along with a physical demonstration or a visual chart is helpful for understanding the dance terminology, such as, "When we move we can travel in three directions: forward, backward, and sideways." The students practice the dance target in many ways. For example, the teacher may ask students to tiptoe forward, hop backward, slide sideways, gallop forward, jump sideways, crab-walk forward, skip sideways, and slither backward. Although the dance target is *directions*, students use a variety of locomotor movements and levels to learn about it. The teacher verbally reinforces the concept of directions through the movement exploration.

Once students have practiced the dance target, it is helpful to engage in a formative assessment. This often occurs through a room scan in order to answer the question, "Can the students clearly demonstrate the target (e.g., three directions)?" If the teacher feels the students understand, she continues to the next part of the lesson; if not, more reinforcement of the concept is needed. Ideally at least 90 percent of the students understand the dance concept before the teacher introduces the content area.

Connect

This is the exciting moment when the dance concept merges with the content area and full integration occurs. Direct connections are made showing the interrelatedness of the two areas. The challenge for the teacher is to make a natural connection between the two areas.

Finding the Elegant Fit

For dance integration to be effective, a synergy develops between dance and the other content area. When each area is enriched by the other, the experience offers exciting opportunities for learning. How does the teacher find this synergy? As described in *Renaissance in the Classroom* (Burnaford, Arnold, & Weiss, 2001), "An elegant fit implies that separate pieces of the curriculum have been brought together to create a new and more satisfying whole" (p. 24). An integrated curriculum works best when the integration is not forced or artificial. It often takes hard work; planning integrated activities is a rigorous intellectual activity that is also exhilaratingly creative (Botstein, 1998).

How are the elements of dance connected to the mathematics or science theme? The movement teacher first decides whether the mathematics or science theme is most suggestive of body, action, space, time, or energy. Then the specific movement concepts are selected that will support and enhance the mathematics or science theme. This is a good time to review the elements of dance chart (figure 2.1) in order to determine which movement concepts are the most relevant. Sometimes the elegant fit is discussed by a team of educators who engage in an exchange of ideas; other times it's an individual dance specialist who finds this connection. The most important thing is for the teacher to *feel and understand* the connection.

For example, a lesson plan on magnets is connected to the dance concept of body parts and touch as the lesson teaches the concepts of *attract* and *repel* between two *body parts*. A mathematics lesson on angles and lines may lead to dance connections with individual, partner, and group *shapes*. It's important to remember that there is no right answer! There are many ways to connect dance with the learning targets, and each teacher may discover a different connection. This stage of the planning process takes critical and creative thinking. Usually the teacher just knows when a strong connection is made.

Combining Domains

After exploring the knowledge of dance, the teacher then introduces the math or science concept, making a direct connection to the dance concept. This part of the lesson forms the core of the experience. Students practice the combined learning activity, using dance in relation to the other content area. Vocabulary from both content areas is used. For example, in a lesson on the plant life cycle, students use the sizes and levels they've been exploring and relate them to the plant life cycle. Students practice using low levels and small shapes for the seeds, medium levels and shapes for the seedlings, and high levels and big shapes for the strong stems and big leaves. Students dance the pollen moving from flower to flower by moving through the space, gently touching elbows with other dancers.

Another formative assessment occurs now: Can the students demonstrate the correct levels and sizes in the plant life-cycle dance? Can the students answer questions about the plant life-cycle dance? Once again, if 90 percent of the students are making the connection, the teacher can move on to the next part of the lesson. If not, more practice and reinforcement of the integrated themes is needed. If the majority of students do not make the connection, it is important to spontaneously revise the lesson plan so that it involves further practice of the integrated concepts.

Create and Perform

The next part of the lesson is exciting, because it is time for students to take the material they have learned and apply it creatively in dance. The teacher gives the assignment to the whole class and then divides the class into partners or small groups for work time. The activity is designed to allow students to make something original with the integrated content theme and share their understandings with the class. This activity leads easily into performance and discussion.

Consider this example on dancing liquids, solids, and gasses. The second-graders spend 7 minutes working together, creating their dances. The teacher visits each group, keeping the students on task. It is now time to share. One of the second-graders introduces her group's dance to the class: "The state of water we are dancing is ice, which is a solid." The four dancers take their places close together in a tight bunch. Their bodies stiffly move around one another, keeping in close proximity, symbolizing the close molecules found in solids. At the end the students freeze and the audience applauds.

A summative assessment takes place now. The teacher addresses the viewers: "Those were some wonderful dances on molecules! Raise your hand if you can remember the spatial relationship of molecules in ice." A student responds, "Molecules are close together." "Yes," encourages the teacher, "and did the dance show the close spatial relationship throughout *the entire dance*, for *most of the dance*, *part of the dance*, or *not at all?*" This leads into a peer assessment of the performers' success in conveying the dance concept as it relates to molecules. If the class feels the performance *did not show* the close relationship, or only showed it for *most* or *part of the time*, the performers are invited to perform it again, with encouragement to show it *the whole time*. Thus, students learn that clear skills in performing dance are valued. It is important to discuss the dance performance honestly and make connections again to the original learning target.

Review and Reflect

Teacher and student reflection happens throughout the lesson but occurs intentionally at the close of the lesson. The teacher returns to the learning targets with questions that review both the math or science target and the dance target. In this final section of the lesson, students are encouraged to use the vocabulary of both content areas in their discussion.

Many lessons provide an exciting jumping-off point for further study. The Extensions section provides additional ideas to encourage learning through activities in science, math, and language arts and through music, creative dramatics, and visual art.

Making New Connections: Designing Your Own Integrated Lessons

The lesson plans in this book are intended to give specific examples for teaching dance in the math or science class. They feature primary science and mathematics learning topics taught to children aged 5 to 11. However, no book can cover every learning area that is taught in school. This section thus provides a step-by-step template for designing a new lesson plan.

We no longer think of learning as the acquisition of discrete pieces of knowledge. Instead the teacher develops a web of connections among disciplines, ideas, and people. This "requires analysis—pulling things apart to know and name

The dance educators can meet with the teacher to plan lessons.

them—and synthesis—bringing things together" (Grumet, 2007, p. 121). In the end, exciting new connections can be forged through discovering associations that didn't previously exist. The natural place to begin is to examine this time-honored approach and build it from the ground up.

Backward Design

A strong format for designing curriculum is presented in Wiggins and McTighe's (2005) *Understanding by Design*. Backward design is "an approach to designing a curriculum or unit that begins with the end in mind and designs toward that end" (p. 338). The basic approach goes like this:

1. The teacher begins by considering the desired results he hopes to see at the end of the lesson.

2. Then he determines what kind of evidence would enable him to determine that the results were achieved (assessment).

3. Once the results and assessments are clearly specified, the teacher can determine the knowledge, skills, and experiences the student needs in order to get there.

Instead of developing in a linear fashion from start to finish, the learning activity template is developed circuitously, jumping from the beginning to the end and back to the beginning again. This is because the backward lesson plan is best developed in a nonlinear format. Though it may seem unconventional at first, the educator will soon realize its strength. The advantage of the nonlinear format is that the teacher keeps an eye on the desired results he or she hopes to achieve at the end, while designing earlier activities that lead to this goal.

How to Design a New Lesson: A 10-Step Process

Before developing the lesson itself, the teacher determines the following, which form the backbone and grounding for the learning activity.

1. Select a theme for the lesson. This is usually drawn directly from the local and state curriculums in the content areas. (What is the curricular theme in the mathematics or science area? What vocabulary should the children know by the end of the class? What learning areas are students struggling to comprehend? What might be a fun topic to explore

through dance? What area of the curriculum needs to be infused with energy and excitement?)

2. What is the grade or age level? This determines how much depth and breadth will be developed later.

3. What results do you hope to see at the end of the lesson? (What will the students know, understand, or be able to do at the end? What can you realistically hope to accomplish by the end of this lesson or unit?)

4. How will you know the students understand it? What is the most credible evidence that shows what they learned?

5. What are the learning targets in the academic content area (i.e., mathematics, science)? These should be reasonable and attainable.

6. Find the elegant fit. Review the elements of dance chart (figure 2.1) to select dance content that naturally fits. (What learning targets in dance best fit with this content area? Does the topic suggest spatial relationships? Tempos? Levels? Movement qualities?)

7. Design the lesson. Begin by teaching the dance content. Introduce the dance target and build knowledge about it using a series of open-ended movement prompts that are carefully designed to allow learners to become comfortable with the movement material and gain the fluency and vocabulary to verbalize their comprehension.

8. Connect the dance concept with the other curricular topic. Teachers may find it helpful to design a chart that integrates dance with the theme. Once the connection is evident, the teacher develops a logical sequence of movement prompts that connect to the topic and considers the criteria for whether the students understand the two areas.

9. Design a culminating activity that allows the students to demonstrate their understanding of the two curricular areas using dance creation and performance. Partner or small-group assignments help

students make sense of the material for themselves and share their knowledge with the class. This activity is often a celebratory classroom performance followed by discussion.

10. The lesson ends with a question-and-answer reflection about the science or math topic and the dance topic. Specific questions help teachers ascertain students' knowledge and learning of the theme and vocabulary.

Evidence of Learning

Assessment is an important part of every teacher's job. The purpose of assessment is to gather evidence of learning. It is most important for teachers to be clear about what they are teaching, why they are teaching it, and what they want students to gain. This enables the teacher to identify evidence to ascertain *whether and to what extent* students understand the information.

Dance integration is based on mutual concepts and authentic connections shared by multiple disciplines, yet the assessment processes are somewhat unique to the individual disciplines. Science and mathematics are easily assessable via written quizzes and tests, but dance assessment is insufficient through traditional written tests because the skills and knowledge are most readily expressed through action. Assessment in dance takes place daily and is based on students' demonstration of the skills and knowledge of the art form of dance. Instruction in the arts has moved from mere exposure to the arts to in-depth learning of arts skills, thinking styles, and processes.

A common mistake teachers make is in trying to measure too many things, which makes the process highly laborious. Our strongest advice is to make it manageable. The lesson plans in this book intentionally measure a limited number of criteria that the authors feel is workable in a classroom with 25 students.

Student learning in dance occurs in many domains, including physical, cognitive, and social or affective. Often students make great gains in areas other than what is being measured, such as when a student takes a new risk, makes a new creative discovery, finds a new passion, or works imaginatively. Most teachers know it when they see it. It is important to celebrate and recognize this *intangible* learning in dance as well, even when it is not part of the formal assessment criteria.

The integrated dance model uses three types of formal assessments:

1. Teacher assessments using checklists, reverse checklists, and rubrics

2. Peer assessments

3. Self-assessments

Appendix C provides additional assessment tools such as written tests and quizzes, reflective journaling, and short-answer response sheets to further assess student learning.

Teacher Assessments: Checklists

The teacher must be able to determine each child's progress throughout the dance class. A checklist is useful when observing each student and is particularly useful when the response is *yes* or *no* or *demonstrates* versus *doesn't demonstrate* (table 2.1). The checklist is oriented toward students performing a task, not the quality of their performance. The lesson plans in chapters 4 through 12 invite the teacher to develop a checklist for specific activities as a summative assessment. Using the questions provided, teachers may make a simple device to check each student's understanding.

Teacher Assessments: Reverse Checklists

According to Seattle dance educator Eric Johnson (2003), the reverse checklist, or room scan, is the most frequent form of assessment in dance; it happens naturally throughout the class. Dance teachers are trained to observe the class and prompt students to express the behaviors and outcomes they are seeking. By scanning the room, the teacher knows who is not performing the desired task. Serving as a generalized assessment, the teacher is able to ascertain whether the majority of the class understands. The room scan allows the teacher to pace the flow of the class, deciding whether it's time to introduce new ideas and move the lesson along or to reteach the material. A room scan serves as the formative assessment tool in the lesson plans in this book. Going beyond a casual view of the class, it involves moving through the classroom, observing students' responses, asking questions, and carefully observing the students. While scanning the room, the teacher asks herself, "Do the majority of students understand the concept of _____? Can they clearly demonstrate _____?"

Teacher Assessments: Rubrics

Rubrics consist of performance characteristics with points or scores that indicate the degree to which the objectives were met. To be most effec-

Table 2.1   Sample Checklist for 8- to 10-Year-Olds

Name	Identifies even and uneven tempos	Accurately performs movement to a steady beat
John	X	
Steve		
Amanda	X	
Luz	X	X
Zachary	X	X
Mei		

tive, the rubric is introduced at the beginning of the culminating activity so that the students understand the performance criteria before they begin. The rubric rating scale is used when students are performing at a more complex level, and the scale uses at least three degrees of performance. When developing a rubric, the more detail that is included, the better, provided it is designed to clearly identify a gradation of performance levels and doesn't restrict learning indicators. The points or numbers associated with each dimension (table 2.2) enable students to make subsequent drafts of their creations, revising them until they are of the highest quality (Johnson, 2003). Specific rubrics are provided in selected lesson plans in chapters 4 through 12 as summative assessments.

Peer Assessments

An important part of dance integration involves students watching one another and learning to accurately assess one another's work. Peer as-

sessments have several benefits for students, who

- learn what it means to conform to a standard and bring it to the highest quality,
- develop skills for articulating their observations clearly and constructively, and
- gain opportunities to deepen their understanding of the learning targets through observing their peers.

Students are directed to focus their comments on the target learning areas and avoid any value judgments. For example, "I'm seeing three different energy qualities" is a useful observation, whereas "I don't like their movement" is a value judgment. Peer assessments may be short checklists or simple rubrics, or they may consist of a show of fingers that indicate the performance level observed (table 2.3). Examples of peer assessments are included in selected lesson plans in chapters 4 through 12.

Table 2.2   Sample Dance Integration Rubric for 5- to 7-Year-Olds

Kindergarten class: reach and plant life cycle				
Name	4—Student demonstrated specified reach and plant stage clearly through the entire dance.	3—Student demonstrated specified reach and plant stage clearly but not through the entire dance.	2—Student's reach or plant stage was not clear.	1—Student's dance was different than what was planned.
Anna	X			
Rose	X			
Graham		X		
Levi		X		
Ryan		X		
Shawna	X			
Isa	X			
Brennan	X			
Shohei	X			
James			X	
Brody			X	

Table 2.3   **Sample Peer Assessment**

"Now that you have watched this small group perform their geometric shapes dance, please let us know how clearly they performed their intended geometric shape. With your hand in the air, hold up 4, 3, 2, or 1 finger to describe their performance."			
4	3	2	1
Clearly and visibly showed their geometric shape throughout the dance.	Showed their geometric shape but did not sustain it throughout the dance.	Geometric shapes were not entirely clear.	Geometric shapes were different than the ones they had planned.

Self-Assessments

Self-assessments are similar to peer assessments in that students are encouraged to reflect accurately and honestly on their own performance, learning to see their continued efforts and drafts as useful and leading to positive change (table 2.4). Ultimately students become empowered as learners as they view their ongoing efforts as leading to success. Examples of self-assessments are included in selected lesson plans in chapters 4 through 12.

Table 2.4   **Sample Self-Assessment**

The strength of my performance was	I used a high level and a curving pathway clearly throughout the dance.
One thing I would like to do next time to improve my performance is	watch the other movers out of the corner of my eye so I know when it is time to freeze at the end.

Summary

The integrated dance class uses dance to teach math and science *and* uses math and science to reinforce dance. The class is carefully designed to maintain the integrity of both disciplines. Drawn from local standards, knowledge of the basics of learning in science and mathematics leads to lesson planning that is thoughtful and inclusive. The movement concepts found in the elements of dance provide the link to the learning targets in math or science. The template for an integrated lesson plan ensures that the lesson progression meets the target learning areas developed for the two content areas. Once the teacher finds the elegant fit between dance and the learning area, students are guided through a process that involves exploration, synthesis, performance, and assessment. Teacher and student assessments are used to evaluate student development and measure student achievement.

References

Botstein, L. (1998). What role for the arts? In W.C. Ayers & I.L. Miller (Eds.), *A light in dark times: Maxine Greene and the unfinished conversation* (pp. 62-70). New York: Teachers College Press.

Burnaford, G., Arnold, A., & Weiss, C. (Eds.). (2001). *Renaissance in the classroom: Arts integration and meaningful learning.* Chicago Arts Partnerships in Education. Hillsdale, NJ: Erlbaum.

Dow, P. (1999). Why inquiry? A historical and philosophical commentary. www.nsf.gov/pubs/2000/nsf99148/ch_1.htm.

Georgia Department of Education. (July, 2011). *Mathematics Common Core Georgia Performance Standards.* http://www.dekalb.k12.ga.us/www/documents/news-and-info/calculus/description-and-standards.pdf

Grumet, M. (2007). Third things: The wondrous progeny of arts integration. *Journal of Artistic and Creative Education, 1*(1).

Johnson, E. (2003). Sharing your art form. Unpublished workshop materials.

National Academy of Sciences. (2007). *Taking Science to School: Learning and Teaching Science in Grades K-8.* http://www.nap.edu/openbook.php?record_id=11625&page=51

National Dance Education Organization. (2009). *Standards for learning and teaching dance in the arts: Ages 5-18.* Silver Springs, MD: Author.

National Governors Association Center for Best Practices, Council of Chief State School Officers. (2010). *Common core state standards for mathematics.* www.corestandards.org/assets/CCSSI_Math%20Standards.pdf Washington, DC: Author.

National Research Council. (2012). *A framework for K-12 science education: Practices, crosscutting concepts, and core ideas.* Washington, DC: National Academies Press.

National Science Education Standards. (1996). The National Academies Press. http://www.nap.edu/openbook.php?record_id=4962&page=2

NGSS Lead States. 2013. *Next Generation Science Standards: For States, By States.* Washington, DC: The National Academies Press.

Wiggins, G., & McTighe, J. (2005). *Understanding by design.* Alexandria, VA: ASCD.

Perpich Center for Arts Education. www.mcae.k12.mn.us/

3

PEDAGOGY: ENLIVENING THE CLASSROOM

Third-grade teacher Brad Maloney is preparing to teach an integrated math–dance activity. His students have been studying bar graphs, learning to visually display data on charts and graphs. He's excited to teach the math lesson using human bar graphs to help students understand the concept kinesthetically. During recess he tapes lines on the floor to represent the horizontal axis. He has collected construction paper and found some upbeat reggae music to accompany the creation of bar graphs. He is trying to estimate how much space he'll need in the room and whether he'll need to move the bookcase. Brad is thinking through the lesson and preparing to teach.

Dance integration transforms the classroom into a space similar to a dance studio and theater, resulting in the learning of new artistic behaviors. This chapter provides practical, hands-on teaching approaches that are useful for dance integration classes. Educators discover how to convert the school environment into a space suitable for creative expression through dance, including ideas for transitioning the space and preparing students for the dance class. Musical accompaniment adds to the dance experience in immeasurable ways and suggestions are provided for building a diverse music library. Classroom management techniques that are specific to dance provide the teacher with usable approaches for maintaining a positive learning environment. A discussion about successfully pairing and grouping students for collaborative work is provided, along with approaches to adaptations for students with special needs. Techniques for dance making and sharing enhance the integrated dance experience artistically and enable the teacher to help students develop into critical thinkers and viewers.

Transforming the Classroom Into the Dance Studio

A few easy classroom changes will greatly enhance the dance experience. Although rearranging the classroom may be temporarily chaotic, the benefits far outweigh the drawbacks. Desks and chairs are pushed aside in order to create a large open space in the classroom. The small act of moving desks and chairs aside is transformational; identifying the classroom as a dance space alters students' experience of the space, leading to new kinesthetic forms of self-expression. With a few simple parameters, teachers can encourage students to participate in a smooth classroom makeover into the dance space: "Friends, in just a moment you'll have 8 counts to push your desk and chair to the edges of the room. By count 8 you'll be standing quietly by your desk. Ready? Begin."

Gymnasiums, lunchrooms, multipurpose rooms, empty classrooms, and libraries are commonly used as dance spaces in schools. Because students are often asked to sit, kneel, or lie down, a clean floor is important. Professional dance studios are built with sprung floors that provide soft, smooth surfaces specially designed for dance. The floors are protected and street shoes are left at the door. Ideally the floor will be compatible with movement; however, in schools dance is often taught on tile, carpet, or concrete. Tile can be cold to lie on, carpet can be nubby, and concrete is a hard, unforgiving surface for dance, but teachers must work with the floor they have. If concrete is the only alternative for the dance class, it is recommended that minimal jumping and leaping take place to avoid injury.

To prepare for dance, students remove their shoes and socks and store them out of the way. Moving with bare feet helps students feel the floor more fully, allowing for more sensitive and nuanced movement. There are fewer injuries when children are grounded; they are connected to the earth and have a better understanding of their own boundaries. Removing shoes also creates a safer environment for small bodies moving in close proximity. Bare feet are ideal on a clean wood floor, but for cold floors and carpets, students can wear socks.

In a large space such as a gymnasium, the teacher may set up boundaries to contain the dancing area to a manageable size. Benches, cones, and even a row of shoes will create a boundary that defines the movement space. Simply set up the boundary and remind students where the movement space begins and ends: "Let's identify our dancing space. Our dancing space goes from the blackboard all the way over to the bookshelves. We won't be moving behind the bookshelves or over by the windows. We'll stay in the big, open area that is our dance space. Find your own personal spot in the dance space and sit with your legs crossed."

When defining the dancing space, a central front focus may be established. Teachers can display charts and pictures on a bulletin board or display the classroom etiquette rules at the front of the space. Music can be played from the front of the room as well, which creates a central location for the teacher. Although the front area is used for displays, the teacher walks throughout

Identifying the classroom as a dance space alters students' experience of the space.

To prepare for dance, students remove their shoes and store them out of the way.

the space during students' explorations, bringing a 360-degree experience to the space. Students are encouraged to use the whole space while moving in order to fully experience the changing configurations in the room.

Transitioning to the Dance Class

The teacher makes a thoughtful transition from the previous activity to the dance class. Whenever possible, students prepare in advance for the dance class: "We're going to take a short bathroom break and when we return we'll walk to the multipurpose room to dance the water cycle."

To complete the transition, students are led through a movement warm-up. Warming up is a tradition practiced by dancers around the world, and it serves several purposes. Designed to get the

kinks out after sitting at desks, a warm-up generally includes stretching, bending, and twisting activities led by the teacher. Students ease gently into the integrated dance class both mentally and physically, transitioning from seated learning to active learning. The warm-up intentionally puts students in their bodies and encourages students to pay attention to themselves, moving with control, intentionality, and sensitivity. Ideally a warm-up integrates the body and mind, allowing for fuller cognitive understandings and the ability to embed the learning kinesthetically. The warm-up also prepares the students for what's coming later in the integrated dance class.

Some teachers develop a single warm-up that they repeat each day, serving as a ritual that begins the class. Others design the warm-up around the learning targets. A typical warm-up in a school class lasts 1 to 5 minutes. Some effective warm-up and relaxation activities are included in appendix A.

Teaching Tools

Teaching dance differs from teaching other disciplines because it's active, dynamic, and experiential, requiring some pedagogical practices unique to dance. Those who are new to teaching dance will learn effective ways to incorporate music into the mathematics or science theme. A roomful of active, moving bodies requires specific classroom management approaches designed to maximize student learning and minimize injuries and off-task behaviors. The culminating activity in the integrated dance class usually involves pairing students or placing them in small groups. This can result in a variety of group dynamics, often requiring assistance from the teacher. Rather than simply giving the students the directions and letting them work for a length of time, the teacher continually provides feedback to the class. The teaching tools in dance are easy to use with a little forethought.

Musical Accompaniment

In an ideal world, all students would dance to live music; however, that is unrealistic for the integrated classroom. Recorded music greatly enhances the dance experience. Music provides motivation, sets a tone, and supports the movers. Dancers often speak of being moved by the music; it helps them to experience the movement more deeply.

Using Music in Class

Generally the teacher gives verbal directions to the class without music playing, setting up the next part of the experience before sound is added. The music starts when students begin to dance and stops when the dance ends. However, sometimes the teacher finds it useful to prompt students while the music is playing, necessitating a volume that allows students to hear verbal instructions. Thus the music is used in relation to the particular needs of the dance experience. The teacher adjusts the volume accordingly.

Music for dance integration is generally used in three ways.

1. *As support and enrichment.* Used as a backdrop to the class or to provide a baseline environment, music can enhance students' dance experience. Select music that does not have lyrics or draw attention and focus.

2. *As an audible component of the movement (e.g., 4/4 or 3/4 meter).* Select music with a strong downbeat so students can easily count the musical phrases.

3. *As texture, quality, or tempo.* Select music based on its mood (e.g., upbeat, pleasant, reflective), dynamic shifts (e.g., soft to loud, sparse to busy), or tempo (e.g., fast, slow).

Building a Collection of Suitable Music

Many musical genres are suitable for the integrated dance class. Teachers may consult their own music libraries and set up a creative movement playlist to use in the classroom. Instrumental music (without words) is most frequently used in creative dance classes. Many online music sources (e.g., Amazon, iTunes) allow you to browse samples before purchase. When in doubt, talk with a musician! Appendix B contains music selections that fall under the categories of contemplative, pleasant, and driving musical qualities. For teachers interested in building their own libraries, here are several useful Internet music sources.

- Stereomood (www.stereomood.com) allows the teacher to search for a specific mood or tone. Searches are based on the quality of the music desired, such as dreamy, calm, energetic, party, jazzy, tango, and so on. Consult this site to collect and purchase music for the dance playlist.

- Pandora (www.pandora.com) allows the teacher to search for specific music genres, such as instrumental, classical, environmental, rock, blues, jazz, and new age.

- Google music (https://play.google.com) requires the user to sign in with a password. Once logged in, the teacher can search genres such as jazz, blues, Latin, reggae, ambient, electronica, and world music.

- iTunes (www.itunes.com) is a free application that is a popular source for purchasing music. The app allows the user to hear a selection before purchasing.

Listen to each chosen song in its entirety and imagine how it fits with the movement concept. Generally music without lyrics is best because there's no competing narrative. A note of warning: Hip-hop is engaging, upbeat, and appealing to young people, but it often includes inappropriate lyrics. When using music with lyrics, be sure to preview the songs carefully.

Classroom Management Techniques

Students deserve a safe environment where the rules and expectations of the class are clear. Because children aged 5 to 11 spend a great deal of time seated at desks, when they are invited to move they can take advantage of the opportunity and act out. According to Seattle dance educator Eric Johnson (2008), there are four causes of off-task behavior:

1. The student is tired, hungry, or distracted (physical cause).

2. The student is angry, upset, or excited (emotional cause).

3. The student is focused on friends (relational cause).

4. The student doesn't understand the instructions or the material is uninteresting, too easy, or too difficult (instructional cause).

It is the teacher's job to manage the class and keep the students engaged and empowered as learners. Ideally the teacher clearly communicates the classroom expectations from the start and repeats these rules frequently. From the first class on, the dance class rules are listed and discussed, with students joining in the discussion of why the rules are important and how they are designed to lead to student success. Rules and

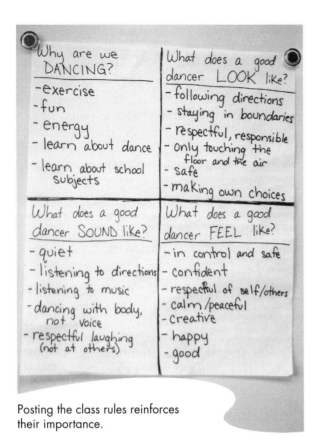

Posting the class rules reinforces their importance.

expectations are repeated each class thereafter until no longer necessary. Posting the class rules provides visual support.

For children who are new to dance, it can be helpful to have a discussion about the experience of a dancer. In the first class, the teacher can ask, "What does a good dance learner look like? What does a good dance learner sound like? What does a good dance learner feel like?" Students begin by envisioning the role of the dancer in the studio and the entire class sets the criteria. As students brainstorm, the collective ideas and classroom expectations are listed on a large chart. In this way the students help develop the class rules that are used in the weeks and months ahead. This activity also gives the teacher the opportunity to overcome stereotypes that students may have about dance. For example, if students think dance is primarily for girls, or if they only know dance as ballet with dancers wearing tutus, the teacher can lead a discussion to broaden their understanding and more effectively set up the experience they're embarking on.

It can be helpful to envision the ideal classroom environment. Students learn most readily when they feel their teachers like them and care about

them. The integrated dance teacher seeks to establish an atmosphere that is positive, encouraging, fair, and responsive. To accomplish this, the teacher develops an engaging and motivating tone of voice. Time is budgeted appropriately so that students have ample time to complete each step of the lesson, ensuring that other distractions do not keep the class from progressing through the lesson.

The teacher keeps her instructions clear and brief. She manages interpersonal difficulties immediately and deals with inappropriate behaviors as (or even before) they begin. When needed, the directions are repeated, simplified, or reframed. The teacher is constantly moving about and scanning the room with her eyes, remaining cognizant of how the class is going. The eye will almost always pick up the one off-task behavior! It's also important to not overlook the other 19 students who are following directions beautifully. Redirecting students, clarifying the directions, and, when needed, stopping the class and completely refocusing the students will help keep the class progressing successfully (Johnson, 2008).

Three classroom management reminders at the beginning of every class (and as needed throughout the class) will prepare students for success:

1. "Remember our freeze signal? You get to freeze in a fantastic shape and hold it completely still."

2. "We touch only the floor and the air, unless we are asked to touch something or someone."

3. "Dancers move with their bodies, not their voices."

Pairing and Grouping Students

Integrated dance lessons enable students to work with a partner or in a small group. In addition to learning math, science, and dance, students also learn a highly important social skill: group dynamics. Working with one's peers provides several benefits as students learn to listen to and respect others' ideas and work collaboratively. The successful teacher discusses the group process with the class. Sometimes working in a group is challenging; other times it's rewarding. This is true for both children and adults! Throughout the integrated dance unit, students will work with every other student in the class in several configurations. An effective group process involves listening to one another's ideas, respecting each person in the group, and trusting one another. The underlying premise is that the whole is greater than the sum of its parts. Students learn that collaboration means they sometimes let their ideas go and try something new.

Benefits of Working in Groups

Groups enable children to form bonds with peers in a structured environment. They learn that people have diverse thinking processes while also recognizing that one's peers share similar problems and concerns. Children exhibit a wide range of cognitive, emotional, and interpersonal skills in groups. Effective group interaction is a lifelong developmental process in which people improve their interaction skills.

Effective Grouping of Students

Young children aged 5 to 6 begin by working with a single partner. At ages 6 to 7 and older, they may be placed in groups of three and four to work together. Students' maturity and developmental readiness determine when they are ready for group work. As most teachers know, some students work better with their peers than others. There are no specific rules for grouping

students together and many approaches can be used. Asking students to count off in fours will quickly create four random groups mixed with boys and girls at all academic levels. Another approach is to pass out color-coded cards and form groups based on the color each student receives.

With classrooms consisting of a wide range of students with special needs, some teachers prefer to handpick groups, combining students who will work well together. Some teachers place lower-functioning students with higher-functioning students to help the lower-functioning students move ahead, while others feel that is detrimental and slows the learning of the advanced students. Some teachers match students with peers at similar levels. For students who tend to dominate in groups, grouping them together encourages them to work successfully with others and prevents them from simply taking over. There are no specific rules for choosing groups; teachers are encouraged to use their best judgment, and when a problem arises, they can use it as a teachable moment.

Secrets to Successful Group Work

When setting up the group project, the teacher needs to be clear and specific to ensure each stu-

Working in groups can be challenging but rewarding.

dent participates. Group work can be challenging, and it works best when the task is clearly delineated for students. Writing the directions on the board is helpful so students understand their tasks. Another approach is to ask each student to create one part of a four-part dance and then teach it to the group. This allows each student to have a creative role in the final dance. It's also helpful to ask the students to begin by sitting in a circle and describing their ideas to the group without deciding anything. This gives each student an opportunity to be heard. Once everyone has weighed in, the merits of the ideas can be discussed and a plan can be formed.

Giving Feedback to Students

Throughout the movement class, the teacher delivers ongoing feedback to students in the form of side coaching, both while students are moving and as a summative response after the dance ends. *Side coaching* is a technique whereby the teacher offers continual suggestions or comments while the students are moving. The students receive descriptive feedback about their ongoing work in the class. The most effective language a teacher can use is clear, vivid, and direct, such as, "This group was dancing so close together without touching, and everyone was moving at a quick tempo! And we all know it's difficult to move quickly while close together, right? Raise your hand if you can tell me what dancers need to remember to perform quickly and close together."

The goal of feedback is to enable the movers to better understand how they are interacting with the dance objectives. Through using the movement vocabulary, students begin to recognize that they are demonstrating the desired objectives, finding personal variations within the movement language, and interacting with their peers appropriately. Thus the teacher provides a mirror, realistically reflecting the work back to the students. When students are not paying attention or appear uncommitted, the teacher gives feedback as well, encouraging them to focus and try harder. When students are acting silly, they are quickly encouraged to take the assignment seriously, identifying other groups who show that commitment. It's extremely important that students know that their peers' less desirable behaviors will be recognized as unacceptable and that they will be asked to improve their behavior. Feedback to students is always honest and direct,

giving the students opportunities to change their behavior and grow to meet the next challenge. Teachers should provide feedback and direction throughout the entire lesson, with few gaps in verbal instruction.

Here are some more tips for teaching dance integration:

- Be encouraging, positive, and enthusiastic.
- Bring your own body into your teaching! Move with your students.
- Be willing to experiment with your students.
- Remain adaptable throughout your lesson plan. Let the class evolve as it needs to.
- Repeat the learning targets frequently so the point of the lesson is clear to students.
- Stay committed to both the mathematics or science objectives and the dance objectives.
- Focus your attention on the students doing well.
- Ask clearly for the behaviors you want, even if it means repeating the requests over and over again.
- Treat your students as artists. Refer to them as *dancers*.
- Acknowledge your students' development as dancers, choreographers, and performers.
- Allow your students to give you feedback, and listen to them.

Dance Making and Choreography

The Create and Perform section of the integrated dance class allows students to engage in dance making. "The term *dance-making* refers to an organized series of shapes, movements, phrases, studies, or complete dances created by students" (Kaufmann, 2006, p. 39). Daily lessons enable students to demonstrate their learning by creating original dances that explore the learning targets. The dances enable students to take the science and math vocabulary and play with it in new ways, resulting in the creation of a dance: an artistic product. Applying the material deepens understanding and leads to long-term retention. Curricular dances are often selected for end-of-year performances and informances (informational demonstrations) for parents because they are such effective modes of performance review and sharing.

Beyond Pantomime: Principles of Abstraction

An intentional distinction is made between dance, which is abstract, and pantomime, which is literal. Creative dance is grounded in principles of abstraction. In dance, the goal is to find a unique and artistic expression of an idea, as opposed to performing a stereotypical representation of an idea. When students create dances about animals, it can sometimes lead to pantomime. For example, when studying butterflies, the dance teacher provides prompts to lead students beyond simply flapping their arms like wings. Words such as *flutter lightly*, *dip*, *glide*, *fold*, and *unfold* describe the movement of butterflies, leading students to a deeper understanding of the species and a more in-depth creative movement expression. Similarly, when studying animal adaptations, students are encouraged to go beyond the stereotypical movements of elephant trunks, lion claws, and fish fins to a movement study that involves analysis and specificity using the elements of dance.

Performing Dance

One of the lifelong skills learned in the school dance class involves becoming comfortable in front of others. Dance integration provides opportunities in virtually every class to perform in front of an audience of peers. These performance opportunities are informal, yet they serve as the culmination of a learning activity and provide a way for students to share their understanding with others.

Performing teaches students to be fully in the moment. They learn to be attentive and responsive to other dancers, listen to musical cues, maintain concentration, and attend kinesthetically to the requirements of the dance. Regular performing opportunities also teach students to trust their own ideas and commit to them fully.

In addition to the skills learned through sharing their dances, students learn the value of the hard work that leads to a performance. They understand the importance of the entire process, beginning with creation, leading to fine-tuning and rehearsing, and culminating in performance.

They become better at interacting cooperatively with others, which builds respect and admiration for their peers' special gifts. Students find themselves grouped in diverse combinations and end up working closely with many individuals. Students learn to remain quiet and orderly as they wait for their turn to perform, underscoring the importance of each person's role in the whole.

Audience etiquette is reinforced: sitting still and showing respect, watching quietly, and clapping at the end. Thoughtful, informed audience members develop when students are invited to look for something specific in the dance; for example, "Make your hands into a fist. Every time you see the dancers stretch out into their far-reach kinesphere, give a thumbs-up." Young children are often more attentive when they're given a hands-on task in addition to watching the performance, assuming it doesn't take the focus away from the performers. Ultimately dance performances illuminate the uniqueness of each person, celebrating individuality and reinforcing both the commonalities and differences among people.

Reflecting on Dance

Following the performance, students learn the skills necessary to positively critique their peers' dances, describing what they felt was most successful and providing suggestions for a possible next draft. Observing one another's performance builds dance literacy and critical thinking. It celebrates diversity as students learn to appreciate dance expressions that are different from their own.

Oftentimes teachers ask specific questions after viewing a dance. These questions are useful for discussion, journaling, and comprehensive writing assignments for ages 7 through 11.

- Describe how the dance began. What happened next? How did it end?

- Describe a memorable moment in the dance. Why was it memorable?

- What did you appreciate most about the choreography (or the performance)?

- Describe what levels you saw in the dance (or reach space, locomotor movements, axial movement, and so on depending on the learning target)?

- How did the dance use the science or mathematics theme?

- If one part of the dance were to be repeated or emphasized, what would you want to see again?
- What suggestions would you give the choreographers for revision? What would these revisions accomplish? Why would you like to see these changes?

Dance is an ephemeral art form; it exists in the moment and then is gone. In order to preserve a dance, teachers may record it, which allows the experience to be viewed again and celebrated. Watching a video recording of their dance lets students critique their own work from a distance. It also provides an excellent way to build a portfolio and allows students to view the progression of their work over time.

Sharing With Parents

It is important to notify parents about the integrated dance classes their children are experiencing. Because many parents are not familiar with dance integration, we recommend sending a note home with information about the instructional approach and the active learning experiences and inviting them to observe the class in action. Teachers can also send home short slips of paper after dance class with reflections about specific lessons in order to spark conversations between parents and children. For example, each child can fill in the blanks and take home a slip of paper with the following: "I danced the water cycle today! I learned _____ and enjoyed _____. Ask me about my group's dance that we performed today in class!" In addition, parents can be invited to attend final performances to see the creative work in action.

Adapting for Special Populations

Today's classrooms consist of students with a wide range of abilities, including students with special needs. Students with mixed abilities can provide additional challenges to classroom teachers who are already juggling many curricular and assessment mandates. The dance class offers excellent opportunities for students with diverse learning approaches, because creative movement emphasizes individuality and personal expression. All students, including those with disabilities, have the right to participate in the integrated dance experience. Ideally the teacher identifies the student's abilities and discovers the instructional adaptations most useful to the individual student. Students in today's classrooms exhibit a wide range of skills and levels, from basic to developing to emerging to accomplished. The teacher provides some simple adaptations and supports so students at all levels can be included in the dance integration class (Kaufmann, 2006).

- *Students with learning disabilities and attention-deficit/hyperactivity disorder (ADHD)* respond well to physical demonstrations, tactile manipulations, peer or teacher supports, and simplified auditory instructions.
- *Students with developmental disabilities* benefit from simplified verbal instructions and physical and tactile demonstrations that are visual. Reminders about personal space boundaries are useful. Students are often uninhibited about dancing and highly responsive to music. They may be challenged to make connections between the science and mathematics integration with dance. Frequently repeating the learning targets will reinforce interdisciplinary curricular learning.
- *Students with hearing impairments* are often highly skilled dancers with well-developed motor skills. Ideally a sign language interpreter will convey directions to the students, or the teacher may wear an amplification device. Students will rely heavily on visual examples. Teachers should attempt to stand directly in front of students in order to facilitate lip reading.
- *Wheelchair users* are encouraged to modify the movements in relation to their abilities. Students are encouraged to move whatever body parts they can and to make substitutions whenever necessary. High, middle, and low levels are viewed from the position of the student in the chair. Because chairs cannot move sideways, the student may reach toward the sides to demonstrate those directions. Teachers, aides, and peers can provide assistance to the dancer in a wheelchair.

Sample Parent Letter

Dear Parents,

I am pleased to serve as your child's creative dance teacher at _____ School! My classes integrate dance into the core curriculum. The goal is to get students excited about math and science and improve student learning using active, kinesthetic approaches to learning.

We believe that students don't need to be seated at desks to learn; in fact, they learn more easily when they are moving! So, we push the chairs and desks aside and bring the curriculum alive through intentional learning approaches that connect the right and left hemispheres of the brain. Dance integration personalizes the curriculum and develops creative, thoughtful, motivated people.

Our Dance Curriculum

Students learn basic skills in creative dance (locomotor and axial movements, levels, pathways, shapes, rhythms and tempo, and movement qualities). They have numerous opportunities to dance individually, together with a partner, and in small groups. Students make solo, duet, and group dances and share them with their peers during informal classroom performances. They also learn to be critical viewers of dance, responding to their peers and talking about choreography using dance vocabulary. Our curriculum enables students to become *dance literate* through moving, choreographing, viewing, and responding.

Dance Integration With Math or Science

Daily activities contain clearly identified learning targets in both dance and math or science. These objectives meet educational standards and contain embedded assessments to help us evaluate student learning.

Class begins with short warm-up, and then we introduce knowledge about one area of dance (e.g., high, middle, and low levels or straight, curved, and angular shapes). Next we introduce a connection to math or science, such as whole numbers or fractions (math) or atoms and molecules or the moon phases (science). I guide students through movement experiences that connect to the content area. Now the students are encouraged to play with the movement material and math or science content in their own way, creating something new that synthesizes both the dance and math or science learning targets. Students share their dances with one another and we discuss what we are seeing using both dance and math or science vocabulary. The classes are enlivening, artistic, and educational.

I am pleased to have the opportunity to work with your child and am always interested in learning more about my students, especially things that will help me better meet their needs and assist in their development. Please feel free to contact me during the school year with any information you think would help me do this (_____ phone number; _____ e-mail address). Finally, you are always welcome to observe the dance integration class to see it in action!

Signed,

• *Students with emotional disabilities* often benefit from a classroom aide to keep them on a positive track and to facilitate positive partner and group interactions. Students are encouraged to express themselves nonverbally in an appropriate manner. With plenty of individual support, the dance class can be a highly effective place to learn appropriate expression.

Summary

A student's experience of the classroom is enlivened when it becomes a dance studio, an artistic space experienced with bare feet. The transition into active learning begins with a movement warm-up and uses teaching tools suitable for dance. Music is chosen to enhance the experience and classroom management techniques are used to support a group of active movers. Respect for other thinkers and movers develops as students practice working with a partner or a small group. Specific feedback to students helps them understand how they are interacting with the desired learning objectives. Regular dance-making and performing opportunities allow students to demonstrate their artistic understanding of the daily theme. Finally, students learn to discuss and write about their own and others' dances, building critical-thinking skills and learning about the process of revision. The dance integration class provides equal opportunities for students with mixed abilities through adaptations designed to enable each student to succeed.

References

Johnson, E. (2008). Sharing your art form. Unpublished workshop materials.

Kaufmann, K. (2006). *Inclusive creative movement and dance*. Champaign, IL: Human Kinetics.

PART

II

DANCE AND MATHEMATICS LEARNING ACTIVITIES

4

COUNTING AND CARDINALITY

*L*earning to count and understand cardinality is an important developmental achievement and is a student's first introduction to mathematics. This chapter provides three lessons designed for students aged 5 to 7. First, locomotor and axial movements are used to teach counting to 100 by ones and tens. Then students learn to compare whole numbers between 1 and 10 and identify numbers that are greater than, less than, and equal to one another through dancing a variety of levels in space. Finally, ordinal numbers are reinforced as students learn that choreographers develop sequences of movements. Each lesson enables students to share their learning through original dances that use the dance language and the counting and cardinality content in an integrated format.

COUNTING

Counting is the most essential skill for learning in mathematics. It is often used in other content areas such as science and dance.

AGES
5-6

LEVEL
Basic

MATERIALS
- Number chart (table 4.1) and whiteboard
- Pieces of paper with a number between 1 and 20 and a movement written on the front (vary the number and type of movement on each paper; make one paper for every student)

MUSIC
Contemplative selection (see appendix B)

ESSENTIAL QUESTION
Why do we count numbers?

ENDURING UNDERSTANDING
Counting finds out the answer to the question, "How many?"

	Dance	Mathematics
Learning target	Students become familiar with various locomotor and axial movements.	Students practice counting and cardinality.
Evidence of student learning	The student demonstrates a specified movement.	The student demonstrates a specified number of movements.
Dance elements and mathematics vocabulary	Locomotor movements (skip, step, jump, march, hop, gallop), axial movements (twist, sway, reach, stretch, kick, balance, turn)	Numbers 1-100, ones, tens

(continued)

	Dance	Mathematics
Standards	• Demonstrate and identify non-locomotor or axial movements. • Demonstrate and identify loco-motor movements (*Standards for Learning and Teaching Dance in the Arts*, p. 23).	• Count to 100 by ones and by tens (*Common Core State Standards for Mathematics*, K.CC.1). • Understand the relationship between numbers and quantities; connect counting to cardinality (*Common Core State Standards for Mathematics*, K.CC.4).

Warm-Up

"Please make a circle as a class with all dancers standing. We are going to send a movement around the circle. Each person will do the same movement that I do and only do it once. Immediately after the person next to you finishes the movement, it is your turn to do the movement. We will move quickly around the circle, practicing taking turns, standing frozen while we are waiting, and observing others as they move. I will go first. When the movement goes all the way around the circle and comes back to me, then I will change the movement."

Begin with a jump and go counterclockwise around the circle with each student doing one jump. After each student has jumped, change the movement to a gentle kick. Continue with three more movements, such as a turn, jumping jack, head circle, or wiggle. Remind students to wait until the person before them has finished before they go and that each student only does the movement one time. The last time around, direct the students to count off: The teacher says "One," the next person says "Two," then "Three," and so forth. At the end say, "We have _____ people in class right now."

Build Knowledge

"Dancers can do many different movements. Some are movements that stay in one place. Imagine you paint an *X* on the floor—*X* marks the spot. When you do actions that are axial, you stay over your *X*. Locomotor actions move throughout the dancing space. Locomotor has the word *motor* in it. Imagine that you have a motor that moves you to a new place, just like a car."

EXPLORE AXIAL AND LOCOMOTOR MOVEMENTS

"Let's practice some axial movements. Are we going to leave our imaginary *X*? Not at all! Begin by stretching your body in a variety of ways. Make sure you are respecting your body; nothing should hurt! Now, twist to look behind you. Can you twist in other ways? What about bending? How many different ways can you bend your body? Now let's kick. Only kick the air, not anything or anyone around you. Now we are going to turn. Please turn slowly and in control. Stop before you get dizzy. Remember that because we are axial, as we turn, we will stay over our imaginary *X*. Is balancing axial? Yes, balancing is axial—it stays on your imaginary *X*. Try a new balance. Can you balance in a new way? Now, let's sway. Swaying is a soft side-to-side rocking action. Make sure to stay over your imaginary *X*.

"Now we are going to do some locomotor movements. Are you going to leave your *X*? Yes! Watch out for other dancers and make sure to look for the empty spaces between other dancers. Walk through the room. This is a locomotor movement you do every day! Now skip through the room. Hop on one foot. Can you hop on your other foot? Let's gallop. Use your eyes and make sure to keep moving into those empty spaces! Jump on two feet through the dancing space. March with high knees."

FORMATIVE ASSESSMENT

Room scan: Can the student perform various axial and locomotor movements?

Connect

Ask all but one student to sit down. Tell the standing student to jump slowly 10 times. "We are going to count how many jumps he (or she) does." With the class, count the 10 jumps aloud. "This time, I am going to count the jumps by myself. Watch to see if I am counting accurately. The dancer is going to count the number of his jumps in his head and try to not listen to my counting." As the student jumps 10 times again, count much faster than he is jumping, therefore ending with a greater number. Ask the class, "Did I count the correct number of jumps? No, I did not count the jumps; I was counting faster than he was jumping. I need to make sure that when I count how many jumps, I count one number for one jump."

COUNTING 100 MOVEMENTS

"We are going to do 100 movements! We will do 10 different movements 10 times each, which equals 100 movements." Fasten the number chart to the whiteboard. Next to the 10, write the word *step*. (If students are not proficient in reading, review each word as you write it on the board.) "We will begin with 10 steps. Make sure to count one number for one step. Let's count aloud together." As a class, count and move 10 steps. "How many movements have we done? One movement 10 times!" Write *hop* next to the 20. "We are going to hop 10 times now. One hop for each number, and we are going to start at number 11 because we have already counted to 10." Hop 10 times counting from 11 to 20. "How many movements have we done? We have done 2 movements 10 times each, which makes 20. Ten, 20." (Point to the number chart as you count by tens.) Continue by writing the actions next to the number chart, counting the movements as the class does them, and then counting by tens before moving on to the next movement. The 10 movements are stepping, hopping, reaching, kicking, jumping, swaying, marching, twisting, turning, and galloping (table 4.1).

FORMATIVE ASSESSMENT

Room scan: Can the student connect one number to one movement (cardinality)?

Students kick together while counting.

Create and Perform

Divide the students into pairs. Give each pair one piece of paper that has a number between 1 and 20 and a movement written on the front.

"In your group, your task is to practice doing your movement that is written on your card the number of times that your card indicates. One student will be the mathematician, and the other student will be the dancer. The mathematician will count out loud the number of movements the dancer does, making sure the dancer does the correct amount of the movement. Once the dancer has done the correct amount of the movement, switch roles. The mathematician will become the dancer and the dancer will become the mathematician."

The teacher should move through the room assisting students, reading actions, helping to count, and assessing student progress. Once the first movement has been achieved, the teacher may wish to hand out additional papers with numbers and movements.

Table 4.1 **Numbers Corresponding to Movements**

Numbers	Movements
1-10	Step
11-20	Hop
21-30	Reach
31-40	Kick
41-50	Jump
51-60	Sway
61-70	March
71-80	Twist
81-90	Turn
91-100	Gallop

SUMMATIVE ASSESSMENT

Use a checklist to assess the following:

- Can the student demonstrate a specified movement?
- Can the student demonstrate a specified number of movements?

Review and Reflect

Reflect on dance target	Reflect on mathematics target
"Do you use any of the axial or locomotor movements that we practiced today outside of dance class? Raise your hand if you can tell me a time when you use one of the movements we practiced today at home or school." Call on several students. "Your homework for tonight is to find an example of when you use one of the actions at home. You can tell me about it tomorrow."	"What other things can we count? Do you think you could count the number of steps you take to get to the lunchroom? Why is it important for us to count?"

EXTENSIONS

- Students count the number of steps they take to get to the lunchroom or recess.
- Students count the number of swings forward they do on the playground swing during 1 minute.

COMPARING WHOLE NUMBERS

Comparing whole numbers between 1 and 10 and identifying whether a number is greater than, less than, or equal to another number is an important skill in understanding counting and cardinality. Comparing numbers is necessary for mathematics at every level and promotes understanding of real-world applications.

AGES
5-7

LEVEL
Basic

MATERIALS
One index card per student with one whole number between 1 and 10 written on the front

MUSIC
Pleasant selection (see appendix B)

ESSENTIAL QUESTION
How can numbers be compared?

ENDURING UNDERSTANDING
The comparison of numbers helps people to communicate and make sense of the world.

	Dance	Mathematics
Learning target	Students learn high, middle, and low levels and compare levels that are higher and lower.	Students compare numbers to identify values that are more and less than.
Evidence of student learning	The student demonstrates high, middle, and low levels.	The student demonstrates a number level. The student orders numbers and levels from least value to most value.
Dance elements and mathematics vocabulary	Levels (high, middle, low)	More, less, greater, lower, value, number, 1, 2, 3, 4, 5, 6, 7, 8, 9, 10
Standards	Dance on high, middle, and low levels with clear focus and transitions (*Standards for Learning and Teaching Dance in the Arts*, p. 23).	• Identify whether the number of objects in one group is greater than, less than, or equal to the number of objects in another group, such as by using matching and counting strategies (*Common Core State Standards for Mathematics*, K.CC.6). • Compare two numbers between 1 and 10 presented as written numerals (*Common Core State Standards for Mathematics*, K.CC.7).

Warm-Up

"Find your own space where you are only touching the floor and the air. Follow me as we warm up our bodies. Take one deep breath in and out. Clap twice. Roll your shoulders three times. Reach down and up four times. Twist five times. Circle one ankle six times. Circle the other ankle six times. Gently kick only the air seven times. Bend and stretch your knees eight times. Reach with your arms in nine different directions. Jump 10 times. Freeze!"

Build Knowledge

"When I reach for a glass in the cupboard, I am using a high level (demonstrate high level with body). When I bend over to pick up a pencil on the floor, I am using a middle level (demonstrate middle level). When I am reaching for my cat under the bed, I am using a low level (demonstrate low level). Everything we do is at a specific level. In dance we use high, middle, and low levels to make our dance more interesting to an audience."

EXPLORE LEVELS

"Make a high-level frozen shape with your body. Make a new high-level shape. Make a low-level shape with your body. Can you make a different low-level shape? Now make a middle-level shape with your body—not too high, not too low. Make a new middle-level shape. Begin walking through the room at a high level. Make sure to look for empty spaces between other dancers. Crawl through the room with a low level. You are going your own way through the dancing space. Now stomp through the room at a middle level. You are not too high or too low but right in the middle. Try your own new way to move at a high level. How many different ways can you move at a low level? Now create your own way to move at a middle level." Practice each level two more times each, checking for student understanding.

"Dancers are artists who make choices among all three levels. Continue moving through the room making dance choices, changing among all three levels."

FORMATIVE ASSESSMENT

Room scan: Can the student clearly demonstrate high, middle, and low levels?

Connect

"We can move on many levels within high, middle, and low. We are going to move with 10 different levels! We will be using all of our levels to show the numbers 1, 2, 3, 4, 5, 6, 7, 8, 9, and 10. Our highest level is 10. Our lowest level is 1 (if students ask about zero, you can say that a zero would mean that you were not there at all). Our middle-most level is 5. What level do you think 8 should be? Eight is less than 10 but more than 5, so it is a high middle level. What level is 2?"

PRACTICE WHOLE-NUMBER VALUES WITH LEVELS

"Make a shape for 10, your highest level. Now make a shape that would be a 1 level, your lowest level. Make a shape that is a 5 level. Remember where your 5 level is—right in the middle. Make your 10 level again. Get a little lower and make a 9-level shape. And an 8-level shape. A 7-level shape! Make sure you are not as low as your 5 yet because 7 is greater than 5. Make a 6-level shape. And now your 5-level shape right at your middle-most level. Now get even lower to your 4 level. And your 3 level. Do you still have room to get lower for your 2 and 1? Make your 2-level shape. And your 1 level, your lowest level.

"Now we are going to move through the room at our various number levels. Move through the room, looking for empty spaces between dancers, using a 4 level. Try to remember where the 4 level is. It's lower than your 5 because 4 is less than 5. Use an 8 level through the room. Eight is less than 10 but more than 5, so it is a high middle level. Move with a 2 level." Continue practicing all number levels, encouraging the idea of more and less in relation to higher and lower.

After practicing each number level, pass out an index card to each student. "When the music begins, you will move at the number level that is on your card. If you are being clear with your level, other dancers should be able to estimate what number you have on your card." Start the music. As the students are dancing, comment on specific students' levels; for example, "You must have a 1 on your card because you are so low to the ground." Stop the students and have them switch cards periodically.

FORMATIVE ASSESSMENT

Room scan: Can the student clearly demonstrate a number level?

Create and Perform

Ask the students to keep their current cards. Divide them into groups of three to six students depending on their maturity level.

"In your group, you will each keep your own card. Your task is to arrange your bodies in order from the least amount of value to the greatest value. Once you are in the correct order, make your level shapes. The audience should be able to see who has more or less value based on your levels. When I am done counting to 10, you will be frozen in your level shapes in the correct order with your group."

Begin counting slowly to 10 out loud. As the students work, observe and assist as needed. Once all of the groups are ready, they each show their line of shapes to the other groups. As they are showing, ask the audience questions such as, "Who do you think has the most value? Who has the least? What numbers do you think they are?" If there is time remaining in the dance lesson, create two groups and repeat this same exercise with larger groups. This is more easily done with the assistance of other teachers or adults. This can also be done with the entire class as one large group with the teacher assisting.

Students display number levels in order from lowest to highest value: 1, 4, 5, 9, 10.

SUMMATIVE ASSESSMENT

Use a checklist to assess the following:

- Can the student demonstrate high, middle, and low levels?
- Can the student demonstrate a number level?
- Can the student order numbers and levels from least value to most value?

Review and Reflect

Reflect on dance target	Reflect on mathematics target
"I use a low level when I sit on the floor during story time. When do you use a low, middle, or high level at home or school? Your sentence should be like this: 'I use a _____ level when I _____.'" Call on several students. "When you go home tonight, your task is to identify an activity where you use a particular level. I will ask you to describe your level and your activity tomorrow."	"Which has more value, a 5 or a 2 (5)? Which has less value, a 6 or a 7 (6)? Which has more value, a 9 or a 1 (9)? Which has less value, an 8 or a 3 (3)? Why is it important for us to know if something is more or less?"

EXTENSION

Teachers prepare paper plates that each have a different quantity of marbles, crackers, blocks, or other objects. Students compare the objects on the plates and determine which plates have the most and least objects.

ORDINAL NUMBERS

Ordinal numbers indicate position or order in relation to other numbers. First, second, third, fourth, and so on are ordinal numbers that children must learn in order to understand what comes next in a sequence.

AGES
5-6

LEVEL
Basic

MATERIALS
- Paper bag with 10 index cards (write one locomotor or axial movement on each card)
- Paper bags with four index cards (write one locomotor or axial movement on each card; make one bag for every four students)
- Whiteboard or easel
- Masking or painter's tape (before class, make a tape line through the center of the dancing space)

MUSIC
Driving selection (see appendix B)

ESSENTIAL QUESTION
How can numbers be ordered?

ENDURING UNDERSTANDING
Numbers can help us do things in a specific order.

	Dance	Mathematics
Learning target	Students learn and memorize a sequence of movements.	Students learn ordinal numbers and connect them to cardinal numbers.
Evidence of student learning	The student performs a choreographic sequence from beginning to end without stopping.	The student performs a choreographic sequence using ordinal numbers to remember the order in which the movements are performed. The student observes and identifies the first, second, third, and fourth movements of another group's dance.
Dance elements and mathematics vocabulary	Locomotor and axial movements, choreographic sequence	Ordinal numbers, first, second, third, fourth, fifth, sixth, seventh, eighth, ninth, tenth
Standards	Sequencing: Demonstrate the ability to sequence a series of movements and to remember them in a short phrase (*Standards for Learning and Teaching Dance in the Arts*, p. 23).	Know number names and the count sequence (*Common Core State Standards for Mathematics*, K.CC.1-3).

Warm-Up

"Please make a circle as a class with all dancers standing. We are going to go around the circle with a variety of movements. Each person will do the same movement that I do and only do it once. Immediately after the person next to you finishes the movement, it is your turn to do the movement. I will go first. When the movement goes all the way around the circle and comes back to me, then I will change the movement. All together we will say the order, first, second, third, fourth person and so on."

Begin with a jump and go counterclockwise around the circle with each student doing one jump and saying the ordinal numbers as you go around. After each student has jumped, change the movement to a gentle kick. Begin by saying "First" when you start a new movement. Continue with various movements such as a turn, jumping jack, head circle, wiggle, and so on. Encourage the students to wait until the person before them has finished before they go, and remind them that each student only does the movement one time. The last time around, ask the students to count off—the teacher says "First," the next person says "Second," then "Third," and so forth. At the end say, "_____ was the last person to go and she (or he) went _____."

Build Knowledge

"We are going to practice a dance today with certain movements done in order. We are going to start by exploring some of these movements."

EXPLORE TWO-MOVEMENT SEQUENCES

"All dancers come to one side of the room (indicate which side). We are going to do two movements to get to the other side of the room. When I say your name, you will skip until you pass the tape line and then crawl to get all the way to the other side." Say each student's name, making sure that the student does the first movement and then the second movement to get across the room. "This time, we will roll to the line and then gallop the rest of the way across." After each student does this task, continue with two more passes, such as jumping then tiptoeing and hopping then marching.

Remove the tape. Repeat the two-movement sequences without the tape, encouraging the students to switch movements in approximately the same place.

FORMATIVE ASSESSMENT

Room scan: Can the student demonstrate two separate movements in the specified order?

Connect

"We are going to create a dance that has a specific order to it. We will remember which movement comes first, second, third, and so on."

LEARN AND MEMORIZE THE SEQUENCE

Write the numbers 1 through 8 on the whiteboard or easel. "I am going to draw the first movement from the paper bag. Do we say this is our 1 movement? No, we say this is our

Students skip to the tape line and then crawl.

first movement, even though we are going to write it next to the number 1." Draw the first movement out of the bag and either tape or write it next to the one on the board. For students who are not proficient in reading, review each word as it is added to the board. "Let's practice our first movement." Practice that movement with music.

"Now I'm going to draw our next movement from the bag. I am going to write it next to the 2. Is it our first movement? No, it is our second movement." Write or tape it next to the 2. "Let's practice our first movement, then our second movement." Practice the first and then second movements with music. "Next to the number 3 I am going to write our third movement." Draw the third movement from the bag. "Let's practice the first, second, and third movements. What movement is first? What movement is second? What movement is third?" Continue in this fashion. As you get to the sixth and seventh numbers, begin asking questions about the ordinal numbers out of order, such as, "What was the fourth movement? What about the seventh movement?"

Practice the whole dance with up to eight movements. Eight movements may be too many for some classes, so teachers should adapt the number to suit the students. If you only do five movements the first day, you can continue this lesson another day, adding more movements.

After the students have practiced with the teacher several times, step out and say, "I am going to watch to see if you are remembering the order. I will tell you when to change by saying 'First,' 'Second,' 'Third,' and so on as you do the movements." Watch the students practice the dance and call out the ordinal numbers to indicate for them to switch to the next movement.

FORMATIVE ASSESSMENT

Room scan:

- Can the student demonstrate the sequence of the movements in the correct order?
- Can the student identify the ordinal number that relates to each movement?

Create and Perform

Divide the class into groups of four and give each group a paper bag with four movements written on index cards in it.

"You are going to create a dance as a group with the movements in your bag. The order that you pull them out of the bag is the order you will do your dance. Your dance will have four movements and you will always do the movements in the same order. Once you know what your dance will look like, practice as a group and try to memorize it so you do not have to look at your cards. You should be able to perform your dance from beginning to end without stopping."

In their groups, the students draw their movements out of their bags and practice their dance with first, second, third, and fourth movements. Teachers should go to each group and assist as necessary. After they have practiced for a few minutes, groups perform the dances for the class. Before the dance, remind the audience to watch for the first, second, third, and fourth movements while the group is performing. After each performance, ask the group, "What was your third (or first, second, or fourth) movement?" Ask the audience, "What was their second (or first, third, or fourth) movement?"

SUMMATIVE ASSESSMENT

Use a checklist to assess the following:

- Can the student perform a choreographic sequence from beginning to end without stopping?
- Can the student perform a choreographic sequence using ordinal numbers to remember the order in which the movements are performed?
- Can the student observe and identify the first, second, third, and fourth movements of another group's dance?

Review and Reflect

Reflect on dance target	Reflect on mathematics target
"Dancers arrange movements into an order to create dances. Every choreographed dance has a specific sequence. Can you think of a time outside of dance when you do things in a specific order? When I am making pancakes, first I make the batter, second I cook the pancakes in a pan, third I put them on a plate, fourth I put syrup on them, and fifth I eat them! Raise your hand if you can tell me something that you do in a certain order." Call on several students. "Your task tonight is to find an activity that you do in a particular order. You can describe the sequence tomorrow in class."	"Let's say our ordinal numbers all together in order. First, second, third, fourth, fifth, sixth, seventh, eighth, ninth, tenth. Why is it important for us to know ordinal numbers?"

EXTENSIONS

- Students tell a partner actions to do in a specific order, such as "First, go to the water fountain; second, get a drink of water; third, walk back to me," and so on.
- Students follow a teacher's instructions in order.

5

OPERATIONS AND ALGEBRAIC THINKING

entral to mathematics are the four basic operations of arithmetic: addition, subtraction, multiplication, and division. This chapter includes three lessons that focus on these operations. The first lesson integrates addition with axial movements. Locomotor movements are counted and taken away to reinforce subtraction in the second lesson. The third lesson combines timing in choreography using canon and unison with multiplication and division. Each lesson emphasizes the dance and mathematics concepts equally and uses the roles of dancer and mathematician.

ADDITION

Computation involves combining numbers using a variety of approaches. This lesson provides a moving, kinesthetic, hands-on approach to solving number problems and mastering addition. Dancers add axial movements with a partner to find the total sum of movements.

AGES
5-7

LEVEL
Basic

MATERIALS
- Whiteboard or easel
- One index card for each child with a number from 1 to 10 and *kicks*, *turns*, or *twists* written on it (for example, *4 kicks*)

MUSIC
Driving selection (see appendix B)

ESSENTIAL QUESTION
Why do we add numbers?

ENDURING UNDERSTANDING
Fluency with addition helps us find answers to important questions.

	Dance	Mathematics
Learning target	Students practice three axial movements: twist, turn, and kick.	Students practice counting and cardinality.
Evidence of student learning	The student identifies and demonstrates a twist, turn, and kick.	The student identifies the total quantity of movements performed with a partner.
Dance elements and mathematics vocabulary	Axial actions (twist, turn, kick)	Add, plus, equal

(continued)

(continued)

	Dance	Mathematics
Standards	Nonlocomotor or axial movement: Demonstrate and identify nonlocomotor or axial movements (*Standards for Learning and Teaching Dance in the Arts*, p. 23).	• Represent addition and subtraction with objects, fingers, mental images, drawings, sounds, acting out situations, verbal explanations, expressions, or equations. Solve addition and subtraction word problems, and add and subtract within 10 by using objects or drawings to represent the problem (*Common Core State Standards for Mathematics*, K.OA.1-2). • Use addition and subtraction within 20 to solve word problems involving situations of adding to, taking from, putting together, taking apart, and comparing. Solve word problems that call for addition of three whole numbers whose sum is less than or equal to 20 (*Common Core State Standards for Mathematics*, 1.OA.1-2).

Warm-Up

"Follow me to warm up our bodies. Jump three times: 1-2-3. Reach up and then down four times: 1-2-3-4. March seven times in place: 1-2-3-4-5-6-7. Swing twice: 1-2." Repeat three more times, making sure to count the number of each movement aloud.

Build Knowledge

"During our warm-up, did we move through the dancing space or stay in one place? We stayed in one place. When we stay in place, it is called *axial*. Axial has an *X* in it. Draw an imaginary *X* on the floor. *X* marks the spot. To do an axial movement, you must stay over your imaginary *X*. We are practicing three axial movements today: turning, twisting, and kicking."

EXPLORE TWISTING, TURNING, AND KICKING

"Find your own space, only touching the floor and the air. Draw your imaginary *X* on the floor. *X* marks the spot. Make sure you stay over your *X*. Begin by twisting. There are many ways to twist. While remaining axial, explore the many ways that you can twist your body. Later, we will count the number of twists that we do. While we are counting it is helpful if we are twisting in similar ways. Try twisting with me. Plant your feet firmly on the floor and bend your knees slightly. Use your arms and head to gently twist your spine to look behind you. Now twist the other direction. Keep twisting one direction and then the other. When you are twisting, your feet do not move at all. One twist is looking behind you in only one direction and then coming back to the front. Let's perform and count 7 twists all together: 1-2-3-4-5-6-7."

"Now we are going to practice turning. It is important to be safe and in control. We do not want to spin fast, and if we ever feel dizzy we should stop turning immediately. Turning can be both axial and locomotor, but today we are practicing axial turning, which means that we stay over our imaginary X. One turn is one rotation all the way around to end where you began. Make sure to turn both directions. Freeze!" Students should only make a few rotations at one time, then stop and practice a new activity before practicing turning again. "Let's count and perform 3 turns all together: 1-2-3. When we are turning, our feet need to move to turn our whole body around. This is different than twisting, in which our feet stay planted on the floor and we do not twist our whole body all the way around. We are going to practice 2 more turns: 1-2.

"Kicking can be powerful or soft. Dancers only kick the air; they do not kick anything or anyone. They have to use their eyes to make sure that they are kicking only empty space. Practice kicking. Kick with one leg. Kick with the other leg. Now let's count 4 kicks." Practice kicking, turning, and twisting 4 more times each, giving a number for students to count with each movement.

FORMATIVE ASSESSMENT

Room scan:

- Can the student clearly and safely demonstrate a twist, turn, and kick?
- Can the student count her movements with the rest of the class?

Connect

Ask all but two students to sit down. One standing student will be the mathematician and one student will be a dancer. The teacher will also be a dancer in this example.

"I am going to kick 8 times and the mathematician will count out loud the number of kicks that I do. Each time a leg goes out, he will count it as 1 kick." Kick 8 times. "The mathematician counted 8 kicks. The mathematician now will count the other dancer's twists. What number comes after 8? We will start counting the twists beginning with 9 so we can learn how many movements there are all together. This dancer will do 4 twists, but the mathematician is going to start counting at 9 because we want to know how much 8 kicks plus 4 twists equals. We want to know how many movements there are all together." The mathematician counts the 4 twists, counting 9, 10, 11, 12. Write on the whiteboard, *8 kicks + 4 twists = ____movements*.

"If I did 8 kicks and my partner did 4 twists, how many movements did we do total? Our equation is 8 plus 4 equals 12 movements."

ADDITION DANCES

Form the students into groups of three and assign one student to be the mathematician first. Write *3 turns* on the whiteboard. "If you are the mathematician, you are going to choose one partner to turn first. Then the mathematician will count the dancer's turns. Dancers are going to turn around 3 times safely and in control." While the students are turning and counting, write on the whiteboard, *3 turns + 6 twists =____movements*.

"Now the other dancer will twist 6 times. Mathematicians are going to count beginning with the number 4 because you already counted 3 movements." After the students have twisted, "If one partner did 3 turns and the other partner did 6 twists, how many movements did they do all together? And 3 plus 6 equals how many? That's right, 9! You and your partner did 9 movements total.

"If you did the turns, you are now the mathematician. Mathematician, choose one partner to do the kicks and one partner to do the turns. The mathematician will first count the kicks and then continue

counting with the other dancer turning." Repeat the activity with the equation *7 kicks + 4 turns =*
____*movements.* "If one partner did 7 kicks and the other partner did 4 turns, how many movements
did they do all together? Yes, they did 11 kicks."

Switch roles one last time and repeat the activity with the equation *5 twists + 8 kicks = _____*
movements.

FORMATIVE ASSESSMENT

Room scan: Can the student identify the sum of movements?

Create and Perform

Arrange the class into pairs. Give each student an index card with a number and an axial movement.
"With your partner, your first task is to find the sum of your movements. How many movements will
you do total? Your next task is for one person to do the movements while the other person counts with
a whisper. Then the next person performs the movements while the first person counts with a whisper.
The audience will need to watch and identify the total number of axial movements."

Give the students 1 minute to practice, and then have each pair perform for the class. After each
group performs, write the corresponding equation on the board as you ask questions: "What movement
did the first person do? How many did he do? What movement did the second person do? How many
did she do? How many movements did this group do in total? _____ + _____ = _____. How did you
calculate the total?"

SUMMATIVE ASSESSMENT

Use a checklist to evaluate the following:

- Can the student identify and demonstrate a twist, turn, and kick?
- Can the student identify the total quantity of movements performed with a partner?

Review and Reflect

Reflect on dance target	Reflect on mathematics target
"Can you think of a time outside of dance when you kick, twist, or turn? This week, notice if you twist, kick, or turn at home or at school. You can describe it to me during our next dance lesson."	"How many pieces of food is 5 crackers plus 5 pieces of cheese (10)? What does 4 grapes plus 3 peanuts equal (7)? Can you think of a time when addition can be used at home? Tonight, use addition while you are eating dinner. Maybe you eat 8 green beans, 3 orange slices, and a piece of chicken. How many pieces of food did you eat? 8 + 3 + 1 = 12 pieces of food. I will ask you to describe what you were adding and how many total pieces of food you ate during our next dance lesson."

EXTENSIONS

- Complete an addition worksheet or answer a series of equations written on the board.
- Create a short dance that includes twists, turns, and kicks.

SUBTRACTION

Subtraction is one of the four basic operations of arithmetic and is used in situations of taking away and comparing quantities to find the difference. It is the inverse of addition, meaning that if a number is added to another number and then the same number is subtracted, the result will be the original number; for example, 3 + 4 = 7, and 7 – 4 = 3. This lesson requires a basic knowledge of subtraction facts and is meant to reinforce subtraction learning. It is not meant to be an introductory lesson.

AGES
6-8

LEVEL
Basic

MATERIALS
- Whiteboard or easel
- Index cards (on half of the cards, write a number from 11 to 20 and *marches*, *gallops*, or *jumps*, such as *13 marches*, and on the other half, write a number from 1 to 10; make one card for every two students)

MUSIC
Pleasant selection (see appendix B)

ESSENTIAL QUESTION
What is subtraction and how is it used?

ENDURING UNDERSTANDING
Fluency with subtraction helps us find answers to important questions.

	Dance	Mathematics
Learning target	Students practice the locomotor actions of marching, jumping, and galloping.	Students use subtraction within 20 to find solutions to problems involving situations of taking away quantities of movements.
Evidence of student learning	The student identifies and clearly demonstrates marching, galloping, and jumping.	The student identifies the difference in a given subtraction problem and performs the solution as the quantity of marches, jumps, or gallops.
Dance elements and mathematics vocabulary	Locomotor actions (march, gallop, jump)	Subtraction, difference

(continued)

	Dance	Mathematics
Standards	Locomotor movement: Demonstrate and identify locomotor movements (*Standards for Learning and Teaching Dance in the Arts*, p. 23).	Use addition and subtraction within 20 to solve word problems involving situations of adding to, taking from, putting together, taking apart, and comparing, with unknowns in all positions, such as by using objects, drawings, and equations with a symbol for the unknown number to represent the problem (*Common Core State Standards for Mathematic*, 1.OA.1).

Warm-Up

"Form one line behind me. You are going to follow the leader in this line, doing as I do." Lead the students through the dancing space using movements of your choosing, which can include skipping, walking, floating, swaying, wiggling, crawling, and so on. Use locomotor movements only.

Build Knowledge

"When you were following the leader, did you stay in one place or move through the dancing space? You moved through the dancing space. When you move through the dancing space it is called *locomotor* movement. Notice that *locomotor* has the word *motor* in it. Like a car that has a motor, locomotor movements move you from one place to another. We are going to practice three locomotor movements today: marching, jumping, and galloping."

EXPLORE MARCHING, JUMPING, AND GALLOPING

"Stand up and find your own space, only touching the floor and the air. When dancers move through the room, they go their own ways, making their own choices. Dancers also look for empty spaces between bodies to avoid running into other dancers. Begin by marching through the room. Your bent knees go up and down strongly, at a steady pace. Dancers step onto the floor softly and quietly when they are marching. Marching is a locomotor step that moves you through the room.

"Now begin jumping through the room. Jumping takes off from the floor with two feet and lands on two feet. Jumping can be either locomotor or axial, meaning staying in one place, but we will be locomotor jumping today, which means we are moving our jumps through the dance space. Make sure that you are landing softly and watching for other dancers. Only jump into empty places.

"Begin galloping through the room. Galloping is a step-together-step action, but when the feet are together, they are off the ground. It is like one foot is chasing the other. Is galloping locomotor? Yes, galloping is locomotor. Marching, jumping, and galloping can all be locomotor, meaning they move through the dancing space like a car with a motor. March through the dancing space. Gallop through the dancing space. Jump through the dancing space." Practice marching, galloping, and jumping three more times each.

"Dancers are artists who make choices using many locomotor actions. Continue your locomotor movements and make your own dance choices. Switch between marching, galloping, and jumping without stopping."

FORMATIVE ASSESSMENT

Room scan: Can the student clearly demonstrate marching, galloping, and jumping?

Connect

"We've been working on subtraction problems in math. Today we're going to review the same subtraction problems from math class using dance." Ask all but one student to sit down. The standing student acts as the teacher's mathematician. "I am going to march and the mathematician will count the number of marches that I do. Each time that a knee comes up, she will count it as 1." March 8 times. "The mathematician counted 8 marches. If I subtract 5 marches, how many marches should I do?" Hold up 8 fingers. Put down 5 fingers. "How many are left over if I start with 8 and take away 5? That's right, 3! I should do 3 marches this time. My mathematician will count to make sure that I do 3 marches." March 3 times.

SUBTRACTION DANCES

Divide the students into pairs. Assign one student in each pair to the role of mathematician. "Mathematicians will watch their partner, the dancer, and count the number of movements that the dancer does. Raise your hand if you are the dancer. Dancers will march 12 times. Each time they lift one leg off the floor, the mathematicians will count it as 1 march. Remember that we are practicing locomotor marching."

As the students are marching and counting, write *12 marches* on the whiteboard. "Dancers just did 12 marches. Subtract 6 marches. Mathematicians, raise your hand if you can tell your partner how many marches they need to do if they subtracted 6 from 12." Call on a mathematician to tell a dancer how many marches to do. "Yes, the dancer needs to do 6 marches this time. Mathematicians, count your partner's marches." Write on the whiteboard *12 marches – 6 marches = 6 marches*. "We know that 12 marches minus 6 marches equals 6 marches."

Teachers may wish to use a number line or hundreds chart throughout this lesson because many students may not be proficient in mental math. The mathematicians can point to the first number of actions, subtract using the number line or chart, and tell their partners how many actions to do in the next step.

"Switch roles. If you were the mathematician, you are now the dancer, and if you were the dancer, you are now the mathematician. Dancers are going to do 15 gallops. Mathematicians, you will count 1 gallop each time the first foot touches the floor." As the students are galloping and counting, write *15 gallops* on the whiteboard. "The dancers did 15 gallops. Subtract 9 gallops. Mathematicians, raise your hand if you can tell your partner how many gallops to do." Call on a mathematician to tell a dancer how many gallops to do. "Yes, 15 gallops minus 9 gallops equals 6 gallops. Mathematicians, count your partner's 6 gallops." Write on the whiteboard *15 gallops – 9 gallops = 6 gallops*. "We know that 15 gallops minus 9 gallops equals 6 gallops."

One student counts another student's marches.

Room scan: Can the students identify and demonstrate the difference in the given subtraction problem using marches or gallops?

Create and Perform

Distribute the index cards. For each pair of students, give one student the card with the number from 11 to 20 and the movement, and give the other partner the card with the number from 1 to 10.

"Your first task with your partner is to subtract the smaller number from the larger number. Once you know the difference, if you have the card with the larger number and a locomotor action, you will go first. Your partner will count as you perform the number of movements on your card. Then, the partner with the smaller number will perform the difference. For example, if I have a card that says *18 marches*, I will march 18 times while my partner counts my marches. If my partner has a card that says *2* on it, she will march 18 minus 2, which is 16. My partner will then march 16 times while I count. Practice your movements, making sure that you are clearly showing marching, galloping, or jumping and that your partner is counting the correct number of movements."

Allow the students 2 minutes to practice and then have each pair perform for the rest of the class (for larger classes or if you have less time, have several pairs go at once with students assigned to watch one group only). After the students perform, ask the following questions and write the equations on the whiteboard: "What locomotor movement did the students do? How many movements did the first partner do? How many movements did the second partner do? How many movements did they subtract?" The equation on the whiteboard should follow this format: (number of movements the first partner performed) – ____ = (number of movements the second partner performed).

SUMMATIVE ASSESSMENT

Use a checklist to assess the following:

- Can the student identify and clearly demonstrate a march, gallop, and jump?
- Can the student identify the difference in a given subtraction problem and perform the solution as the quantity of marches, jumps, or gallops?

Review and Reflect

Reflect on dance target	Reflect on mathematics target
"How are marches, jumps, and gallops similar? How are marches, gallops, and jumps different? Can you think of a time outside of dance when you march, gallop, or jump? This week, notice a time at home when you march, gallop, or jump and be prepared to tell me about it."	"What is 19 minus 8 (11)? Why is subtraction important? Your task this week is to use subtraction at home while helping a parent cook, building a model or making a craft, tidying your bedroom, or doing something in another situation that you discover. For example, you may be helping a parent cook. You start with 8 eggs in the carton and you use 4. How many eggs do you have left? Eight minus 4 is 4."

EXTENSIONS

- Complete a subtraction worksheet.
- Create an obstacle course that includes marching, galloping, and jumping.

MULTIPLICATION AND DIVISION

Multiplication and division have an inverse relationship. The basic operation of multiplication finds the product of two factors. The operation of division finds an unknown factor by dividing the product by the other factor. By knowing 6 x 5 = 30, one can determine that 30 ÷ 5 = 6.

AGES
8-11

LEVEL
Intermediate

MATERIALS
- Whiteboard or easel
- 10 index cards with one number from 1 to 10 written on each

MUSIC
Driving selection (see appendix B)

ESSENTIAL QUESTION
How can multiples be used to solve problems?

ENDURING UNDERSTANDING
Fluency with multiplication and division helps us find answers to important questions.

	Dance	Mathematics
Learning target	Students explore timing relationships within groups.	Students use multiplication and division to solve problems using equal groups.
Evidence of student learning	Timing relationship (canon, unison, before, after)	The student performs a dance that demonstrates a multiplication or division equation. The student successfully states the unknown variable in the equation.
Dance elements and mathematics vocabulary	Locomotor and axial movements, choreographic sequence	Multiply, divide, factor, product, quotient, equation

(continued)

	Dance	Mathematics
Standards	Tempo: Dance with a steady beat in different tempos. Patterns: Repeat a rhythmic pattern of movement (*Standards for Learning and Teaching Dance in the Arts,* p. 24).	• Use multiplication and division within 100 to solve word problems in situations involving equal groups, arrays, and measurement quantities (*Common Core State Standards for Mathematics,* 3.OA.3). • Understand division as an unknown-factor problem (*Common Core State Standards for Mathematics,* 3.OA.6). • Fluently multiply and divide within 100, using strategies such as the relationship between multiplication and division (e.g., knowing that 8 x 5 = 40, one knows 40 ÷ 5 = 8) or properties of operations. By the end of grade 3, know from memory all products of two one-digit numbers (*Common Core State Standards for Mathematics,* 3.OA.7).

Warm-Up

"Please make a circle as a class with all dancers standing. We are going to send a movement around the circle. Each person will do the same movement that I do and only do it once. When the person next to you has started the movement but not quite completed it, then it is your turn to do the movement. I will go first. When the movement goes all the way around the circle and comes back to me, then I will change the movement."

Begin with a jump and go counterclockwise around the circle with each student doing one jump. After each student has jumped, change the movement to a gentle kick. Continue with various movements such as a turn, jumping jack, shoulder shrug, wiggle, and so on. Remind students to begin their movement after the person before them has started the movement but before that person is done in order to create a wavelike effect.

Build Knowledge

"A person who creates dances is called a *choreographer*. Choreographers often use timing relationships to create meaning, make patterns, or make their dances more engaging. Today we are going to practice two timing relationships—unison and canon."

EXPLORE UNISON AND CANON

"I am going to teach you a short dance phrase that we can repeat. We are going to practice all together. Our dance starts with three jumps. Jump! Jump! Jump! Then we do a full turn. Turn around!

Next we reach up and then down. Up and down! Then we start again. Jump! Jump! Jump! Turn around! Reach up! Reach down!"

As you lead the students, make sure to speak the movement words rhythmically so the students all move simultaneously (in dance, this is called *unison*). Teachers who have previously worked with counts may wish to introduce counts: 1-jump, 2-jump, 3-jump, 4- and 5-turn, 6-reach up, 7- and 8-reach down. Practice the dance eight times to promote memorization.

"When dancers move in unison, it means that they are doing the same movements at the same time. We have been practicing in unison. We are going to practice the dance three more times making sure we are in unison—we are doing the same movements at the same time." Practice three times as an entire group, encouraging unison.

"Canon is similar to a round in music. One person or group starts and then another joins in, starting at the beginning. Sometimes choreographers create canons with many parts—perhaps 10 dancers dancing in canon! We are going to start with a two-part canon." Divide the room in half by walking through and indicating to students whether they are on side 1 or side 2. "If you are on side 1 (indicate which side of the room), you are going to begin the dance and only do it once. Side 2 will start the dance after side 1 dancers do the three jumps and are beginning their turn. Only do it once" (table 5.1). Practice the dance in canon. (It is helpful, but not required, to have a teacher or aide in each group.) Choose a student leader for each group who has been performing the movement accurately and with clarity.

Table 5.1 Movements Written as a Canon

Count	1	2	3	4	5	6	7	8	1	2	3
Group 1	Jump,	jump,	jump,	turn	around,	reach up,	reach	down,	freeze,	freeze,	freeze.
Group 2	Freeze,	freeze,	freeze,	jump,	jump,	jump,	turn	around,	reach up,	reach	down.

Quickly divide the class into two more groups to make four groups total. "This time we are going to try a four-part canon. Group 1 (indicate the groups as you refer to them; group order should move across the room from one side to the other) will begin. After group 1 jumps three times, group 2 begins. After group 2 jumps three times, group 3 begins. After group 3 jumps three times, group 4 begins. When you have done the phrase one time, freeze so you can see the canon in the remaining groups." Choose two more students to lead the new groups and practice the four-part canon.

"We are going to practice the canon with new timing. Keep these four groups. Everyone will begin frozen. Group 1 will begin. Group 2 will not start until group 1 is just finishing the reach down. Group 3 will remain frozen until group 2 is finishing the reach down. Group 4 will start the phrase when group 3 is finishing the phrase. Only one group will be moving at a time." Practice this version of the four-part canon.

FORMATIVE ASSESSMENT
Room scan: Can the student perform a clear four-part canon?

Connect
"We are going to use multiplication and division to create dances that use canon or unison."

MULTIPLICATION AND DIVISION DANCES

Divide the class into pairs. "If you and your partner each kick 7 times, how many kicks will you do all together between the 2 of you? Yes, 14! We know that 2 people times 7 kicks equals 14: 2 x 7 = 14. One partner, the dancer, is going to kick first, and the other partner, the mathematician, is going to count the kicks. Then switch roles. After both partners have kicked, the two of you will have done 14 kicks total. If one partner does 7 kicks, then the other partner does 7 kicks, is it in unison or in canon? Canon!"

After the students have done their kicks, make groups of four by grouping two pairs. (If you need to adjust numbers based on how many students you have in your class, change the following numbers appropriately.)

"If the 4 people in your group each do 5 jumps, how many jumps will you have done all together in your group? That's right, 20! We know that 4 x 5 = 20! Five, 10, 15, 20! In your group, do your jumps in canon with the rest of the group counting the jumps. After each person jumps, say the number of jumps that have been done all together. For example, the first person would say '5,' the next person would do 5 more jumps and say '10,' then '15,' then '20.'" The students do their jumps in canon. "You have 4 people in your group. If everyone in the group does an equal number of marches and you need to do 36 total marches, how many marches should each person do? Nine marches! We know that 36 ÷ 4 = 9. We also know that 9 x 4 = 36. This time, try your marches in unison. You must work together to do your marches at the same time. Count out loud so you can stay together."

FORMATIVE ASSESSMENT

Room scan: Can the student move clearly in unison or canon?

Create and Perform

Arrange the students into groups of three to six depending on the maturity level of the students. Groups do not need to be equal in size; the number of students in each group may vary. One person in each group randomly draws an index card with a number from 1 to 10.

"In your group, you will be making a multiplication dance. You have a card with a number on it. That number is the amount of a specific movement that each person in your group will do. Your first task is to determine how many total movements you will do in your group. You must multiply the number of people in your group times the number on your card. Your second task is to select a movement that you can clearly count. You will each do this movement the specified number of times. Then you must decide if you will be moving in canon or in unison. Lastly, you will practice your dance."

Teachers may find it helpful to write the following directions on the board or on easel paper where the students can reference it:

- Multiply: number of people x number on card (movements).
- Choose a movement.
- Canon or unison?
- Practice.

After the students have completed the directions, each group performs for the class. After each group, peer assess by asking the audience, "How many dancers were in the group? How many movements did each person do? What is the multiplication equation? How many movements did the group do all together? Did they dance in canon or in unison? If the 4 dancers did 24 movements total (use the numbers appropriate for each group), and each dancer did an equal amount, how many movements did each person do? This is division!" Teachers may wish to repeat or modify this activity by telling each group a total number (product) of movements that the group must do with each person doing an equal amount. Students would then need to use division to determine how many movements each student would need to do in order for the group to do a total of the specified amount.

SUMMATIVE ASSESSMENT

Use a checklist to determine the following:

- Can the student demonstrate a clear timing relationship within a group?
- Can the student perform a dance that demonstrates a multiplication or division equation?
- Can the student successfully state the unknown variable in the equation?

Review and Reflect

Reflect on dance target	Reflect on mathematics target
"Outside of dance, can you think of something that happens in unison? In canon? This week, your task is to find one thing that happens in canon and one thing that happens in unison. I'll be interested to know if you find things that people do in canon and if you discover that there is more unison or canon movement in the world as well as what the movements were."	"If 9 dancers do 8 turns each, how many turns do they do in total (72)? This week, notice if you come across groups of equal objects. Try to use multiplication to determine the total number of objects. For example, in my kitchen, there are 5 rows of ceiling tiles and each row has 7 tiles. I can determine how many tiles there are all together by multiplying 5 times 7, which equals 35 tiles."

EXTENSIONS

- Students create a classroom task that can be done in canon and in unison.
- Students use multiplication to determine how many times they have recess in one week.
- Students find the solution to this question: If you eat 3 meals a day, how many meals will you eat in 4 weeks?

6

NUMBERS AND
OPERATIONS

As students progress through mathematical studies, understanding of numbers, representations, relationships, and number systems is imperative. This chapter includes two lessons. The first lesson is designed for students aged 6 to 8 and focuses on movement levels and place value of the ones, tens, and hundreds place. The second lesson is designed for students aged 8 to 11 and integrates size, or kinesthetic reach, with fractions. Both lessons present clear applications of mathematical concepts while engaging students with suitable dance vocabulary.

PLACE VALUE

Comprehending place value is central to understanding the value of a number. Place value enables students to perform operations in mathematics and compare number values. In base 10, place value is the position of a single digit within the number. These positions include the ones place, tens place, hundreds place, and so on. Students learn that place value is based on groups of 10.

AGES
6-8

LEVEL
Basic

MATERIALS
- One index card for each child plus several extra (before class write *1*, *10*, or *100* on each)
- Three pieces of paper with *100* written on one, *10* on another, and *1* on another (before class, hang them on the wall or place them on the floor in the following order from left to right, approximately 2-4 ft or 60-120 cm apart: 100, 10, 1)
- Whiteboard or easel paper
- Masking tape

MUSIC
Pleasant selection (see appendix B)

ESSENTIAL QUESTION
How can I solve double-digit problems?

ENDURING UNDERSTANDING
Place value is based on groups of 10.

	Dance	Mathematics
Learning target	Students learn to dance with high, middle, and low levels.	Students understand the place value of ones, tens, and hundreds.
Evidence of student learning	The student demonstrates a specified level.	The student identifies a three-digit number using correct place value.

(continued)

(continued)

	Dance	Mathematics
Learning target	Level (high, middle, low)	Place value, ones place, tens place, hundreds place, ones, tens, hundreds
Standards	Levels: Dance on high, middle, and low levels with clear focus and transitions (*Standards for Learning and Teaching Dance in the Arts*, p. 23).	• Understand that the three digits of a three-digit number represent amounts of hundreds, tens, and ones (*Common Core State Standards for Mathematics*, 2.NBT.1). • Count within 1,000; skip count by fives, tens, and hundreds (*Common Core State Standards for Mathematics*, 2.NBT.2). • Read and write numbers to 1,000 using base 10 numerals, number names, and expanded form (*Common Core State Standards for Mathematics*, 2.NBT.3).

Warm-Up

"For our warm-up, we will be making many frozen shapes. We will practice freezing, making interesting and unique shapes, and counting the number of shapes. We will start by making 10 shapes that are near to the floor, and we will count by ones. Try to create as many different shapes that are low to the floor as you can: 1-2-3-4-5-6-7-8-9-10. Now we are going to make 10 shapes that are high off the ground, but we will count by hundreds this time. Make sure you are reaching as high as you can: 100-200-300-400-500-600-700-800-900-1,000. Now we will make 10 shapes that are in the middle, not too high and not too low, and count by tens: 10-20-30-40-50-60-70-80-90-100." As the students make shapes, encourage balance, stability, and unique shapes.

Build Knowledge

"When I place books on the top shelf, I use a high level (demonstrate high level with body); I'm on my tiptoes! When I help you at your desks, I use a middle level (demonstrate middle level); I'm bending over. When I take my shoes off for dance, I use a low level (demonstrate low level); I'm sitting on the floor. Everything we do uses a specific level. In dance we choose high, middle, and low levels to make our dance more interesting to an audience."

EXPLORE LEVELS

"Make a high-level frozen shape with your body. Make a new high-level shape. Make a low-level shape with your body. Can you make a new low-level shape? Now make a middle-level shape with your body—not too high, not too low. Make a new middle-level shape. Begin skipping through the room at a high level. Make sure to use your eyes to find the empty spaces between other dancers. Slither through the room with a low level. You are going your own way through the dancing space. Now bear crawl through the room with a middle level. You are not too high or too low but right in the middle. Create your own movement at a high level. How many different ways can you move at a low level? Now create your own movement at a middle level." Practice each level two more times each, checking for student understanding.

"Dancers are artists who make choices using all three levels. Move through the room making choices and keep changing your dance to include high, middle, and low levels."

FORMATIVE ASSESSMENT

Room scan: Can the student clearly demonstrate high, middle, and low levels?

Connect

Write the number *752* on the whiteboard. "We are going to use levels today to represent place value. Look at this number on the board. What number is in the hundreds place? Seven. This number has 7 hundreds. What number is in the tens place? Five. This number has 5 tens. What number is in the ones place? Two. This number has 2 ones. Seven hundreds plus 5 tens plus 2 ones equals 700 plus 50 plus 2 equals 752.

"Let's try another example. Our number is 346. Who can tell me which number is in the hundreds place? How many hundreds are there in 346?" Invite a student up to the whiteboard to write *300 +*. Invite other students to continue adding to the expanded number by writing *300 + 40 + 6 = 346*.

PLACE-VALUE LEVELS

"We are going to use a low level for ones, middle level for tens, and high level for hundreds. Stand up and find your own personal space, only touching the floor and the air. When you are at a low level, you are a one. Create your own one dance, traveling through the room. You are using a low level. When you are at a middle level, you are a ten. Practice your ten dance. I see middle levels! When you are at a high level, you are a hundred. Practice your hundred dance. I see high levels!" Repeat the place values four more times each, using both the dance language of high, middle, and low levels and the mathematics language of ones, tens, and hundreds. "Now make a level shape that shows me your value—hundred, ten, or one."

Distribute one index card to each student. "When you receive your card, begin moving with the value indicated by your card. If you are a one, you will move with a low level. If you are a ten, you will move at a middle level. If you are a hundred, you will move at a high level." After each person has a card, say, "Continue moving with your value, but move toward the wall with the 1, 10, and 100. If you are a one, you will move toward the 1 on the wall and then make a low shape. If you are a ten,

Students form place-value lines.

you will move toward the 10 on the wall and then make a middle shape. If you are a hundred, you will move toward the 100 on the wall and make a high shape. You have 5 counts to move toward the wall to your value's place and make a shape: 1-2-3-4-5-freeze!"

On the whiteboard, write three blanks: __ __ __. "How many low-level ones do we have?" Count aloud for each student in a low-level shape. "We have ___ ones. We are making a number all together as a class. On the board I have three blanks for our number. Where should the ones go? The ones place is on the right." Write in the number of ones.

"How many tens do we have?" Count aloud the dancers making middle-level shapes. "We have ___ tens. Where is the tens place? The tens place is the middle blank, second from the right." Write in the number of tens.

Count aloud the number of dancers making high-level shapes. "We have ___ hundreds. Where is the hundreds place? The hundreds place is the remaining position, third from the right." Write in the number of hundreds.

"How many ones do we have in this number? How many tens? How many hundreds? Raise your hand if you can read the number we have made." If, for example, there are more than 10 tens, the teacher should choose 10 students and skip count the tens (10, 20, 30, 40, 50, 60, 70, 80, 90, 100). Then the teacher should swap the 10 ten cards with a hundred card that the 10 tens hold together and share and move into the hundreds place. This can be done for ones and hundreds as well.

Ask the students to switch cards to obtain a new place value. Be sure to switch with a few children with the extra cards in order to create a new number. "Begin dancing your new place-value level throughout the room. You have 5 counts to move toward the wall to your place value and freeze in your level shape: 1-2-3-4-5-freeze!"

Count aloud the number of dancers in each place and fill in the blanks on the whiteboard. Ask the students to raise their hands if they can read the number.

FORMATIVE ASSESSMENT

Room scan:

- Can the student demonstrate a level based on a place value?
- Can the student answer questions about the number of students in each place value in order to read a three-digit number?

Create and Perform

"Switch cards and keep your new card. In just a moment I am going to arrange you into groups. In your group, your first task is to determine how many ones, tens, and hundreds you have in your group. Next, determine what number your group will make by identifying the place value for each person. Third, review what level each person will dance. Finally, practice your dance. When you perform your dance, you will dance with your level in the area in front of your place-value poster."

Divide the students into groups of five to eight depending on maturity. Groups do not need to be evenly sized. Teachers may find it helpful to write the following directions on the whiteboard or on easel paper:

- How many ones, tens, and hundreds do you have in your group?
- What number will your group be displaying?
- Review what level each person should use.
- Practice dancing your level in your place value.

Teachers may also find it helpful to use masking tape to create sections for each place value to help students know where their positions are.

Perform each dance for the rest of the class. After each group performs, ask the audience, "How many ones were there? How many tens? How many hundreds? What number was this group dancing?"

SUMMATIVE ASSESSMENT

Use a checklist to determine the following:

- Can the student demonstrate a specified level?
- Can the student identify a three-digit number using the correct place value?

Review and Reflect

Reflect on dance target	Reflect on mathematics target
"When do you use a high, middle, or low level in your daily life? Raise your hand if you can complete this sentence: 'I use a _____ level when I _____.'" Call on several students. "This week, your task is to notice when you use a high, middle, or low level at home and be ready to tell me about it in class."	Write the number *378* on the board. "How many ones are in this number? How many tens? How many hundreds? This week your task is to listen to the numbers you hear described at home, at school, and on television; for example, 'There are 365 days in the year.' See if you can identify the ones, tens, and hundreds in the numbers you encounter in your life. I will ask you to describe an example during our next dance lesson."

EXTENSION

Students are given a list of three-digit numbers and must write how many ones, tens, and hundreds are in each number.

FRACTIONS

Adapted from a lesson by Eric Johnson.

Fractions describe how many parts of a certain size there are or any number of equal parts. Students learn that the whole can stay the same even though the number of parts can change.

AGES
8-11

LEVEL
Basic

MATERIALS
- Masking or painter's tape (before class, tape a single line through the middle of the dancing space)
- Index cards with one fraction written on each (one for each student)

MUSIC
Driving selection (see appendix B)

ESSENTIAL QUESTION
How can I use fractions in my life?

ENDURING UNDERSTANDING
Fractions express a part of a whole.

	Dance	Mathematics
Learning target	Students explore far and near reach (size) and dance with their full kinesphere.	Students understand fractions as part of a whole and compare fractions.
Evidence of student learning	The student demonstrates near, far, and medium reach (small, large, and medium size).	The student demonstrates a specified fraction using reach (a fraction of the student's entire reach or kinesphere). The student places her fraction shape into an order with others from smallest to largest value.
Dance elements and mathematics vocabulary	Size (large, small, narrow, wide, medium), reach (near, medium, far), kinesphere	Fraction, part, whole, denominator, numerator, more, less, equal

(continued)

(continued)

	Dance	Mathematics
Standards	• Articulation of movement: Demonstrate ability to move with clarity of motion and definition of intent. • Shapes: Form shapes and create designs with the body. • Personal space: Define one's personal space in relation to the personal space of other dancers (*Standards for Learning and Teaching Dance in the Arts*, pp. 23-24).	• Understand a fraction 1/*b* as the quantity formed by 1 part when a whole is partitioned into *b* equal parts; understand a fraction *a/b* as the quantity formed by *a* parts of size 1/*b* (*Common Core State Standards for Mathematics*, 3.NF.1). • Explain equivalence of fractions in special cases, and compare fractions by reasoning about their size (*Common Core State Standards for Mathematics*, 3.NF.3). • Explain why a fraction *a/b* is equivalent to a fraction (*n* x *a*)/(*n* x *b*) by using visual fraction models, with attention to how the number and size of the parts differ even though the two fractions themselves are the same size. Use this principle to recognize and generate equivalent fractions (*Common Core State Standards for Mathematics*, 4.NF.1). • Compare two fractions with different numerators and different denominators, such as by creating common denominators or numerators or by comparing with a benchmark fraction such as 1/2. Recognize that comparisons are valid only when the two fractions refer to the same whole. Record the results of comparisons with symbols >, =, or <, and justify the conclusions, such as by using a visual fraction model (*Common Core State Standards for Mathematics*, 4.NF.2).

Warm-Up

"Find your own space. Decide for yourself, without saying it out loud, if you are going to crawl or roll. When the music starts, begin crawling or rolling, but do not change between the two. Only do the one movement that you chose." Start the music and let students move for about 30 seconds. "Now choose between skipping or jumping. Only choose one and show it clearly with your body." After 30 seconds, freeze the class. "If you are on this side of the line, you are going to watch the other side dance. If you are on the dancing side, skip or jump very clearly with your body so that the audience knows exactly which one you chose."

While the first group is dancing, ask the audience, "The total number of dancers is the denominator. What is the denominator? The number of dancers skipping is the numerator or the number above the fraction bar. What is the numerator? What fraction of the dancers are skipping? What fraction of the dancers are jumping?" Switch roles for each group and repeat the activity.

Build Knowledge

"Dancers move within a kinesphere. A kinesphere is the space around our body that we can reach by extending our limbs. It is sometimes called our *personal space* or *reach space*. Within our kinesphere, we can dance using a near reach or a small size, a far reach or large size, or somewhere in the middle—a medium reach or size." Demonstrate the three reaches.

EXPLORE REACH

"Make a far-reach shape with your body. You are very large and wide with your bodies, reaching into the far edges of your kinesphere. Make a new far-reach shape. Make a near-reach shape. You are very small and close to your body. Can you make a new near-reach shape? Make a medium-reach shape. One more medium-reach shape! Now we're going to move through the room using a near reach in our small kinesphere. Now move through the room with a far reach, a very large kinesphere. Watch out for other dancers and make sure to stay in control of your body. Now use a medium reach through the room. You are not too big or too small, not too near or too far." Move using near, far, and medium reaches three more times each.

"Dancers are artists who make choices using all three reaches. Move through the room changing among near, far, and medium reaches."

FORMATIVE ASSESSMENT

Room scan: Can the student demonstrate near-, medium-, and far-reach kinespheres?

Connect

"Imagine your whole kinesphere. This is 1 whole. We are going to use fractions of our kinesphere or total reach space. Show your 1 whole. It is your farthest reach! Now show 1/2 of your reach. This is a medium reach. What about 1/4? You are becoming nearer. And 3/4? You are larger than 1/2 but smaller than 1 whole."

FRACTION EXPLORATION

"Moving through the room, you will hear me say a fraction. You will use that fraction of your kinesphere as you are moving, showing how near or far or medium reach that fraction of your kinesphere is. Begin by using 1/2 of your reach through the room. You use a medium reach." Continue for several minutes, using 1/2, 3/4, 1/4, 1/8, 7/8, 5/8, 1/10, 4/10, 2/5, and so on. Choose the fractions that directly relate to the fractions being studied in mathematics. While directing the students through the various fractions, comment on and encourage size and reach of the kinesphere as well as commenting on equivalent fractions and more and less than.

FORMATIVE ASSESSMENT

Room scan: Can the student clearly demonstrate specific fractions using a fraction of the kinesphere?

Create and Perform

Pass out one index card with a fraction written on it to each student. "When the music starts, move through the room using the fraction on your card as the fraction of your reach. When the music stops, freeze. If you are being very clear with your reach, other dancers should be able to estimate the fraction that is on your card." Start the music. Let it play for 20 seconds. Stop the music and remind the students to freeze.

"Find a partner who is close to you. Determine which one of you has a greater fraction and which one of you has a lesser fraction. Or maybe you are equivalent. Once you know how you compare, freeze in a shape next to your partner that shows your fraction of reach. Other dancers should be able to see which dancer has a greater value. You have 8 counts to freeze next to your partner: 1-2-3-4-5-6-7-8-freeze!"

When the students are frozen, choose one group and ask the remaining students questions, such as "Which dancer has more value? What fractions do you think they are?"

Instruct the students to swap cards with their partners and repeat the activity, this time instructing them to find a group of three and line up in order from smallest to largest. Continue with groups of four, then groups of five. When the students are working in groups of five, show each group to the rest of the class to ask questions and to observe the students' abilities to compare and order the fractions.

Five students with fraction cards form a line in order: 1/10, 3/8, 1/2, 3/4, 9/10.

SUMMATIVE ASSESSMENT

Use a checklist to determine the following:

- Can the student demonstrate near, far, and medium reach (small, large, and medium size)?
- Can the student demonstrate a specified fraction using reach (a fraction of the student's entire reach or kinesphere)?
- Can the student place his fraction shape into order from lesser to greater value?

Review and Reflect

Reflect on dance target	Reflect on mathematics target
"I use a near reach when I am in a crowded room and a far reach when I am stretching in the morning. When do you use a near, middle, or far reach outside of dance?" Call on several students. Remind them to use full sentences: "I use a _____ reach when I _____." "Your homework this week is to notice when you use a specific reach. Next dance class you can describe an activity when you used near, middle, or far reach in your life."	"When I bake a pie, I cut the pie into 6 slices. Each slice is then 1/6 of the pie. I eat only 1/6 of the pie, but my brother eats 2 slices. He eats 2/6, which simplified is 1/3 of the pie. How many slices are left? When are other times that we can use fractions in our daily life? Your homework this week is to notice when you are using a fraction of something at home or at school and be ready to tell me about it.""

EXTENSIONS

- Create a word problem and solution involving fractions.
- Draw or paint a picture that is separated into four parts. Make each 1/4 only one color.

7

MEASUREMENT AND DATA

earning to measure and interpret data is an important skill used in every level of mathematics. Measuring is crucial for using life skills outside of the classroom, comparing objects, and understanding relationships of objects, and interpreting data promotes connections and comparisons as well as understanding. This chapter includes five lessons. First, students learn to calculate the values of pennies, nickels, and dimes using high, middle, and low levels. In the second lesson, shapes and levels are used to study time and analog clocks. In the third and fourth lessons, jumps and hops become nonstandard units to measure lines and to calculate area and perimeter. Finally, tempo and levels are used to interpret data with bar graphs. Students are able to embody the mathematics content and use clear dance vocabulary to integrate movement with learning in measurement and data.

PENNIES, NICKELS, AND DIMES

Counting coins promotes real-world applications of math skills. Counting pennies is associated with cardinality: 1 penny for 1 cent. Counting and calculating the value of nickels requires skip counting by fives or multiplication by 5. Calculating the value of dimes requires skip counting by tens or multiplication by 10. Finding the value of a varied set of coins increases proficiency in mathematical operations. These skills enable students to understand monetary values they encounter in their lives.

AGES
6-8

LEVEL
Basic

MATERIALS
- One index card for each student (before class, print the words *penny*, *nickel*, or *dime* on each card)
- Whiteboard or easel

MUSIC
Driving selection (see appendix B)

ESSENTIAL QUESTION
Why is it important to understand the value of coins?

ENDURING UNDERSTANDINGS
Coins have distinct values.

	Dance	Mathematics
Learning target	Students perform movement at high, middle, and low levels.	Students understand the monetary value of pennies, nickels, and dimes, and they calculate the value of a set amount of coins.
Evidence of student learning	The student identifies and demonstrates high, middle, and low levels.	The student correctly calculates the value of a specified set of coins while observing and identifying other dancers' levels.
Dance elements and mathematics vocabulary	Levels (high, middle, low)	Value, penny, nickel, dime, cents, coins, money
Standards	Levels: Dance on high, middle, and low levels with clear focus and transitions (*Standards for Learning and Teaching Dance in the Arts*, p. 23).	Work with money to solve word problems involving dollar bills, quarters, dimes, nickels, and pennies, using $ and ¢ symbols appropriately (*Common Core State Standards for Mathematics*, 2.MD.8).

Warm-Up

"Find your own space where you are only touching the floor and the air. You are my mirror. As I move, you move as I do." Begin a short warm-up of bending, twisting, rolling shoulders, shaking hands and feet, and reaching up and down. Make sure to move low to the floor, high off the ground, and at a middle level as the students follow.

Build Knowledge

"When I hang my coat on the rack, I am using a high level (demonstrate high level with body); I'm reaching up high. When I use the drinking fountain, I am using a middle level (demonstrate middle level) because I need to bend over. When I am sitting on the floor with you, I am using a low level (demonstrate low level). Everything we do is at a specific level. In dance we use high, middle, and low levels to make our dance more interesting to an audience."

EXPLORE LEVELS

"Make a high-level frozen shape with your body. Make a new high-level shape. Make a low-level shape with your body. Can you make a new low-level shape? Now make a middle-level shape with your body—not too high, not too low. Make a new middle-level shape. Begin skipping through the room at a high level. Make sure to look for empty spaces between other dancers. Slither through the room with a low level. You are going your own way through the dancing space. Now float through the room with a middle level. You are not too high or too low; you are right in the middle. Create your own movement at a high level. How many different movements can you do at a low level? Now create your own movement at a middle level." Practice each level four more times, checking for student understanding.

"Dancers are artists who make choices using all three levels. Dance through the room moving among high, middle, and low levels without stopping."

Room scan: Can the student clearly demonstrate high, middle, and low levels?

Connect

"We are going to use levels to show the value of pennies, nickels, and dimes. Which of these coins has the least value? A penny has the least value. A penny is 1 cent. We will use a low level to show a penny. Which coin—penny, nickel, or dime—has the most value? A dime is 10 cents. We will use a high level to show a dime. Which coin do you think will be a middle level? A nickel is 5 cents and we will dance with a middle level" (table 7.1).

Table 7.1   Coins and Levels

Coin	Value	Level
Dime	10¢ 10 cents	High
Nickel	5¢ 5 cents	Middle
Penny	1¢ 1 cent	Low

PENNIES, NICKELS, AND DIMES EXPLORATION

"Dance through the room with a penny level. A penny is a low level and is worth 1 cent. Move through the room with a nickel level. A nickel is a middle level and is worth 5 cents. Continue moving through the room with a dime level. A dime is a high level and is worth 10 cents." Practice the coin levels four more times each, prompting the levels using coin vocabulary, monetary value, and dance levels (table 7.1).

On the whiteboard, write the following:

3 dimes =

6 nickels =

4 pennies =

Total =

"I have 3 dimes, 6 nickels, and 4 pennies. I need to calculate how much money I have. As a class, we are going to jump at a dime (high) level three times while skip counting by tens to determine the amount of money we have in dimes. Here we go at a high level: 10! 20! 30! We have 30 cents in dimes." Write *30¢* next to the dimes.

"Now we will jump at a nickel (middle) level six times while skip counting by fives to determine how much money 6 nickels are worth: 5! 10! 15! 20! 25! 30! We have 30 cents in nickels." Write *30¢* next to the nickels.

"Now we will jump at a penny (low) level four times while counting by ones: 1! 2! 3! 4! We have 4 cents in pennies." Write *4¢* next to the pennies. "Who can explain how much money these coins make (64¢)? We must add the value of dimes plus the value of nickels plus the value of pennies." Repeat three or four times with varying quantities of each coin.

FORMATIVE ASSESSMENT

Room scan: Can the student dance the three coins showing the correct levels?

Create and Perform

Divide the class into groups of five to eight students depending on maturity level. Pass out one index card to each student. Each group should have a mix of pennies, nickels, and dimes.

Dancers demonstrate pennies (low level), nickels (middle level), and dimes (high level).

"Your first task is to determine how much money you have in your group. Then, review what level each dancer will use. If you have a penny card, what level do you use (low)? What level do you use if you have a nickel card (middle)? What level do you use if you have a dime card (high)? Once you know how much money you have in your group and what level each person will dance, practice dancing with everyone moving at your own level."

As the students get started, it may be helpful to write the following questions and directions on the board and then walk around helping the groups as they work:

- How much money do you have in your group?
- What level should each dancer use (high, middle, or low)?
- Practice dancing with each person moving at the appropriate level.

Once the students have completed the questions and have practiced, direct each group to perform for the rest of the class. When the group performs, the students begin frozen at their own levels, dance with their own levels while the music is on, and then freeze at their own levels when the music is off. While they are performing, the audience watches in order to calculate how much money is in each group.

After each group performs, write on the whiteboard how many pennies, nickels, and dimes were observed in each group. Then ask the students to calculate the total amount of money in each group.

SUMMATIVE ASSESSMENT

Use a checklist to assess the following:

- Can the student identify and demonstrate high, middle, and low levels?
- Can the student correctly calculate the value of a specified set of coins while observing and identifying other dancers' levels?

Students may also write the number of each coin and the total value on paper for each group and turn them in for evaluation.

Review and Reflect

Reflect on dance target	Reflect on mathematics target
"Raise your hand if you can name three levels we use in space while dancing (high, middle, and low). Can you describe a time in your daily life when you use a specific level? Your sentence should follow this format: 'I use a _____ level when I _____.'" Call on three to five students to explain their levels. "You use high, middle, and low levels all the time at home and at school. This week notice activities that use different levels. At our next class, you can tell me a time when you used a high, middle, or low level in your daily life."	"What is the monetary value of a penny (1 cent)? A nickel (5 cents)? A dime (10 cents)? Your homework this week is to ask a parent or grandparent for a handful of coins to calculate the value."

EXTENSION

Solve the following problem: While cleaning up the living room, you find 2 quarters, 9 pennies, 3 nickels, and 2 dimes.

- What is the total value of all your coins?
- List three things you think you could buy with the money you found.
- Now list three things you cannot buy for that amount.

TIME

Clocks are used to measure time. Telling time is important in order to sequence events, follow a schedule, and understand many mathematics concepts. We read the hour, minute, and second hands on a clock to help us tell time.

AGES
7-9

LEVEL
Basic

MATERIALS
- Whiteboard or easel (before class, draw an analog clock without hands)
- Analog clock to reference
- Index cards with times written on one side (one for every two students)

MUSIC
Pleasant selection (see appendix B)

ESSENTIAL QUESTION
Why is telling time important?

ENDURING UNDERSTANDING
We measure time in our daily life.

Analog clock.

	Dance	Mathematics
Learning target	Students practice clarity of shapes and high and low levels.	Students read analog clocks.
Evidence of student learning	The student clearly demonstrates a time using a body shape at a high or low level.	The student identifies and demonstrates a given time using a body shape and high or low level.
Dance elements and mathematics vocabulary	Level (low, high), shape	Time, clockwise, counterclockwise, minute, hour, seconds, minute hand, second hand, a.m., p.m.

(continued)

(continued)

	Dance	Mathematics
Standards	• Articulation of movement: Demonstrate ability to move with clarity of motion and definition of intent. • Levels: Dance on high, middle, and low levels with clear focus and transitions. • Shapes: Form shapes and create designs with the body (*Standards for Learning and Teaching Dance in the Arts*, pp. 23-24).	Tell and write time from analog and digital clocks to the nearest 5 minutes using a.m. and p.m. (*Common Core State Standards for Mathematics*, 2.MD.7).

Warm-Up

"Make a circle as a class. Walk around the circle in a clockwise direction. Now walk around the circle in a counterclockwise direction. Without letting our circle shrink, skip in a counterclockwise direction. Now gallop in a clockwise direction. Continue clockwise using your own movement, maintaining the space between the dancers on either side of you. Freeze.

"On an analog clock, the hands move in a clockwise direction. On an analog clock, it takes an hour for the hour hand to move one number. It takes 12 hours to go around the whole clock. Is that fast or slow? It is moving slowly. Dance with very slow steps clockwise in our circle, imagining how slowly the hour hand is moving. The minute hand takes 5 minutes to go from one number to the next and 1 hour to go all the way around the clock. Does it move faster or slower? It moves faster, but still not extremely quickly. Continue moving clockwise around the circle, but march at a medium tempo, imagining the minute hand. Some analog clocks have second hands. A second hand goes around the clock in 1 minute. Is this faster or slower than the minute hand? Faster! Maintaining the space around your body, prance with a fast tempo in a clockwise direction. Freeze."

Build Knowledge

Demonstrate levels while describing them: "I use a high level when I wash the top of my car. I have to stretch and reach high! I use a low level when I sit on the ground pulling weeds. I use high and low levels every day. Dancers use high and low levels of space to make their dances more interesting to watch."

EXPLORE LEVELS

"Freeze in a high-level shape. Freeze in a new high-level shape. Freeze in a low-level shape. Make a new low-level shape. Skip through the dancing space using a high level. Create a new movement to dance at a high level. Crawl through the dancing space at a low level. Watch for other dancers and make sure you are finding the empty spaces between bodies. Dance with your own movement at a low level. You can roll, slither, scoot, crawl, or crab walk. Are there other ways?" Repeat high and low levels throughout the room three more times for each level.

FORMATIVE ASSESSMENT

Room scan: Can the student clearly demonstrate high and low levels?

Connect

"We will use levels again in a few moments. On the whiteboard I have drawn an analog clock. We use hands on the clock to tell time. The hour hand indicates the hour of the day. The minute hand indicates the number of minutes past the hour. There are 60 minutes in an hour. To determine the minutes, we need to skip count by fives at each of the numbers on the clock in a clockwise direction. Practice with me." Point to the numbers as you skip count aloud: "Five, 10, 15, 20, 25, 30, 35, 40, 45, 50, 55, 60, or 1 hour. The minute hand is longer than the hour hand. Sometimes we call the minute hand the *long hand* and the hour hand the *short hand*. Some clocks do not have a second hand. Usually when people read time, they only read the hour and minute hands."

TIME SHAPES

Next to the whiteboard clock, write *3:30* (do not write *a.m.* or *p.m.* yet). "Staying in your own space, use your whole body to demonstrate the hands of the clock for 3:30. You can use many body parts—your back, arms, legs, head—to make a shape that shows where the hands of the clock should be. Imagine that your body is on this clock, even though you are staying in your own space. Where should the short hand—the hour hand—be pointing? Between the 3 and 4. Where should the long hand—the minute hand—be pointing? At the 6." Draw attention to one or two students who are clearly demonstrating 3:30.

Write *11:45* on the board. "Now use your whole body to demonstrate 11:45. Decide where the minute and hour hands should go, make your shape, and then freeze. You have 8 counts: 1-2-3-4-5-6-7-8-freeze!" Once the students have made their shapes, choose some students to show their shapes.

"We practiced levels earlier. I am going to tell you a few more times. If the time is a.m., make your shape at a low level, as if your clock is on the floor. If the time is p.m., make your shape at a high level, as if your clock is on the board. It is 7:25 p.m. Make a shape with your body to show 7:25 p.m. What level should you be at? Where do your long and short hands point?" Showcase a student who is clearly demonstrating 7:25 p.m. at a high level. Practice time shapes several more times, choosing times to the nearest 5 minutes and using a.m. and p.m.

FORMATIVE ASSESSMENT

Room scan: Can the student clearly demonstrate the clock times with shapes and levels?

Create and Perform

Group the students into pairs. Give each pair an index card with a time written on one side. Choose a student to act as the teacher's partner as an example. "With your partner, use your bodies to show the time that is on your card. You can each be your own clock side by side, or you can work together to make one clock with each other. For example, my partner and I have the time *9:35 a.m.* We need to make our shape at a low level. I will be the minute hand pointing in the direction of the 7, and my partner will be the hour hand pointing in the direction of the 9. You have 12 counts to freeze in your shape with your partner: 1-2-3-4-5-6-7-8-9-10-11-12-freeze!" Once the students have made their shapes, ask each pair to state what time they are and then show their shape.

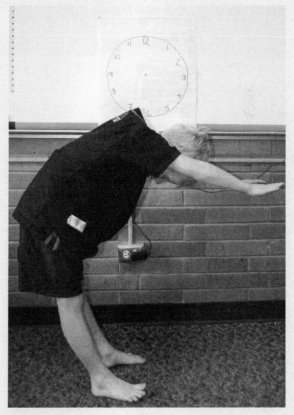

Student demonstrates 3:30 in front of the clock.

SUMMATIVE ASSESSMENT

Use a checklist to assess the following:

- Can the student demonstrate high and low levels?
- Can the student identify and demonstrate a given time using a body shape and high or low level?

Review and Reflect

Reflect on dance target	Reflect on mathematics target
"When do you use a high or low level outside of dance? Raise your hand if you can think of an example. Your sentence should be like this: 'I use a _____ level when I _____.' Your homework this week is to identify an activity that you do at a low level and an activity that you do at a high level and be prepared to share it when I see you again."	"What time is it right now? What time does school start in the morning? What time do you go to lunch? What time does school let out? Why is it important to be able to read an analog clock? Your homework this week is to look for analog clocks at home or in public places and determine the time when you are doing something. When we meet again I'd like you to tell me a time when something happened; for example, 'I went to a movie that started at 1:00 p.m.'"

EXTENSIONS

- Students draw clocks for the times they usually wake up, go to school, go to sport practice, eat dinner, and go to bed.
- On a sheet of paper, students draw a particular time on a clock. They then swap papers with a partner and describe an activity they do at that time of day.

MEASUREMENT

Measurement is important for comparing objects, understanding relationships between objects, and using life skills outside of the classroom. This lesson focuses on length measurement using nonstandard units.

AGES
5-7

LEVEL
Basic

MATERIALS
- Masking tape secured to the floor in four sets of three lines (one short, one medium, and one long)
- Whiteboard or easel

MUSIC
Driving selection (see appendix B)

ESSENTIAL QUESTION
How do I use measurement in my life?

ENDURING UNDERSTANDING
Measurement helps us understand and describe the world.

	Dance	Mathematics
Learning target	Students learn and compare a hop and a jump.	Students use nonstandard units to measure and compare various lines.
Evidence of student learning	The student clearly executes a hop and jump.	The student counts the number of hops or jumps needed to measure a line and predicts and then identifies lines that are shorter or longer in length.
Dance elements and mathematics vocabulary	Locomotor movements (hop and jump)	Unit, measure, longer, shorter
Standards	Demonstrate and identify locomotor movements (*Standards for Learning and Teaching Dance in the Arts*, p. 23).	Express the length of an object as a whole number of length units by laying multiple copies of a shorter object (the length unit) end to end; understand that the length measurement of an object is the number of same-size length units that span it with no gaps or overlaps (*Common Core State Standards for Mathematics*, 1.MD.2).

Warm-Up

"Find your own space where you are only touching the floor and the air. Shake one foot. Shake the other foot. Circle one ankle. Circle the other ankle. Shake your knees. Circle your hips. Circle your hips the other direction. Gently circle your spine. Shake your shoulders. Shake your hands. Circle your hands. Shake your head gently. Circle your head. Skip through the room watching for other dancers. Freeze. Sit down."

Build Knowledge

"A hop pushes off the floor from one foot and lands on the same foot (demonstrate as you are describing). A jump pushes off from two feet and lands on two feet. There are many springing movements that dancers can do, but today we are going to explore the differences between hopping and jumping."

EXPLORE HOPPING AND JUMPING

"Practice hopping on one foot throughout the room. Switch feet and hop on your other foot. A hop takes off from one foot and lands on the same foot.

"Jump on two feet. Jumping takes off from two feet and lands on two feet. Do you move through the room farther while jumping than while hopping?"

Continue practicing jumps and hops, alternating which action you are doing until most students are clearly demonstrating the locomotor movements.

FORMATIVE ASSESSMENT

Room scan: Can the student clearly demonstrate hops and jumps?

Connect

"How can you measure the tape lines on the floor? What tools could be used to measure length (rulers, yardsticks, tape measures)? Using these tools, you can find the length in numbers of inches, feet, or meters. These are standard units. An inch is always the same size. You could also measure the lines in numbers of apples. Are all apples the same size? All apples are not the same size, just like all children are not the same size. You will be using hops and jumps to measure the lines, but because not all students are the same size, each dancer's jumps and hops will be different than those of the other dancers. Each of you will try to make all of your hops the same size and all of your jumps the same size because they are the nonstandard units you are using for measuring."

MEASURING WITH NONSTANDARD UNITS

Divide the students into four groups and assign a set of three lines to each group. "You are each going to measure your smallest tape line with hops. Count your hops and remember your number when you are done." Teachers and students waiting their turns should act as mathematicians and count the hops aloud for the student to hear. After all of the students have measured the smallest line, point to the middle-length line and ask, "Do you think you will have more hops or fewer hops for the next line?"

Each student then measures the middle line with hops. "Which line had more hops? Is this line shorter or longer than the first line? Do you think you will have more hops or fewer hops for the last line?" Each student measures the last line with hops. "Which line had the most hops?" Teachers may also wish for the students to measure their lines in standard units, such as inches or feet, and then record their nonstandard measurements in a T-chart with their standard units.

Student jumps on the line to measure it.

FORMATIVE ASSESSMENT

Room scan:

- Can the student make predictions based on results?
- Can the student demonstrate hops and jumps to measure the lines?

Create and Perform

"You will be measuring all three lines with jumps. Which line do you think will have the most jumps? Is this the longest line?" Direct the students to measure all three lines with jumps. Teachers may wish to record the results on the board. After all students have measured all lines, refer back to their predictions. "Which line had the most jumps? Is this the longest line?" Lead a discussion about how they know which line is longest.

SUMMATIVE ASSESSMENT

Teachers may wish to have older students record their results on paper, which can then be used to assess whether the student was able to measure appropriately using jumps and make accurate comparisons. For younger students, this can also be done while recording student results on the board.

Use a checklist to assess the following:

- Can the student clearly execute a hop and a jump?
- Can the student count the number of hops or jumps needed to measure a line?
- Can the student predict and then identify lines that are longer in length based on the student's findings?

Review and Reflect

Reflect on dance target	Reflect on mathematics target
"Describe a time when you would choose a hop but not a jump (examples: jumping to reach something high, hopping when you hurt one leg). Your homework this week is to notice if you use a hop or jump outside of dance. When I see you again, I will ask you to describe an activity where you used a hop or a jump."	"How did you measure these lines? Were each student's jumps the same length as the other students' jumps? How is this different than measuring in centimeters or yards? Your homework this week is to measure the length of an object using standard or nonstandard units."

EXTENSION

Make a map of your playground. Using your new units of measure (hops or jumps), draw the map to guide the mover from place to place. Each clue should include the distance to cover using one or more of your units and the direction to travel.

PERIMETER AND AREA

Objects have distinct attributes that can be measured. *Perimeter* is the total distance around the outside of a two-dimensional shape and is calculated by adding the measurements of all the sides. *Area* is the amount of surface that makes up a two-dimensional shape and is measured in square units. The area of rectangles is found by multiplying length by width.

AGES
7-10

LEVEL
Basic

MATERIALS
- Masking or painter's tape (before class, use the tape to make a large rectangle and four smaller rectangles on the floor) or variously sized rectangular rugs
- One blank piece of paper and pencil for each student
- Whiteboard or easel

MUSIC
Pleasant selection (see appendix B)

ESSENTIAL QUESTION
How do I use measurement in my life?

ENDURING UNDERSTANDING
Objects can be measured and described in a variety of ways.

	Dance	Mathematics
Learning target	Students practice precision of movements.	Students use nonstandard units of measurement to explore area and perimeter.
Evidence of student learning	The student clearly demonstrates locomotor jumps that are equal and consistent length.	The student uses jumps as a unit to measure two sides of a rectangle and correctly determines the perimeter and area of the shape.
Dance elements and mathematics vocabulary	Locomotor jumping	Unit, area, perimeter, rectangle

(continued)

(continued)

	Dance	Mathematics
Standards	Articulation of movement: Demonstrate ability to move with clarity of motion and definition of intent (*Standards for Learning and Teaching Dance in the Arts*, p. 23).	Multiply side lengths to find areas of rectangles with whole-number side lengths in the context of solving real-world and mathematical problems, and represent whole-number products as rectangular areas in mathematical reasoning. Solve real-world and mathematical problems involving perimeters of polygons, including finding the perimeter given the side lengths, finding an unknown side length, and exhibiting rectangles with the same perimeter and different areas or with the same area and different perimeters (*Common Core State Standards for Mathematics*, 3.MD.7-8).

Warm-Up

"We will be doing quite a bit of jumping today, so in order to take care of our bodies, we need to warm up our joints. Let's start by circling one foot. Now shake it. Switch feet. Circle and then shake. Bend and stretch our knees four times. March in place. Move our hips from side to side. Reach down and up, down and up." Repeat five times.

Build Knowledge

"Dancers sometimes try to use clear and precise movements. We are going to jump through our dancing space, but we want to try to make every jump the same distance. It is not about trying to make every jump travel as far as possible but about making every jump manageable and consistent."

EXPLORE JUMPING WITH CLARITY

Practice jumping through the room. Each person tries to make each jump the same distance.

FORMATIVE ASSESSMENT

Room scan: Can the student jump with precision and control?

Connect

"You may have noticed the rectangles on the floor. We are going to measure the perimeter and area of these rectangles. Instead of using inches or meters, we are going to use jumps as nonstandard units."

MEASURE THE LARGEST RECTANGLE

"Make a shape on the perimeter of any of the rectangles. Now make a shape on the area of any of the rectangles. Perimeter is the distance around the outside edge of the shape, and area is how much space the entire shape takes up."

Give each student a paper and pencil. On the board, draw a rectangle that reflects the largest rectangle. Instruct the students to draw the rectangle on their own paper and then leave their paper and pencil on the floor or on a desk out of the way.

One student jumps on the rectangle while another student measures and records his jumps.

"When it is your turn, you are going to measure this long side using your precise, controlled jumps. As you are jumping, make sure to count how many jumps it takes for you to measure the side. When you are done jumping, go back to your paper and write your measurement next to the long side."

After students have measured the long side with jumps and written down the number, ask them to measure a short side and write their measurement next to a short side on their paper.

"We know a long side and a short side. Can we determine the perimeter? Yes! We know that the other long side is the same as the one we already measured and the other short side is the same as the one we already measured! All we need to do now is add the lengths of all four sides to determine the perimeter. Remember that your measurements are each different, so your perimeters may be different, too." Allow the students a few minutes to find the perimeter in jump units.

"Can we find the area of this rectangle in your jump units? Absolutely! Area is length times width. You need to multiply your long side by your short side." Give the students several minutes to determine the area.

FORMATIVE ASSESSMENT

Room scan:

- Can the student measure the rectangle with jumps?
- Can the student determine the area and perimeter?

Create and Perform

Divide the class into four groups and assign each group one of the smaller rectangles. "Your group is sharing a rectangle, but you will each be working individually. Choose a new nonstandard unit to measure your rectangle, such as galloping, skipping, marching, or sliding. Make sure your name is on your paper. On the back, draw your new rectangle. Your task is to measure only two sides and then determine the perimeter and area in your new nonstandard unit. What two sides do you think you will measure? A long side and a short side. We know that the long sides of a rectangle are both the same length and the short sides of a rectangle are both the same length. Measure a long side and a short side and then determine the area and the perimeter of the rectangle." Teachers may have the students perform their rectangle dance by demonstrating their nonstandard unit measurements (e.g., 3 gallops on the long side and 2 gallops on the short side) and explain their calculations.

SUMMATIVE ASSESSMENT

Use a checklist to assess the following: Can the student clearly demonstrate locomotor jumps that are equal and consistent in length?

When students are finished finding the area and perimeter, collect the papers. Evaluate the papers to assess the following: Can the student use jumps as a unit to measure the sides of a rectangle and correctly determine the area and perimeter of the shape?

Review and Reflect

Reflect on dance target	Reflect on mathematics target
"You jumped with extreme precision today. When do you think it is important for dancers to be very precise, accurate, and clear with their bodies? When I add eggs to my cookie batter, I use precision to make sure the eggshells don't fall in. What kinds of movements do you do at home that require body precision? Your homework this week is to identify an activity that uses body precision. You can tell me your movement precision the next time I see you."	"How do you find the perimeter of a rectangle (add all the sides)? How do you find the area of a rectangle (multiply length times width)? Why is it important to be able to determine area and perimeter? Your homework is to measure the area and perimeter of a room in your house and be ready to tell me next week."

EXTENSIONS

- Measure the tape rectangles using standard units such as yards or meters. Then find the perimeter and area and compare with the nonstandard units.
- Measure the classroom using nonstandard units such as bodies lying down shoulder to shoulder or blocks laid end to end.

BAR GRAPHS

In both mathematics and science, children learn to visually interpret and display data in graphs or charts. Bar graphs are one such presentation of data that students can use to communicate information visually.

AGES
7-9

LEVEL
Intermediate

MATERIALS
- One piece of construction paper (12 x 18 in. or 30 x 46 cm) for each student (before class write *fast*, *slow*, or *medium* on each paper, varying the quantity of each)
- Masking or painter's tape
- Whiteboard or easel

MUSIC
Contemplative, pleasant, and driving selections—5 to 10 selections with varying styles and tempos (see appendix B)

ESSENTIAL QUESTION
How can I collect, organize, and display data?

ENDURING UNDERSTANDING
Bar graphs convey data in a concise way.

	Dance	Mathematics
Learning target	Students learn slow, fast, and medium tempos in free rhythm and sensed time. Students explore high, middle, and low levels.	Students practice making bar graphs and interpreting their meanings.
Evidence of student learning	The student demonstrates a slow, fast, or medium tempo. The student demonstrates a high, middle, or low level..	The student correctly models a bar graph and identifies if his bar has the most students, fewest students, or neither.
Dance elements and mathematics vocabulary	Tempo (fast, slow, medium), levels (high, middle, low)	Bar graph, category, column, least (fewest), most, data
Standards	• Tempo: Dance with a steady beat in various tempos. • Levels: Dance on high, middle, and low levels with clear focus and transitions (*Standards for Learning and Teaching Dance in the Arts*, p. 23).	Draw a picture graph and a bar graph (with single-unit scale) to represent a data set with up to four categories (*Common Core State Standards for Mathematics*, 2.MD.10).

Warm-Up

"We are going to freeze dance. When the music is on you will dance, and when the music is off, you will freeze. Dancers are very responsive to music. When you are dancing, listen to the sound of the music and what it suggests to you. If it is bouncy music, you may jump or skip. If it is slow and soft, you may float gently through the room. Dance the way the music tells you to move." Play five 30-second selections, making sure to vary the tempos.

Build Knowledge

"What did you notice about the music selections in the freeze dance?" Call on students, encouraging them to describe characteristics of the music and how those traits influenced their dances. "Did you notice that some songs were fast, some were slow, and some were in the middle? We call that *tempo*. It is the speed or pace of the music. Like music, dancers can use a variety of tempos with their bodies. Dancers can move with slow, medium, or fast tempos."

EXPLORE TEMPO

"Find your own space. Begin by walking with a slow tempo. Use your arms slowly, your head slowly, your legs slowly, and your back slowly. Can you move slowly using a different movement? When I say 'Go,' gallop with a fast tempo. Make sure to watch for other dancers and to stay in control of your body. Go! Dance quickly with your whole body! Freeze! Now march with a medium tempo that is not too fast and not too slow but right in the middle. How many different ways can you dance with a medium tempo?" Practice fast, medium, and slow tempos three more times each.

FORMATIVE ASSESSMENT

Room scan: Can the student dance with slow, medium, and fast tempos?

INTRODUCE LEVELS

"Sometimes dancers use different levels in space. We can move high off the ground, low to the ground, and in the middle (demonstrate the levels while describing them). We call these *high, middle,* and *low levels.*"

EXPLORE LEVELS

"Using a medium tempo, move through the room at a high level. How high can you move? Now use a low level. How low to the floor can you be? You can slither, roll, crawl, and scoot. Find your middle level that is not too low and not too high." Practice high, middle, and low levels three more times each, encouraging the students to find new ways to move at each level.

FORMATIVE ASSESSMENT

Room scan: Can the student dance at high, middle, and low levels?

Connect

"We are going to use our levels and tempos to make a human-sized bar graph. We use bar graphs to visually communicate data."

MAKE A BAR GRAPH

On the floor, make a line of tape to represent the horizontal axis. Use tape to make the letters *F, M,* and *S* where each column will go. "This is our horizontal axis. We have three categories on our axis: *F* for fast, *M* for medium, and *S* for slow. I am going to give you each a piece of construction paper with a tempo written on it. When you receive your paper, move all through the room with that tempo. When I tell you to, continue to dance your tempo, but begin moving to your column. If you have *fast* on your paper, you move toward the *F*; if you have *slow*, you move toward the *S*; and if you have *medium*, you go to the *M*. When you get to your column, you will lay your papers down end to end to make a bar. When your paper is down, stand on your paper and freeze." Review the directions again to promote understanding.

Give each student a piece of construction paper with a tempo written on one side. After they are all moving through the room with their designated tempo, instruct them to move to their column. Once they are all lined up in their bars, ask them the following questions: "Which column has the most students? Which column has the fewest students? Which column has neither the most nor the fewest? If your column has the most students, make a high-level shape to show that you have the most. If your column has the fewest students, make a low-level shape. If your column does not have the most or the fewest, make a middle-level shape."

FORMATIVE ASSESSMENT

Room scan:

- Can the student answer questions about the data?
- Can the student connect her level to the data it is displaying: most students, fewest students, or neither?

Create and Perform

"Pick up your paper and swap it with another student so that you have a new tempo." Divide the class into groups of four to eight depending on maturity level, trying to have a variety of tempos in each group.

Students use levels to make bar graphs with papers and lines.

"In your group, your task is to make a new bar graph. When it is your turn, you will clearly use your tempo to move from this side of the room (opposite the horizontal axis) to your columns. When you get to your columns, you will put your papers down and freeze in a level shape. In order to have everyone freezing in your bar, it may be necessary to keep just one foot on your paper. If you are in the column with the most students, you will make a high shape; if you are in the column with the fewest students, make a low shape; or if you are neither, make a middle-level shape. Your task right now is to make sure you all know what tempo you will be moving at and what level you will be at when you make your bar. You need to figure out which bar will have the most and fewest so you know what level you should be at. Make sure to work together!"

Give the groups 2 minutes and then have them perform for the class. Groups will use their tempos to get to their bars and make their level shapes. After each group performs, ask the audience questions, such as "Which tempo has the most students?"

SUMMATIVE ASSESSMENT

Use a checklist to assess the following:
- Can the student demonstrate a slow, fast, or medium tempo?
- Can the student demonstrate a high, middle, or low level?
- Can the student correctly model a bar graph and identify if his bar has the most students, fewest students, or neither?

Review and Reflect

Reflect on dance target	Reflect on mathematics target
"When do you use a certain tempo outside of dance? I use a fast tempo when I brush my teeth." Call on several students. "When do you use a high, middle, or low level outside of dance?" Call on other students. "Your homework this week is to identify an activity where you use a specific level and tempo. Next time we meet, you can tell me the activity and the level and tempo."	"What other sorts of data could we use a bar graph to display? Bar graphs convey data. Your homework is to locate a bar graph that helps us understand data. Next time we meet, you can describe the data displayed on the bar graph."

EXTENSION

Choose a question to ask a group of students, such as "What is your favorite type of cookie?" Analyze and display the results with a bar graph. You may wish to incorporate technology by making a bar graph on the computer.

8

GEOMETRY

Geometry is the mathematical study of lines, points, shapes, and the spatial relationship of objects. Learning in geometry begins with basic two-dimensional shapes and continues into much more complex studies. This chapter provides four lessons that integrate dance with geometry. In the first lesson, two-dimensional shapes are explored with body shapes and pathways. Relationships, touch, and body shapes are used to learn three-dimensional shapes in the second lesson. In the third lesson, symmetry and asymmetry are discovered using body shapes as individuals, pairs, and groups. And in the fourth lesson, pathways and shapes are integrated with angles and parallel and perpendicular lines. The format of each lesson enables students to embody the mathematical principles while creatively exploring the dance vocabulary.

TWO-DIMENSIONAL SHAPES

Before entering formal education, children begin learning about shapes through games, puzzles, and toys. In school, children use math vocabulary to identify, describe, and compare shapes.

AGES
5-7

LEVEL
Basic

MATERIALS
- Construction-paper cutouts (one each of a triangle, square, rectangle, and circle or additional shapes the class is studying such as a trapezoid, rhombus, or hexagon)
- Whiteboard or easel

MUSIC
Contemplative selection (see appendix B)

ESSENTIAL QUESTION
How can I identify and describe shapes?

ENDURING UNDERSTANDING
The world is made up of many different shapes.

	Dance	Mathematics
Learning target	Students create body shapes and pathways through space.	Students identify and model two-dimensional shapes.
Evidence of student learning	The student clearly demonstrates a specified geometric shape with the body. The student clearly demonstrates a specified pathway through space.	The student clearly identifies and demonstrates a specified geometric shape with the body. The student clearly identifies and demonstrates a pathway that models a specified two-dimensional shape.

(continued)

	Dance	Mathematics
Dance elements and mathematics vocabulary	Shape, pathway (curvy, straight, circular, zigzag)	Shape, circle, triangle, rectangle, square, sides, corners (additional shapes may also be used, such as rhombus, trapezoid, hexagon, and pentagon)
Evidence of student learning	• Pathways: Dance through space in straight, curved, circular, diagonal, zigzag, and combinations of pathways. • Shapes: Form shapes and create designs with the body (*Standards for Learning and Teaching Dance in the Arts*, pp. 23-24).	• Correctly name shapes regardless of their orientation or overall size (*Common Core State Standards for Mathematics*, K.G.2). • Analyze and compare two- and three-dimensional shapes in various sizes and orientations using informal language to describe their similarities, differences, parts (e.g., number of sides and vertices or corners), and other attributes (e.g., having sides of equal length) (*Common Core State Standards for Mathematics*, K.G.4). • Model shapes in the world by building shapes from components (e.g., sticks and clay balls) and drawing shapes (*Common Core State Standards for Mathematics*, K.G.5).

Warm-Up

"Imagine that you have paint on your hands. Paint a design or picture in the air with your hands. Now imagine that you have paint on your feet. Paint a design with your feet in the air. Paint a design with your feet on the floor. Now you have paint on your head. What kinds of lines can you paint in the air with your head? Choose a new body part and imagine it has paint on it. Show me how you can paint the air and floor with that body part."

BUILD KNOWLEDGE

Ask the students to sit down. "Imagine that I have paint on the soles of my feet." Move through the room with a curvy pathway. "Did you see my pathway? What sort of paint marks did I make? Curvy lines! Dancers use pathways when they dance. Pathways are the trails we move through the dancing space. Even though the paint is imaginary, we can still notice the pathway. We can use curvy pathways, straight pathways, and zigzag pathways." Demonstrate the pathways as you are talking about them. Then draw a curvy line, straight line, and zigzag line on the whiteboard.

EXPLORE PATHWAYS

"We will be using pathways throughout our dancing space, and it is important to watch out for other dancers so we do not collide. When you practice your pathways, make sure you continue to look for empty spaces between bodies. Sometimes you may need to pause in your pathway and allow

Students skip in a curving pathway with the pathway drawn behind.

someone to pass before you continue. Find your own space where you are only touching the floor and the air. Begin by skipping in a curvy pathway. Curvy pathways have no sharp corners and the lines are not straight. Imagine that you are painting curved lines through the dancing space.

"March in a straight pathway. Use a sharp corner when you need to change directions. Straight pathways have no curvy lines.

"Tiptoe with a zigzag pathway. Zigzag pathways have straight lines and sharp corners. There are no curvy lines in a zigzag pathway.

"Gallop in a straight pathway. Crawl in a curvy pathway. Jump in a zigzag pathway."

FORMATIVE ASSESSMENT

Room scan: Can the student clearly demonstrate curvy, straight, and zigzag pathways?

Connect

Ask the students to sit down. "Now we will use frozen body shapes and pathways to make dances about geometric shapes."

SHAPES AND PATHWAYS

Hold up the paper circle. "What shape is this? A circle. How many sides does it have? None! How many corners does it have? None! A circle has no sides or corners. Is it made with a curved line or straight lines? A curved line. Please make the shape of a circle with your hands. Stand up and make a circle shape with your whole body. Make a new circle shape with your body. Are there any straight lines or corners? No! Now imagine that you have paint on your body. Let's skip in a circle pathway in the dancing space. Are you painting a circle on the floor? Skip in your own circle pathway. Maybe it is a big circle, or maybe it is a smaller circle. If you are spinning in one place, though, you are not making a circle pathway; you are just making a dot! Pathways are locomotor, which means that you are moving through the dancing space, not staying in one place. Freeze in a circle shape. Sit down."

Hold up the paper triangle. "What shape is this? A triangle. How many sides does a triangle have? Three! How many corners does a triangle have? Three! A triangle has three straight sides and three sharp corners. Make a triangle with your hands. Stand up and make a triangle shape with your body. Make a new triangle shape with your body. Tiptoe in your own triangle pathway. Make sure your pathway has three straight sides and three sharp corners. Imagine that you are painting a triangle on the floor with your body. There are no curvy lines. Freeze in a triangle shape with your body. Sit down."

Hold up the paper square. "What shape is this? A square. How many sides does a square have? Four! How many corners does a square have? Four! What do we know about a square's sides? How is a square different than a rectangle? The sides are all the same length. Are there any curved lines in a square? No! Just straight lines and sharp corners. Make a square with your hands. Stand up and make the shape of a square with your whole body. Please understand that it is difficult to make an actual square with your body, but you are trying to make your own representation of a square. Make a square in a new way with your body. March in a square pathway. We know that the sides of a square are the same length, so we need to do the same number of marches for each side of the square. Let's do five marches for each side of the square: five marches and then a sharp corner, five marches and then a sharp corner. There are no curvy lines in a square! Freeze in a square shape. Sit down."

Hold up the paper rectangle. "What shape is this? A rectangle. How many sides does a rectangle have? Four! How many corners does a rectangle have? Four! A rectangle is a stretched out square. It has two long sides and two short sides. It does not have any curvy lines; just straight lines and sharp corners. Make a rectangle with your hands. Stand up and make a rectangle with your body. You are making your best demonstration of a rectangle. Make a new rectangle with your body. Gallop in a rectangle pathway. There are no curvy lines. You are galloping with straight lines and sharp corners to make your own rectangle pathway. Freeze in a rectangle shape. Sit down."

FORMATIVE ASSESSMENT

Room scan: Can the student clearly demonstrate specific pathways and shapes?

Create and Perform

Divide the students into groups of four. Assign each group a shape (circle, triangle, square, or rectangle). Hold up the paper shapes. Ask each group to point to the shape that they have been assigned.

"When it is your group's turn, you will perform a shape dance. Your dance will start with everyone in your group making your shape together. When I see that you are frozen in your shapes, I will start the music. When the music begins, you will use your shape as your own individual pathway. When the music ends, you will come back to your group and freeze in your shape all together. If you are in the triangle group, you will start with all four dancers making one frozen triangle together. When the music starts, you will each make your own triangle pathway. When the music stops, you will quickly move to your group and freeze in your first triangle shape. Practice with your group." Allow the groups to practice for 1 to 2 minutes and then have them perform for the class.

SUMMATIVE ASSESSMENT

Use a rubric (table 8.1) to assess the performances. Use a checklist to assess the following:

- Can the student clearly identify and demonstrate a specified geometric shape with the body?
- Can the student clearly identify and demonstrate a pathway that models a specified two-dimensional shape?

Table 8.1   Rubric for Pathways

The student's pathway was	
4	clear and continued throughout the entire dance.
3	clear but not continued throughout the dance.
2	not clear.
1	different than what was planned.

Review and Reflect

Reflect on dance target	Reflect on mathematics target
"I use a straight (or curvy, zigzag, or circular) pathway when I walk down the hall to the lunch room. When do you use a straight, curving, circular, or zigzag pathway outside of dance? Your sentence should sound like this: 'I use a _____ pathway when I _____.' Your homework tonight is to identify the pathway that you use to get home from school. Tomorrow, be prepared to describe your pathway."	Call on four students and ask them to draw the four shapes (triangle, square, rectangle, and circle) on the whiteboard. "Your homework is to identify objects that are triangles, circles, rectangles, and squares. Tomorrow, I will ask you to tell me one object for each shape."

EXTENSIONS

- Use construction-paper cutouts of various shapes to create a picture.
- Go on a scavenger hunt and write down all the objects in the room that are triangles, squares, rectangles, and circles.

THREE-DIMENSIONAL SHAPES

Young children often learn two-dimensional shapes first, and then identify and classify three-dimensional shapes. Manipulatives are useful for teaching three-dimensional objects. In this lesson, students use their bodies to create three-dimensional shapes.

AGES
5-7

LEVEL
Basic

MATERIALS
Three-dimensional models of a cube, cone, cylinder, and sphere

MUSIC
Pleasant selection (see appendix B)

ESSENTIAL QUESTION
How can I identify and describe three-dimensional shapes?

ENDURING UNDERSTANDING
The world around us contains solid, three-dimensional shapes.

	Dance	Mathematics
Learning target	Students work cooperatively with others and use appropriate touch to create group shapes with other dancers.	Students identify and classify the three-dimensional shapes: cone, cylinder, sphere, and cube.
Evidence of student learning	The student demonstrates group shapes. The student uses appropriate touch.	The student clearly demonstrates a specified three-dimensional shape with a group.
Dance elements and mathematics vocabulary	Shapes, touch, relationships	Three-dimensional, solid, cone, cylinder, cube, sphere
Standards	• Shapes: Form shapes and create designs with the body. • Relationships: Dance in a defined spatial relationship to others. Work cooperatively (*Standards for Learning and Teaching Dance in the Arts*, p. 24).	• Correctly name shapes regardless of their orientation or overall size. Identify shapes as two-dimensional (lying in a plane, flat) or three-dimensional (solid) (*Common Core State Standards for Mathematics*, K.G.2-3). • Model shapes in the world by building shapes from components (e.g., sticks and clay balls) and drawing shapes (*Common Core State Standards for Mathematics*, K.G.5).

Warm-Up

"Find your own space where you are only touching the floor and the air. For our warm-up, we are going to practice making frozen shapes with our bodies. I will count out loud. You have 8 counts to move into a fabulous frozen shape with your whole body. Then you will freeze for 8 counts without moving at all! Next you will have 8 counts to slowly change into a new shape and 8 counts to freeze in that shape. We will keep repeating the pattern: 8 counts to move into a shape, and 8 counts to freeze in your shape. Try to make a new shape each time." Count aloud with music, clapping, or a hand drum. Practice 10 shapes.

BUILD KNOWLEDGE

"Sometimes dancers move closely with one another, and sometimes we even touch while we are dancing. We respect other people's bodies, so we always touch in a respectful and safe way, without pushing or pulling. It is appropriate to touch someone gently on the feet, hands, back, arms, knees, or head. If we are uncomfortable with how we are being touched, we ask the other dancer to stop or change the way the dancer is touching us."

EXPLORE TOUCH

Divide the students into pairs and choose one person in each pair to be first. "If you are the first person, you are the sculptor. Your partner is your clay. You are going to work together. Using respectful touch, you will mold your partner into shapes. Your partner will try to hold the shapes as you mold them like clay. If you notice that your partner is struggling to balance or hold a shape, please mold a new shape that your partner can hold more easily." Give the first partners 1 minute to mold their partners, and then switch roles. This exercise can be done two to four times.

FORMATIVE ASSESSMENT

Room scan:

- Can the student use gentle, respectful, and appropriate touch with a partner?
- Can the student work cooperatively with a partner?

Connect

"There are flat shapes and solid shapes. We know flat shapes such as circles, triangles, rectangles, and squares. Solid shapes are not flat; they are three-dimensional, meaning they have length, width, and depth. Some solid shapes are cones, cubes, spheres, and cylinders. We are going to model three-dimensional shapes with our bodies. Please understand that it is very difficult to make some of these shapes, and your task is to make your best representation of the shape."

THREE-DIMENSIONAL SHAPES

Hold up the model of the sphere. "What shape is this? A sphere. Is it flat or solid? Solid. A sphere has no edges, just one curved surface. A ball is a sphere. Make a solid sphere shape with your body. Make a new sphere shape. And another sphere shape."

Hold up the model of the cylinder. "What shape is this? A cylinder. Is it flat or solid? Solid. A cylinder has two circular faces and one curved surface. A soup can is a cylinder. Make a solid cylinder shape with your body. Make a new cylinder shape."

Hold up the model of the cone. "What shape is this? A cone. Is it flat or solid? Solid. A cone has one circular face and one curved surface that comes to a point. An ice-cream cone is a cone shape. Make a solid cone shape with your body. Make a new cone shape."

Four students make a cube shape.

Hold up the model of a cube. "What shape is this? A cube. Is it flat or solid? Solid. A cube has six square faces. Dice are cubes. Make a solid three-dimensional cube shape with your body. Make a new cube shape with your body. Make a cone shape. Make a cylinder shape. Make a sphere shape. Make a cube shape."

Practice each shape two more times each.

FORMATIVE ASSESSMENT

Room scan: Can the student demonstrate the four geometric shapes with the body?

Create and Perform

Divide the class into groups of three to four students. "In a moment, I am going to assign each group one of the three-dimensional solid shapes. Your task is to find a way to make your solid shape cooperatively with your whole group using respectful touching and working together." Assign each group one shape—cone, cube, cylinder, or sphere. Allow the students to work for 2 minutes and then show each group shape to the class. If there is time, repeat the activity with new shapes for each group.

SUMMATIVE ASSESSMENT

Use a checklist to assess the following:

- Can the student use appropriate touch?
- Can the student clearly demonstrate a specified three-dimensional shape with a group?

Review and Reflect

Reflect on dance target	Reflect on mathematics target
"How do we use respectful touching at home or in school? Your homework this week is to use respectful touch with a parent, sister, brother, or friend, and be prepared to describe the experience when we have dance class again. For example, I use a handshake when I am meeting a new person, and I give a respectful hug when I see an old friend."	Ask the students to identify each three-dimensional model. "Today, notice all the three-dimensional spheres, cubes, cylinders, and cones you encounter at home and at school. Tomorrow, please identify the objects and their shapes."

EXTENSIONS

- Go on a scavenger hunt to find spheres, cylinders, cones, and cubes that are everyday objects in the classroom or at home.
- Mold clay into a sphere, cone, cube, and cylinder.

SYMMETRY AND ASYMMETRY

AGES
7-11

LEVEL
Basic

MATERIALS
Whiteboard or easel

MUSIC
Pleasant selection (see appendix B)

ESSENTIAL QUESTION
Where do I find symmetry in my everyday life?

ENDURING UNDERSTANDING
The world is made up of symmetrical and asymmetrical designs.

	Dance	Mathematics
Learning target	Students use body control while creating clear personal and group shapes.	Students understand symmetry and asymmetry.
Evidence of student learning	The student clearly demonstrates symmetrical and asymmetrical shapes as an individual. The student clearly demonstrates symmetrical and asymmetrical shapes with a group.	The student clearly demonstrates symmetrical and asymmetrical shapes as an individual. The student clearly demonstrates symmetrical and asymmetrical shapes with a group.
Dance elements and mathematics vocabulary	Shapes, relationships	Symmetry, asymmetry, line of symmetry, shape
Standards	<ul><li>Articulation of movement: Demonstrate ability to move with clarity of motion and definition of intent.</li><li>Shapes: Form shapes and create designs with the body.</li><li>Relationships: Dance in a defined spatial relationship to others. (*Standards for Learning and Teaching Dance in the Arts*, pp. 23-24).</li></ul>	Recognize a line of symmetry for a two-dimensional figure as a line across the figure such that the figure can be folded along the line into matching parts. Identify line-symmetric figures and draw lines of symmetry (*Common Core State Standards for Mathematics, 4.G.3*).

Warm-Up

Do the BrainDance (see appendix A). Be sure to emphasize body sides, which are relevant to this lesson.

BUILD KNOWLEDGE

"Dancers use their bodies to create many shapes. Sometimes dancers start and end dances in frozen shapes or even hold still shapes in choreography as other dancers are moving. We try to be very clear about the shapes we make and we know how to control our bodies. We are going to make clear and controlled shapes with our bodies today."

EXPLORE SHAPES

"Make a frozen shape with your arms. Make a shape with your arms and your legs. Form a shape with your arms, legs, and back. Make a new shape with your entire body. Create a shape that is curvy. Now create an angular shape. Now a round shape. Can you make a twisted shape? Make a small shape. Make a big shape. Make your own fantastic and unique shape!"

FORMATIVE ASSESSMENT

Room scan: Can the student create and hold a frozen shape with clarity and control?

Connect

"What does it mean if a shape is symmetrical? A symmetrical shape can be folded in half and both sides are the same, as if the fold or line of symmetry were a mirror. An asymmetrical shape is not the same on both sides." Demonstrate this by drawing an imaginary line down the center of a student's shape and discussing the two sides. Repeat several times with symmetrical and asymmetrical shapes.

Students show asymmetry and symmetry.

SYMMETRICAL AND ASYMMETRICAL SHAPES

"Make a symmetrical shape with your body. If you draw a line of symmetry down the middle of your body, is each side the same as the other? Make a new symmetrical shape. Can you think of a different symmetrical shape that you can make with your body? Make an asymmetrical shape with your body. Both sides are not the same. Create a new asymmetrical shape. Make another new asymmetrical shape."

Divide the students into pairs. "With your partner, you have 10 counts to make a symmetrical shape together side by side. You may use gentle touching, but you do not have to touch: 1-2-3-4-5-6-7-8-9-10-freeze! Make a new symmetrical shape with your partner in 10 counts." Count to 10 again. Repeat as the students make three more symmetrical shapes.

FORMATIVE ASSESSMENT

Room scan: Can the student create symmetrical shapes that are clear?

Create and Perform

Combine each pair of students with another pair to form groups of approximately four students. "Your task in your group is to create one symmetrical shape with your entire group. Make sure that you know where the line of symmetry is and that both sides are the same." Allow the students to work for 2 minutes and then ask groups to show their symmetrical shapes to the rest of the class. The teacher can take digital pictures of each group to view and discuss later.

If there's time, groups can also create an asymmetrical shape. Or, they may create a symmetrical shape and then a moving transition into an asymmetrical shape. The transition could be simply morphing into the new shape, or it could be more complex with the dancers using a locomotor action such as skipping or crawling to move completely out of one shape and into the next.

SUMMATIVE ASSESSMENT

Use a checklist to assess the following:

- Can the student clearly demonstrate symmetrical and asymmetrical shapes as an individual?
- Can the student clearly demonstrate symmetrical and asymmetrical shapes with a group?

Review and Reflect

Reflect on dance target	Reflect on mathematics target
"Why is it important for dancers to create clear shapes? Why do dancers practice moving and freezing in shapes with control? Your homework is to identify a shape that you make with your body at home. Perhaps you sit in a certain way when you watch a movie with your family. Maybe when you are waiting with a parent in line at the grocery store you stand in a specific shape. Or maybe when you sit at your desk you hold a shape. Be prepared to describe a shape that you make with your body outside of dance class when I see you next."	Draw several shapes on the whiteboard and call on students to identify the symmetrical or asymmetrical shapes. "Tonight, identify one object at home that is symmetrical and one object that is asymmetrical, and be ready to describe the objects tomorrow."

EXTENSIONS

- Create a symmetrical sculpture with modeling clay.
- Using crayons, draw five symmetrical shapes and five asymmetrical shapes.

ANGLES AND LINES

Geometric angles and lines can be analyzed and categorized based on their attributes. A right angle is formed when two lines meet at a 90-degree angle. An obtuse angle is formed when two lines meet at more than 90 degrees but less than 180 degrees. An acute angle is formed when two lines meet at less than 90 degrees. Lines are perpendicular when they intersect at 90 degrees, and lines are parallel when they can extend in both directions and never intersect. This lesson should serve as a review and reinforcement of angles and lines previously learned in geometry studies.

This lesson contains a series of activities that may require more than one class session. For more mature students, and with ample time, this lesson may be done in one lesson. To divide it into three lessons, do the following:

1. Explore the Build Knowledge section, introducing individual and group shapes, and the drill introducing angle shapes.

2. Review themes from lesson 1 and introduce the line shapes.

3. Combine angles and lines into choreography, as described in the Create and Perform section.

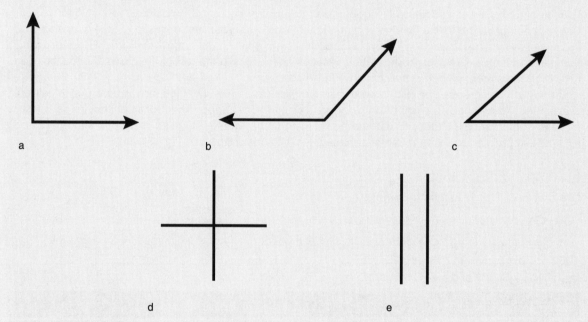

Angles (right, *a*; obtuse, *b*; acute, *c*) and lines (perpendicular, *d*; parallel, *e*).

AGES
9-11

LEVEL
Basic

MATERIALS
- Index cards with one of the following written on each: *acute angle, right angle, obtuse angle, parallel lines, perpendicular lines* (one card for each student)
- Whiteboard or easel

MUSIC
Pleasant selection (see appendix B)

ESSENTIAL QUESTION
What is the relationship of two lines?

ENDURING UNDERSTANDING
Objects in the world are made up of angles of various measures.

	Dance	Mathematics
Learning target	Students create clear shapes individually, with a partner, and as a group.	Students identify and classify acute, right, and obtuse angles as well as parallel and perpendicular lines.
Evidence of student learning	The student creates clear angle and line shapes individually and with other students.	The student performs a dance that includes three angles or types of lines, working cooperatively with others.
Dance elements and mathematics vocabulary	Shape	Angle (obtuse, acute, right), line (perpendicular, parallel), intersect
Standards	Shapes: Form shapes and create designs with the body (*Standards for Learning and Teaching Dance in the Arts*, p. 24).	Draw points, lines, line segments, rays, angles (right, acute, obtuse), and perpendicular and parallel lines. Identify these in two-dimensional figures (*Common Core State Standards for Mathematics*, 4.G.1).

Warm-Up

"When the music starts, we're going to tiptoe through the room. When the music stops, immediately freeze in your own creative and unique shape." Give students a new locomotor movement each time (e.g., walk, hop, gallop, jump, skip, prance, crab walk, crawl, slither). Play the music for 10 to 15 seconds and encourage students to freeze in a new and creative dance shape each time the music stops.

BUILD KNOWLEDGE

"While we were freeze dancing, you were making frozen shapes with your body. Dancers are artists who choose unique and interesting shapes. Choose a new creative shape with your body. Taking 8 full counts to transition, change to a new, interesting shape: 1-2-3-4-5-6-7-8-freeze. Change for 8 counts again to an entirely different unique shape: 1-2-3-4-5-6-7-8-freeze. In a moment, we will be creating shapes with more than one dancer."

EXPLORE GROUP SHAPES

Divide the students into pairs. "With your partner, create a new, interesting shape. Your bodies do not need to be making the exact same shape, but you are making one whole shape together. Perhaps you are gently touching. Maybe you are near each other and filling the empty spaces around each other's bodies. Your individual shapes should complement each other in order to create a more complete shape with the two of you. You have 8 counts to create your shape and freeze: 1-2-3-4-5-6-7-8-freeze. You have 8 counts to make a new shape with your partner: 1-2-3-4-5-6-7-8-freeze.

"Leaving your partner, you have 12 counts to find a new group of two or three dancers who are near you and freeze in a group shape: 1-2-3-4-5-6-7-8-9-10-11-12-freeze. You have 12 counts to find an entirely new group of two or three and make a creative group shape: 1-2-3-4-5-6-7-8-9-10-11-12-freeze." Continue directing the students to find new groups of two, three, or four people and create interesting group shapes. Repeat the activity five times.

FORMATIVE ASSESSMENT

Room scan: Can the student cooperatively create group shapes?

Connect

"We know three types of angles. A right angle is an angle that measures 90 degrees. An obtuse angle is an angle that measures greater than 90 degrees but less than 180 degrees. An acute angle is less than 90 degrees." Draw the angles on the whiteboard or easel.

ANGLE SHAPES

"In your own space, make a shape that demonstrates a right angle. Use your body to make a 90-degree angle. Make a shape that demonstrates an acute angle. Your angle is less than 90 degrees. Now make a shape that demonstrates an obtuse angle. Your angle is greater than 90 degrees. Make a new, interesting shape that displays an acute angle. I should be able to clearly see your acute angle less than 90 degrees. Make a new, creative right angle. I should see your clear 90-degree angle. Create a new obtuse angle. Are you making a unique shape that clearly shows your angle greater than 90 degrees?"

FORMATIVE ASSESSMENT

Room scan: Can the student clearly demonstrate right, acute, and obtuse angles with body shapes?

LINE SHAPES

"We know that perpendicular lines intersect at a right angle and parallel lines can continue in their direction forever without ever intersecting. Make a shape with your body that shows perpendicular lines. We should see a 90-degree angle where the lines intersect. Create a new shape that demonstrates parallel lines. There should be two lines that will never intersect, even if they continue on in their directions.

"Go back to your first partner. With your partner, you have 8 counts to work cooperatively to create a shape together that demonstrates perpendicular lines: 1-2-3-4-5-6-7-8-freeze." Choose a pair of students who are clearly demonstrating perpendicular lines in a group shape to showcase to the rest of the class. "Now you have 8 counts to create a shape with your partner that demonstrates parallel lines: 1-2-3-4-5-6-7-8-freeze." Choose a new pair of students to showcase to the class.

"Now choose a new way to make parallel lines with your partner. And a new way. Find one more unique way to make parallel lines. Now make perpendicular lines with your partner. Find a new way to make perpendicular lines. And one more way."

FORMATIVE ASSESSMENT

Room scan: Can the student clearly demonstrate parallel and perpendicular lines with a partner?

Create and Perform

Divide the students into groups of three to five. Give each group three index cards. "Earlier in our dance lesson, we made frozen shapes and then used 8 counts to slowly transition into a new shape. In your group, your task is to create a dance that includes three shapes with transitions between. Your three shapes are the angles or lines that are written on your index cards. Create your shapes cooperatively, with your entire group making one shape all together. You will start in one angle or line shape, transition to the second shape, and then transition to the last shape. The audience should be able to clearly identify your angles and lines. Also, just like when you were working with your partner, there are a lot of ways to make these shapes. Make sure that your lines and angles are not only clear and visible but also really interesting to look at. Make sure you don't copy something you already did or saw." Give the students several minutes to create their dances, and then have them perform for the class.

SUMMATIVE ASSESSMENT

Use a checklist to assess the following:

- Can the student create clear angle and line shapes individually and with other students?
- Can the student perform a dance that includes three angles or types of lines while working cooperatively with others?

Acute and obtuse angles, and parallel and perpendicular lines.

Review and Reflect

Reflect on dance target	Reflect on mathematics target
"When do you sit with a right angle? When do you sit with an obtuse angle? Do you ever sit with an acute angle? When you go to lunch today, identify the angle of your back to your legs when you sit at the lunch table. After lunch, I will ask you to describe your angle."	"Look around the room. Raise your hand if you can identify a right angle in the classroom." Call on one or two students. Repeat with acute and obtuse angles and perpendicular and parallel lines. "When you go home, identify objects at home that have acute, obtuse, or right angles or perpendicular or parallel lines. When we meet again, I will ask you to name one object and its angle or lines."

EXTENSIONS

- Create a drawing consisting only of parallel lines, perpendicular lines, acute angles, obtuse angles, and right angles.
- Locate a street map. Find two streets that run parallel. Find two streets that are perpendicular. Identify an intersection that has a right angle. Are there acute and obtuse intersections in this community?

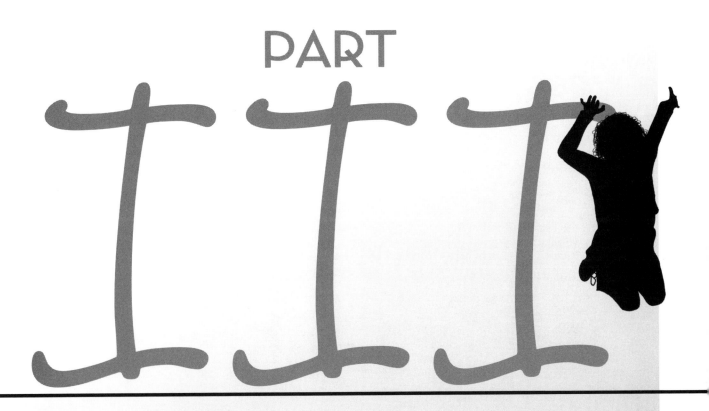

PART

III

DANCE AND
SCIENCE LEARNING
ACTIVITIES

9

PHYSICAL SCIENCE

hysical science is the study of the physical world. It analyzes the nature and properties of energy, physics, and nonliving matter. This chapter contains four lessons. The first lesson brings together the understanding of magnets with shape and respectful touching. The physics of balance and force are explored in individual balances and partner counterbalances in the second lesson. The third lesson combines atoms and molecules with dance energy qualities and spatial relationships. The final lesson of this chapter uses the combined elements of spatial relationships, tempo, and energy qualities to increase understanding of the three states of water.

MAGNETS

Magnets are metal objects, most commonly iron, that have a magnetic field causing an attractive or repulsive force on other magnetic objects.

AGES
6-8

LEVEL
Basic

MATERIALS
One large magnet

MUSIC
Contemplative selection (see appendix B)

ESSENTIAL QUESTION
What is a magnet?

ENDURING UNDERSTANDING
Magnets attract and repel certain objects.

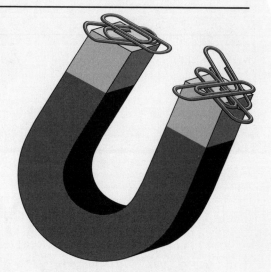

Magnet attracting paper clips.

	Dance	Science
Learning target	Students create shapes using a variety of body parts. Students practice respectful touching of other dancers.	Students learn about magnets, magnetic poles, and the two forces (attracting and repelling) that magnets can have.
Evidence of student learning	The student creates a connected group shape using respectful touch. The student identifies a body part as a point of touch.	The student identifies a body part as a north pole attracted to another student's south pole. The student demonstrates a group shape displaying a magnetic attraction.
Dance elements and science vocabulary	Body parts, respectful touch, shape, group shape, being respectful and safe	Magnet, magnetic field, north pole, south pole, attract, repel

(continued)

(continued)

	Dance	Science
Standards	• Anatomy: Demonstrate isolated and coordinated dance movement for the head, neck, joints, and body parts of the torso and limbs (*Standards for Learning and Teaching Dance in the Arts*, p. 23). • Shapes: Form shapes and create designs with the body (*Standards for Learning and Teaching Dance in the Arts*, p. 24). • Demonstrate respect for one's physical well-being and the well-being of others. • Demonstrate an understanding of and respect for one's personal space and the personal space of others (*Standards for Learning and Teaching Dance in the Arts*, p. 27).	Objects in contact exert forces on each other. Electric, and magnetic forces between a pair of objects do not require that the objects be in contact. The sizes of the forces in each situation depend on the properties of the objects and their distances apart and, for forces between two magnets, on their orientation relative to each other (*Next Generation Science Standards*, PS2.B: Types of Interactions).

Warm-Up

Teachers may wish to precede this lesson with an exploration of magnets. Place a variety of magnets on tables or desks in stations and allow the students to tactilely explore the magnets and their possibilities.

"Find your own space. We are going to warm up our bodies using many different body parts. Start by moving your head. How many ways can you move your head? Can you roll it, shake it, look side to side, up and down? What about your shoulders? Practice moving your shoulders in many ways. Move them up and down, roll them forward and back, and shake them. Move your whole arms. What are some ways that you can move your arms? Now, just move your hands and fingers. What sorts of hand movements can you do? What about your back? Can you move your back by itself, or do other body parts move too? What are some ways you can move your back? Move your hips from side to side, front and back, and in little circles. Staying in place, how can you move your legs? There are many ways that you can move your legs. Now just your feet and toes. Can you make circles? Shake them? Point your toes down to the floor and then flex them up to the ceiling?"

Build Knowledge

"We are using many body parts today. We will also be touching while dancing sometimes. It is important that we are respectful when we touch other dancers. We do not want to hurt other dancers or make them feel uncomfortable. When we touch, we make sure that we are being gentle. We also make sure that we are touching in respectful places, such as shoulders, knees, hands, and backs. As a dancer and as a person, if other people are making us feel uncomfortable, it is important to respectfully ask them to change what they are doing." Demonstrate a few examples of good touch.

EXPLORE BODY PARTS AND TOUCH

Pair off the students. "With your partner, one person will stand still. The second person will practice respectful touch to indicate what body part the first person will dance with. Maybe the second person gently touches the top of the first person's head, and that person then moves the head in any way.

Then, the first person will touch another body part and the second person will practice moving with the new body part. Continue choosing new body parts for your partner to move until I tell you to switch." Practice for a minute for each partner twice.

FORMATIVE ASSESSMENT

Room scan:

- Can the student demonstrate respectful touch?
- Can the student move with clear and specific body parts?

Connect

"We are going to use dance shapes to explore magnets today. Look at my magnet! A magnet is a metal object that has a magnetic field and can attract or repel other magnetic objects. When they attract, it means that they are coming together. When they repel, it means that they are pushing each other away and unable to connect. (Demonstrate the magnets attracting and repelling each other.) Magnets have a north pole and a south pole. Opposites attract! North poles attract south poles and south poles attract north poles. Like poles repel: North poles repel other north poles and south poles repel other south poles."

MAGNET SHAPES AND DANCES

"Imagine that you have a north pole in one hand and a south pole in the other hand. What happens? They attract! What does that shape look like? Now imagine that you have a south pole in one foot and a north pole in your other knee. What does that shape look like? You have a south pole in your ear and a south pole in your shoulder. They repel! What if you have a south pole in your elbow and a north pole in your knee? They attract! And if you have a north pole in that same elbow and a north pole in that same knee, then what? They repel!" Practice for 2 to 3 minutes using a variety of body parts attracting and repelling.

If possible, demonstrate the following with magnets. "If I place a magnet on top of a table and put another magnet right underneath the table, what will happen to the top magnet if I move the bottom one? If they are attracting, the top magnet will move with the bottom magnet. Even though they are not touching, they have a magnetic field that allows them to exert force on each other. Go back to your partner. Imagine that you have a thin wall between you. You are not going to touch, because the wall is there, but your magnetic fields will still attract. We are going to take turns following our partners. One partner will move, attracting the other partner, and the other one will follow. Make sure that you stay close to your imaginary wall so that your magnets do not get too far away!" Students explore this mirroring activity for a minute for each person twice.

FORMATIVE ASSESSMENT

Room scan: Can the student correctly demonstrate shapes using information about the body parts and the magnetic poles?

Create and Perform

Instruct the students to sit down on one side of the room. You may wish to demonstrate the following with a magnet and paper clips. "What happens if you have a jar of paper clips and you drop a magnet into it? The magnet attracts the paper clips! We are going to imagine that one student is a

Students are connected in a group shape.

magnet and the rest of you are paper clips. The magnet will choose any locomotor movement to dance to this side of the room (opposite of where students are seated) and make a frozen shape that she or he can hold for a long time. For the rest of the paper clips, when I say your name, you will use any locomotor action to move toward the magnet. You will then attract and connect using respectful touch and make a group shape. Choose a body part to be your north pole. That is where you will connect to the magnet or another paper clip. Wherever you touch on another dancer is a south pole."

Choose a student to be the magnet and begin the exercise. As each student adds to the group shape, ask that person to identify the body part with the north pole. Remind the students to use respectful touch and to attract with a variety of body parts. Once all students have attracted, you can ask them to repel back to where they were sitting and repeat the exercise with a new student as the magnet. Depending on the maturity of the students, you may wish to divide the class into groups of five or six and repeat the activity in small groups, requiring that each student perform the role of the magnet once.

SUMMATIVE ASSESSMENT

Use a checklist to assess the following:

- Can the student create a connected group shape using respectful touch?
- Can the student identify a body part as a north pole attracting another student's south pole?
- Can the student demonstrate a group shape displaying a magnetic attraction?

Review and Reflect

Reflect on dance target	Reflect on science target
"When do we use respectful touching outside of dance? This week, your homework is to use respectful touch at home with a family member or friend. Next time we meet you can give me an example of when you used respectful touch."	"If I have a north pole and a south pole, will they attract or repel (attract)? What about if I have a north pole and a north pole (repel)? Your homework this week is to find a refrigerator magnet and explore what objects it attracts."

EXTENSIONS

- Provide magnets to the students and encourage them to explore the north and south poles with attraction and repulsion.
- Assign the students to research magnets in order to identify everyday objects that use magnets.

BALANCE AND FORCE

Objects at rest generally have forces acting upon them; however, the forces add to balance each other out. When the forces do not balance, the forces can change the motion of the object.

AGES
9-11

LEVEL
Intermediate

MATERIALS
None

MUSIC
Pleasant selections with a slow or medium tempo (see appendix B)

ESSENTIAL QUESTION
How do forces affect motion?

ENDURING UNDERSTANDING
There are laws that govern the motion of all forces in the universe.

	Dance	Science
Learning target	Students explore force and balance individually and using counterbalancing with a partner.	Students understand that forces act on objects, influencing motion or balance.
Evidence of student learning	The student executes an individual controlled balance while standing on one leg. The student demonstrates a safe and controlled counterbalance with a partner.	The student identifies the forces acting on a pair of dancers in a counterbalance.
Dance elements and science vocabulary	Balance, counterbalance, spatial relationships, push, pull	Counterbalance, balance, push, pull, force
Standards	• Balance: Demonstrate an ability to balance while standing on two legs or one leg. • Styles and genres: Demonstrate basic movements of a particular style or genre of dance (*Standards for Learning and Teaching Dance in the Arts*, p. 23).	Each force acts on one particular object and has both a strength and a direction. An object at rest typically has multiple forces acting on it, but they add to give zero net force on the object. Forces that do not sum to zero can cause changes in the object's speed or direction of motion (*Next Generation Science Standards*, PS2.A: Forces and Motion)

Warm-Up

"Find your own space, only touching the floor and the air. Using your feet, push off the floor. Make sure you use enough force to jump off the floor, then let gravity pull you back down from your jump. Gently move down to a low level. Use your hands to push off the floor, changing the motion and shape of your body. Can you push off the floor with other body parts?"

In classrooms that have wood or linoleum floors, teachers may also direct dancers to use body parts to pull and push themselves along the floor, but this is not recommended on carpet.

Build Knowledge

"Dancers must practice balancing in many ways. Balancing is important for many dance steps in many styles as well as for other sports and activities. When you balance, you oppose the force of gravity and find stability in your body. Even though gravity is pulling you to the ground, your muscles must use an equal amount of force to hold you up."

EXPLORE BALANCE

"Plant your two feet into the floor and stand tall with strength. Right now you are balancing. The forces of gravity and the forces of your muscles are in balance and you are able to stand without falling down. Now stand on one foot and bring your other foot to your knee as if you are marching. Try to hold your balance by standing tall and strong through your spine. Continuing to maintain your balance, gently extend your lifted leg in front of your body. Change legs. Stand on your other foot and bring your lifted foot to your knee. One side is often more difficult than the other. Stand tall and strong. Now extend the lifted leg to the front. Can you find a new way to balance on one leg? Try a new way to balance. Can you balance in other ways?"

FORMATIVE ASSESSMENT

Room scan: Can the student demonstrate stable balance on one foot?

Connect

"An object at rest often has many forces acting on it. These forces add to make zero and cancel each other, providing stability and balance. When you are balancing, you must use the force of your muscles in an amount that is equal to the force of gravity in order to maintain steadiness. Sometimes the body has additional forces acting on it in addition to its own muscles and gravity. We are going to practice a counterbalance in which each dancer's body has an equal amount of force from a partner and from gravity to maintain stillness and balance."

COUNTERBALANCE OF FORCES

Organize the students into pairs. "You must work cooperatively with your partner and remain safe by being respectful to your partner and not becoming silly. Grasp each other's wrists, facing one another. Move your feet in until your toes are almost touching. Gently lean away, trying to maintain a straight body. You are counterbalancing with your partner, meaning you are both balancing but neither of you can continue your balance without the other. In order to sustain your balance, the force of your partner's pull must be equal to gravity. If it is less than gravity, then you will fall backward. If it is more than gravity, then your partner will pull you forward. Find a stable counterbalance with your partner pulling away."

"If you mastered the counterbalance with two hands, start again while only holding right wrists. Start with your feet close and slowly lean away, continuing to keep your body straight. If you struggled with the counterbalance with two hands, continue practicing with two hands. If you achieved the counterbalance with two hands and right wrists, try grasping left wrists."

Students lean their weight away from one another.

Teachers should walk through the room, helping pairs and encouraging safety. If the students are finding stable counterbalances, another challenge for the pulling-away counterbalance is to lift a foot while maintaining the balance.

"Now press the palms of your hands together. Push into your partner as you move your feet away from your partner. The force of your partner's weight must be equal to the force of your weight. The forces must be equal to gravity to prevent you from falling to the ground."

Students lean their weight in toward each other.

Room scan: Can the student demonstrate a counterbalance with a partner?

Create and Perform

"With your partner, your task is to create a dance that includes one counterbalance moment with your partner and an individual balance moment for each of you. Your dance needs to include smooth transitions between balances using dance elements that we have previously explored." You may wish to lead a brief discussion about dance elements that have been previously learned or provide simple examples, such as skip to your partner, float softly away from your partner, and so on. "Create your dance and practice. You should be able to perform your dance without stopping."

Allow the students several minutes to practice. Stop the students and provide one additional direction: "Before performing, identify with your partner the forces acting on your counterbalance to help you maintain your shape."

Students perform the dances for the class. After each performance, ask the performers, "What forces were acting on your counterbalance?"

SUMMATIVE ASSESSMENT

Use a checklist to assess the following:

- Can the student execute an individual controlled balance while standing on one leg?
- Can the student demonstrate a safe and controlled counterbalance with a partner?
- Can the student identify the forces acting on a pair of dancers in a counterbalance?

Review and Reflect

Reflect on dance target	Reflect on science target
"When do you need to balance at home? This week, your task is to identify an activity that requires you to balance."	"What are some of the forces acting on your body when you are still? Are there other forces that can act on your body that change the speed or direction of your body?"

EXTENSION

Write a poem describing the forces acting on a still body.

ATOMS AND MOLECULES

Matter makes up everything that takes up space, including air, water from the faucet, trees, and the human body. All matter is formed by atoms, particles that are too small to see. Atoms combine with other atoms to form molecules, creating new substances.

Science curriculums throughout the United States introduce atoms in varying grade levels. This lesson is meant to provide a general understanding of the structure of atoms and molecules without going into advanced detail about bonds and types of atoms and molecules. The focus of this lesson is the structure of the atom—the nucleus, containing positively charged protons and neutrons with no charge, and the electron cloud, containing negatively charged electrons—and the way atoms can combine to form molecules.

AGES
8-11

LEVEL
Intermediate

MATERIALS
Atom poster (or whiteboard for drawing an atom)

MUSIC
Pleasant selections with a medium or fast tempo (see appendix B)

ESSENTIAL QUESTION
What is the structure of all matter?

ENDURING UNDERSTANDING
All matter is made up of tiny moving particles.

	Dance	Science
Learning target	Students understand energy qualities and dance in a specified spatial relationship to others.	Students understand the general structure of atoms and molecules.
Evidence of student learning	The student demonstrates a heavy, light, or swaying energy quality. The student demonstrates a specific spatial relationship in the atom dance.	The student identifies and models an electron, proton, or neutron using the correct energy quality, tempo, and spatial relationship.
Dance elements and science vocabulary	Energy quality (heavy, light, swaying), spatial relationship	Matter, atom, molecule, nucleus, proton, neutron, electron, charge, positive, negative, neutral
Standards	• Relationships: Dance in a defined spatial relationship to others. • Dance qualities: Explore movement possibilities in dance using a variety of movement qualities or characteristics (*Standards for Learning and Teaching Dance in the Arts*, p. 24).	Substances are made from different types of atoms, which combine with one another in various ways. Atoms form molecules that range in size from two to thousands of atoms (*Next Generation Science Standards*, PS1.A: Structure and Properties of Matter).

Warm-Up

"Make a circle as a class. Maintaining the circle, begin walking around the edge in a clockwise direction. Now walk in a counterclockwise direction. Change directions again, but this time skip around the circle. Change directions. Boys, continue skipping around the outside of the circle, and girls, skip anywhere inside the circle. Boys, make sure to maintain the shape and size of the circle. Now switch—girls come back to the edge and skip along the outside of the circle, and boys skip inside the circle. This time, boys are on the outside galloping, and girls are on the inside twisting. Switch! Girls are galloping on the outside and boys are twisting on the inside. Freeze."

Build Knowledge

"Imagine dropping a baseball-sized rock from shoulder height. Now imagine dropping a feather from shoulder height. They both fall, but they fall very differently. The rock falls heavily, whereas the feather lightly floats to the ground. Dancers can use weight when they are dancing as well. Dancers can move heavily, lightly, or somewhere in the middle. These are called *energy qualities*. We are practicing heavy, light, and swaying energy qualities today."

EXPLORE ENERGY QUALITIES

"Move through the room, imagining every part of your body is heavy. Can you be heavy while standing? Can you be heavy while moving low to the ground? How many different ways can you be heavy? Now move through the room lightly, as if there is very little gravity. Imagine that you are floating away. Can you be light with your head? Your arms? Your legs? Your back? What about bouncy? Can you be light and bouncy? Now be neither heavy nor light. Sway through the room, not too heavy, not too light. Now be heavy and droopy but still move through the room. Change to light and bouncy, almost as if you are so excited that you are flying away! Now sway through the room." Practice heavy, light, and swaying four more times each.

FORMATIVE ASSESSMENT

Room scan: Can the student clearly demonstrate heavy, light, and swaying energy qualities?

Connect

"Matter is everything around us. It is everything that takes up space, including the air, the desks, and you. Matter is made up of tiny particles that are so small that we cannot see them. These particles are called *atoms*. Atoms are in everything around us!"

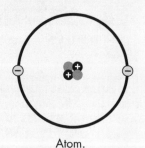

Atom.

Either draw attention to the atom poster or draw an atom on the whiteboard. "Atoms have a nucleus in the center that contains protons and neutrons. Around the outside of the nucleus in what is called the *electron cloud* are the electrons. Protons have a positive electrical charge, neutrons have no electrical charge, and electrons have a negative electrical charge." On the whiteboard, write *Proton (+): positive, Neutron: neutral (no charge), Electron (–): negative.*

ATOM DANCE

"When someone does a positive action at school, what does that mean? Yes, it is a good action. Imagine you are having an amazing day. Everything is positive! You feel excited. Of the three energy qualities we have been practicing, which one do you think is positive? Heavy and droopy, light and bouncy, or swaying? Light and bouncy is definitely positive! Protons have a positive charge. When we are doing the proton dance, our movement is light and bouncy. Practice your proton dance!" Practice moving through the room using a light and bouncy energy quality.

"When something negative happens, what does it mean? Something bad. Maybe you are having a bad day. Negative things just keep happening. How do you feel? Do you feel light and bouncy? I feel heavy and droopy. Electrons have a negative charge. When we do the electron dance, we use a heavy and droopy energy quality. Practice your electron dance." Move through the room using a heavy and droopy energy quality.

"Sometimes we have days that are not positive or negative, just an average day. This is a neutral sort of day. Neutrons have no electrical charge, so we say they are neutral. We will sway for the neutron dance. We're swaying here, having an average, neutral day. Practice your neutron dance." Practice swaying through the room.

Continue by practicing protons, neutrons, and electrons four more times each, checking for student connection of the atom part to the energy quality. When giving directions, use both the dance language and the atom vocabulary.

"We are going to make an atom as a class with our bodies. Look at the atom poster. Where are the protons and neutrons in the atom? They are in the nucleus, or the center of the atom. When we make our atom, protons and neutrons will be in the center of our room. Where are the electrons in the atom? Electrons go around the outside of the atom. I am going to give each student a number—1, 2, or 3. Show your number with your fingers so you don't forget." Number the students so that every student is a 1, 2, or 3. On the whiteboard, write *1 = proton, 2 = neutron, 3 = electron*.

"Look at the board. If you are a 1, you are a proton. Protons are positive, so they will be moving in a light and bouncy way. Protons will be in the center of the room because they are in the nucleus, the center of the atom. If you are a 2, you are a neutron. Neutrons are neutral so you will sway. Neutrons will also be in the center of the room because they are in the nucleus. If you are a 3, you are an electron. Electrons have a negative charge, so they will use a heavy and droopy energy quality. Electrons go around the outside of the atom. When I say 'Go,' protons and neutrons move to the center of the room and begin your dance. Electrons move to the perimeter of the dancing space and begin going around the outside of the nucleus. Go!"

Practice the atom dance, helping the students find their roles. After all of the students have been dancing for 30 to 45 seconds, freeze. On the whiteboard, erase the roles and write new roles: *2 = proton, 3 = neutron, 1 = electron*. "Keep your number. Now you have a new part in the atom dance. Think about where your part is. Are you in the nucleus or going around the outside? Are you positive, negative, or neutral? What energy quality will you be dancing? When I say 'Go,' go to your new part

The electrons circle around the protons and neutrons in the nucleus.

and begin your atom dance. Go!" Practice the new roles. Switch roles again (3 = proton, 1 = neutron, 2 = electron) and have the students go directly to their new part and begin dancing.

FORMATIVE ASSESSMENT

Room scan:

- Can the student dance in the correct spatial relationship to other dancers?
- Can the student move with the energy quality appropriate for the student's role in the atom?

Create and Perform

"When atoms combine, they form molecules. For atoms to combine, the electrons go around both of the nuclei." On the board, draw two atoms with a figure eight for the electron clouds to create a molecule.

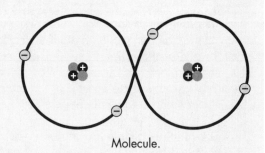

Molecule.

"We are going to make two molecules with two atoms each, so we need four atoms. Raise your hand if you are a 1." Divide the 1s into four groups, indicating where in the room they should go. Continue by dividing the 2s and 3s. "Keep the role that you were dancing last. Practice your atom in your group only." Observe the students. There should be four clear atoms.

Indicate to two groups, "Now if you are an electron in these two atoms, you will make a figure eight around both of the nuclei in these atoms. If you are the electrons in the other two atoms, you will make a figure eight around those two atoms." Practice the two molecules, observing for correct spatial relationships and energy qualities. Then ask each molecule to watch the other molecule perform the dance.

SUMMATIVE ASSESSMENT

Use a checklist to assess the following:

- Can the student demonstrate a heavy, light, or swaying energy quality?
- Can the student demonstrate the specified spatial relationship?
- Can the student identify and model an electron, proton, or neutron using an energy quality and spatial relationship?

Review and Reflect

Reflect on dance target	Reflect on science target
"When do you use certain energy qualities at home? Your homework this week is to identify an activity in which you use a clear energy quality. Next time we meet you can tell me the activity and the energy quality you used."	"What charge does a proton have (positive)? What charge does an electron have (negative)? What charge does a neutron have (no charge)? Where are the protons and neutrons in the atom (nucleus)? Where are the electrons (electron cloud)? How is a molecule formed (two atoms connect)? Where are atoms and molecules in the world (everything that has matter)? This week, your homework is to imagine the atoms and molecules that make up everything inside your home."

EXTENSION

Students draw an atom or molecule.

STATES OF WATER

Water can be a solid, liquid, or gas depending on its temperature. In each state, the molecules are moving with various tempos and relationships to other molecules.

AGES
6-11

LEVEL
Intermediate

MATERIALS
States of water poster (table 9.1)

MUSIC
Pleasant selection (appendix B)

ESSENTIAL QUESTION
What are three forms of water?

ENDURING UNDERSTANDING
Each state of water has unique properties.

	Dance	Science
Learning target	Students move using tempos, spatial relationships, and energy qualities. Students combine elements of dance to make more complex movements.	Students explore the physical changes of water molecules in solid, liquid, and gas states.
Evidence of student learning	The student demonstrates a combination of tempo, energy qualities, and relationships while performing a state of water dance.	The student clearly performs a state of water dance demonstrating the appropriate tempo, energy quality, and spatial relationship corresponding to a solid, liquid, or gas state of water.
Dance elements and science vocabulary	Tempo (fast, medium, slow), energy qualities (stiff, flowing, light), spatial relationships (near, medium, far), combined elements	Molecule, water, freeze, melt, evaporate, condense, state, liquid, solid, gas, ice, water vapor

(continued)

(continued)

	Dance	Science
Standards	• Dance in a defined spatial relationship to others. • Dance with a steady beat in a variety of tempos. • Explore movement possibilities in dance using a variety of movement qualities or characteristics. • Create and share a short dance that demonstrates varied use of the basic elements of dance (*Standards for Learning and Teaching Dance in the Arts*, pp. 24-25).	• Different kinds of matter exist, and many can be solids or liquids depending on their temperature. Matter can be described and classified by its observable properties (*Next Generation Science Standards*, PS1.A: Structures and Properties of Matter). • Matter of any type can be subdivided into particles that are too small to see, but even then the matter still exists and can be detected by other means (*Next Generation Science Standards*, PS1.A: Structures and Properties of Matter).

Warm-Up

"We are going to freeze dance. Start in a frozen shape. When you hear the music, begin dancing through the room. Listen to the music and respond to what you are hearing. If you hear slow and soft music, dance with a slow tempo and soft energy quality. If you hear a fast and bouncy selection, dance with a fast tempo and bouncy energy quality. When the music stops, freeze and stay frozen until the music starts again." Play four or five selections with varying tempos and textures for 20 to 30 seconds each.

Build Knowledge

Ideally, dancers will have already been introduced to tempo and energy qualities (an introduction to tempo can be found in chapter 7 in the lesson on bar graphs, and energy qualities can be found earlier in this chapter in the lesson on atoms and molecules). This lesson will serve as a review of these elements, an introduction to spatial relationships, and a progression into more complex combinations of elements.

"What tempos can we dance with? We can dance using fast, slow, and medium tempos. What energy qualities can we dance with? We can dance with stiff, soft, flowing, bouncy, light, heavy, swaying, and more qualities. We are going to practice spatial relationships and combine some of our dance elements to make more complex dances.

"Dancers can move very near to other dancers, and they can dance far away from other dancers. They can also dance in the middle—not too far and not too near to other dancers. We are going to practice spatial relationships of near, medium, and far."

EXPLORE SPATIAL RELATIONSHIPS

"Making sure that you are staying in control of your body, begin moving slowly as close to each other as you can without touching. Our entire class is using a near relationship. We must use slow and controlled movements so that we do not bump into other dancers. Now, how far away from other dancers can you get while still moving through the dancing space? Try not to get near any other dancers. Because you have more space around your body, you can move bigger and faster. Now practice moving with a medium relationship. You are not too near to other dancers but not too far, either.

"Using a near relationship, dance with a slow tempo and stiff energy quality. Dancers combine many elements of dance in order to make their dances more interesting to an audience. Now dance with a far relationship, fast tempo, and light energy quality. Lastly, dance with a medium relationship, medium tempo, and flowing energy quality."

FORMATIVE ASSESSMENT

Room scan:

- Can the student clearly demonstrate a far, medium, or near relationship with other dancers?
- Can the student combine a tempo, energy quality, and spatial relationship?

Connect

"Raise your hand if you can identify the three states of matter." Call on students to identify solids, liquids, and gasses as the three states of matter. "A solid holds its shape. Can water be a solid? Yes. Water is a solid when it is frozen as ice. A liquid takes the shape of its container. Can water be a liquid? Absolutely. A gas fills its container evenly and completely. Can water be a gas? Yes, water can be a gas when it is heated and it evaporates into water vapor or steam. Water is made up of tiny particles called *molecules*. The motion of water molecules changes as the temperature rises or lowers. As the temperature changes, water changes states."

STATES OF WATER DANCES

"Begin by dancing as near to each other as you can without touching. You are moving with a slow tempo and stiff energy quality. You are the molecules in ice coming together to make an ice cube. The temperature is very cold. The solid state of water is ice. Our ice dance is a slow tempo, stiff energy quality, and near relationship.

Students move stiffly and close together.

"It is beginning to warm up in the classroom and the ice is melting into liquid water. The molecules are moving faster, but not too fast yet. You are using a medium tempo. The molecules are spreading out, but not too much yet. You are using a medium relationship. Dance with a flowing energy quality to show the liquid state of water. Your liquid water dance is a medium tempo, medium relationship, and flowing energy quality.

"The temperature is getting hotter in the classroom and the molecules are evaporating to become water vapor. The dancer molecules are moving very fast now and spreading out to a far relationship to fill the entire dancing space. The molecules are excited and are bouncing through the air. You are dancing with light, airy, bouncy, and excited energy qualities throughout the dancing space to show the gas state of water. The water vapor dance is a fast tempo, light and bouncy energy quality, and far relationship.

"The temperature is cooling down. The water vapor is condensing to liquid water. You are now moving with a medium tempo, medium relationship, and flowing energy quality as liquid water. The temperature continues to cool down even more and the liquid water is freezing into solid ice. You are moving with a slow tempo, near relationship, and stiff energy quality as ice."

Repeat the states using both the dance vocabulary and the science vocabulary to indicate the changes (table 9.1).

Table 9.1   States of Water Poster

State of water	Tempo	Relationship	Energy quality
Water vapor	Fast	Far	Light and excited
Evaporate↑ Condense↓			
Water	Medium	Medium	Flowing and smooth
Melt↑ Freeze↓			
Ice	Slow	Near	Stiff

FORMATIVE ASSESSMENT

Ask questions throughout, such as "What sort of temperature do you think we have?", "The temperature is getting colder. What is happening to the water?", or "We have evaporated, so what is our body doing now?" Observe the students:

- Can the student demonstrate a state of water using a tempo, energy quality, and relationship?
- Can the student identify the tempo, energy quality, and relationship of a solid, liquid, or gas?

Create and Perform

Divide the class into groups of three to six depending on maturity level. For younger students, assign each group one state of water. "With your group, your first task is to review your state of water. What energy quality, tempo, and relationship should you be dancing with? Once you know the three elements of your state of water, practice your movement." Students practice moving with their assigned state of water using the correct tempo, energy, and relationship.

Before performing, ask students to self-assess using a rubric (table 9.2). "Think about what you were just practicing. Using our dance rubric, how well did you practice the dance? Were you a 4, meaning your energy quality, tempo, and relationship were clear and continued throughout the entire performance? Were you a 3, meaning your three dance elements were clear but not sustained throughout the performance? Were you a 2, meaning your dance elements were not clear? Or were you a 1, meaning you were practicing a different dance than what was planned? Practice your dance one more time, trying to give your dance a 4: your tempo, energy quality, and relationship are clear and continue through the entire dance." Students practice one more time and then perform their state of water for the rest of the class or in groups.

Table 9.2 **States of Water Rubric**

The performer's tempo, energy quality, and relationships were	
4	clear and continued throughout the entire performance.
3	clear but not sustained throughout the performance.
2	not clear.
1	different than what was planned.

Older children should use more than one state of water, demonstrating their ability to remember order and sequence as well as multiple states of water. "With your group, you are going to create a dance that includes all three states of water. Be sure to use the appropriate tempo, energy quality, and relationship for each state. You can decide what order to do the states, but be sure to practice your dance and be able to perform it without stopping." After students practice their dances, ask the students to self-assess using the guidelines in the previous paragraph. After the students practice one more time, the groups perform their dances for the rest of the class.

SUMMATIVE ASSESSMENT

Students will peer assess during performances using a rubric (table 9.2). "Without using your voice, hold up the number of fingers—4, 3, 2, or 1—that you think this group achieved. Be sure you can explain why you are giving this rating." Call on several students to use the dance and science vocabulary to describe why they are giving the rating that they are holding up.

Teachers use a checklist to assess the following:

- Can the student demonstrate a combination of tempo, energy qualities, and relationships while performing a state of water dance?

- Can the student clearly perform a state of water dance demonstrating the appropriate tempo, energy quality, and spatial relationship corresponding to a solid, liquid, or gas state of water?

Review and Reflect

Reflect on dance target	Reflect on science target
"Raise your hand if you can describe a time at home when you use more than one element of dance at the same time—for example, using a fast tempo and shaking energy when brushing your teeth." Call on several students. "This week, identify a time when you use more than one element of dance when you are at home. Be prepared to describe the dance elements and the activity during our next dance lesson."	"Describe what happens when water molecules heat up or cool down." Call on several students. "Your task today is to identify water in all three forms at school or at home. When do you come across ice, liquid water, or water vapor? Tomorrow, be prepared to describe the water that you noticed today."

EXTENSION

Write a short story about a water molecule moving among the three states of matter. Begin your story with "I'm a drop of water . . ."

10

LIFE
SCIENCE

*L*ife science is the study of living things and their patterns, processes, and relationships. This chapter contains six lessons. The first lesson explores the classification of vertebrates into the five classes (reptiles, amphibians, mammals, fish, and birds) using dance actions. The second, third, and fourth lessons connect dance with life cycles. Choreographic sequencing combines with the butterfly life cycle, musical counting and memorization of movements connect to the frog life cycle, and the plant life cycle explores size and levels. The fifth lesson focuses on abstraction and choreography of the five senses. Finally, the sixth lesson of this chapter teaches the names of bones and the movement possibilities associated with each bone.

VERTEBRATE CLASSIFICATION

Vertebrates are a class of animals that have spinal cords and backbones. They are some of the most advanced animals on earth. Most vertebrates also have highly advanced nervous systems. The five classes of vertebrates are reptiles, amphibians, mammals, fish, and birds.

The five classes of vertebrates are fish, reptiles, amphibians, birds, and mammals.

From K. Kaufmann and J. Dehline, 2014, *Dance integration: 36 dance lesson plans for science and mathematics* (Champaign, IL: Human Kinetics).

AGES
7-11

LEVEL
Basic

MATERIALS
Vertebrate poster (table 10.1; before class, write poster on easel paper or whiteboard)

MUSIC
Pleasant selection (see appendix B)

ESSENTIAL QUESTION
What is a vertebrate?

ENDURING UNDERSTANDING
Living things can be classified based on their characteristics.

	Dance	Science
Learning target	Students use locomotor actions to abstractly represent ideas.	Students learn the five classes of vertebrates (mammals, amphibians, reptiles, fish, birds).
Evidence of student learning	The student demonstrates an action representing a class of vertebrates.	The student identifies characteristics of a class of vertebrates. The student performs a vertebrate dance using an action.
Dance elements and science vocabulary	Action (float, slither, slide, sway, walk)	Vertebrate, backbone, classification, class, amphibian, reptile, mammal, fish, bird
Standards	Locomotor movements: Demonstrate and identify locomoto r movements (*Standards for Learning and Teaching Dance in the Arts*, p. 23).	There are many different kinds of living things in any area, and they exist in different places on land and in water (*Next Generation Science Standards*, LS4.D: Biodiversity and Humans).

Warm-Up
Lead the students in follow-the-leader using locomotor actions such as crawling, skipping, galloping, tiptoeing, and taking giant steps.

Build Knowledge
"Dancers use actions to convey ideas. We move using many actions every day; we sit, stand, talk, and play. We can also use dance actions; we can float, sway, walk, slide, and slither."

EXPLORE ACTIONS

"Find your own space, only touching the floor and the air. Begin by walking through the dancing space. Allow your arms to hang and swing gently. Your feet are pushing off the floor and landing softly back onto the floor. You are using your eyes to find the empty spaces between bodies.

"Now float through the room. You are moving lightly and softly as if you are floating on air.

"Next, slide through the room. You are dancing as if the room is slippery. Every movement is smooth, sliding, and loose. Nothing is stuck or sharp.

"Sway through the dancing space. Swaying is a side-to-side rocking motion. Your body movement is flowing, smooth, and fluid without any bumps. It is as if you are in water and the current is moving you gently side to side.

"Lastly, slither through the space. Be sure to watch out for other dancers. If you need more space for your body, you can stand up and walk to a new place. Slithering is a low-level crawling action. You are sliding your body along the floor as if you are a snake." Practice sliding, slithering, swaying, walking, and floating actions four more times each.

"Dancers are artists who make dance choices using many actions. Dance through the room without stopping, choosing among the various actions. Try to use all five: walking, floating, swaying, slithering, and sliding."

FORMATIVE ASSESSMENT

Room scan: Can the student demonstrate walking, floating, swaying, slithering, and sliding?

Connect

"Living things can be classified based on their traits. One classification of animals is vertebrates. Vertebrates are animals that have a backbone and spinal cord. There are five types of vertebrates: mammals, reptiles, amphibians, fish, and birds. We will use our dance actions to represent each group of vertebrates. We will not be acting out the animals but will use the characteristics of each class to inspire an action."

VERTEBRATE ACTIONS

"Birds have hollow bones and feathers. Some, but not all, birds fly. The front two limbs are wings. Birds lay eggs and are warm-blooded animals. We will use a floating action to represent birds. Float through the room. Imagine how light birds must be with their hollow bones. Their feathers lightly flutter. Some birds defy gravity by flying. Remember that you are not acting like a bird but are using a floating action to symbolize the bird class of vertebrates.

"Reptiles have dry, scaly skin, and some live in or near water. Reptiles breathe air using lungs. They lay eggs with hard shells on dry land and are cold-blooded animals. Imagine a reptile's scaly skin. It acts like armor to protect the animal! We are using a slithering action to represent reptiles. Snakes and lizards are reptiles. Move through the room slithering low to the ground, imagining that you are dragging your dry, scaly skin along the floor.

"Amphibians begin life in the water, breathing with gills, then grow and develop lungs and breathe air. They return to water to lay eggs and to moisten their skin. Amphibians do not have hair, scales, or feathers. Imagine an amphibian's moist skin. I picture it as being slippery! Use a sliding action for amphibians. Use your whole body to move using slippery, sliding, smooth, and loose movements.

"Fish breathe through gills and live in the water their entire lives. We will use a swaying action to represent fish. Imagine your body moved side to side by the flow of water. Your dancing is flowing, smooth, and fluid without any jolts.

"Mammals give birth to live young, drink their mothers' milk, and have hair or fur on some or all of their bodies. Humans are mammals! Walk through the dancing space. Humans are not the only mammals—there are many other species—but today we are using a walking action to symbolize mammals."

Continue practicing the actions for the five classes using both the dance language and the vertebrate vocabulary (table 10.1). Ask questions such as, "What vertebrate class are we using a walking action for? What action are we using to show birds?"

Table 10.1 **Dancing Vertebrates**

Vertebrates		
Class	**Characteristics**	**Action**
Mammal	Give birth to live young, drink mother's milk, have hair or fur	Walk (human)
Reptile	Have dry and scaly skin, live near water, breathe air, lay eggs with hard shells on dry land, are cold-blooded animals	Slither (scaly skin)
Amphibian	Begin life in water breathing with gills, grow and develop lungs to breathe air, return to water to lay eggs, have moist skin	Slide (moist skin)
Fish	Breathe through gills, live in water entire life	Sway (live in water)
Bird	Front two limbs are wings, some fly, have feathers and hollow bones, lay eggs, are warm-blooded animals	Float (hollow bones, feathers)

FORMATIVE ASSESSMENT

Room scan:

- Can the student identify the action if prompted using vertebrate vocabulary?
- Can the student identify the class of vertebrates if prompted using dance vocabulary?

Create and Perform

Divide the class into groups of four. Assign each group one class of vertebrates. "In your group, first review the characteristics of your vertebrate type. How do you know that an animal belongs in that group? Next, remember what action we were using to represent that class of vertebrates. Then practice moving with that action. For example, if my group has mammals, first we need to review the traits of mammals. We know that mammals give birth to live young, drink their mothers' milk, and have hair or fur. Next we need to remember the action. We will use a walking action. Then we practice walking. Go ahead."

Allow students several minutes to work. Walk through the room asking questions and assisting as necessary. Before each group performs the movement, ask the students in the group to describe the characteristics of their vertebrate class. After each group performs, ask the audience to describe the action that the performers used and to name examples of the class of vertebrates.

SUMMATIVE ASSESSMENT

Use a checklist to assess the following:

- Can the student demonstrate an action representing a class of vertebrates?
- Can the student identify characteristics of a class of vertebrates?

Teachers may also use a rubric for assessment (table 10.2).

Table 10.2 **Vertebrate Rubric**

The student's action was	
4	clear and continued through the entire dance.
3	clear but not continued through the entire dance.
2	not clear.
1	different than what was planned.

Review and Reflect

Reflect on dance target	Reflect on science target
"When you are at school or at home, when do you use one of the five actions we practiced today? For example, I use a sliding action when I am trying to walk through an icy parking lot. Raise your hand if you can give an example of when you use one of the actions." Call on several students. "Your homework tonight is to identify an action that you use during a specific activity. Tomorrow you will be asked to share your action and activity."	"What class of vertebrates is a frog? Raise your hand if you can describe some characteristics of a frog and determine what class it is." Call on students to identify characteristics of a frog that aid in classifying it. For example, a frog lays eggs in the water, begins life in the water breathing with gills, develops lungs to breathe air, and has moist skin. A frog is an amphibian. "Your homework tonight is to think of an animal and determine what class of vertebrates it is based on its characteristics. Maybe on your way home you see a woodpecker. You notice that it has wings and that it flies. It also has feathers. You can identify that the woodpecker is a bird because of its characteristics. Tomorrow you will share your animal and its class."

EXTENSIONS

- Identify one animal from each class of vertebrates.
- Write a story about an animal that includes details about its life that help to determine its class of vertebrates.

BUTTERFLY LIFE CYCLE

Every animal has a life cycle. A butterfly begins in an egg, hatches to a caterpillar in the larval stage, forms a chrysalis in the pupal stage, and becomes a butterfly in the adult stage. It then lays eggs and the cycle continues.

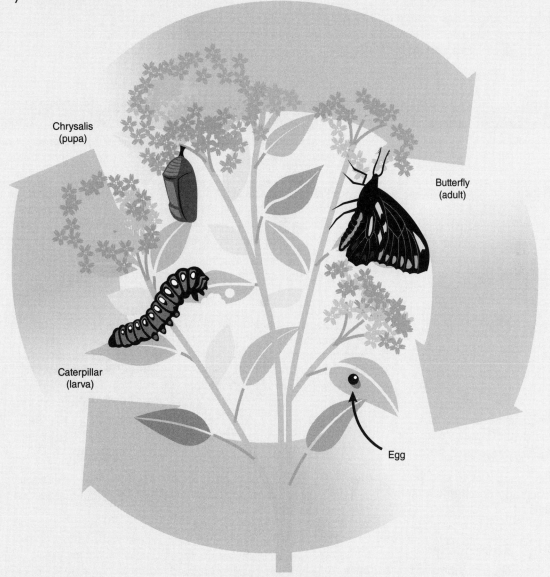

Butterfly life cycle.

From K. Kaufmann and J. Dehline, 2014, *Dance integration: 36 dance lesson plans for science and mathematics* (Champaign, IL: Human Kinetics).

AGES
5-8

LEVEL
Basic

MATERIALS
Butterfly life-cycle poster (included in this lesson; before class, draw on whiteboard or easel)

MUSIC

Contemplative selection (see appendix B)

ESSENTIAL QUESTION

How do living things change as they grow?

ENDURING UNDERSTANDING

All living things have a life cycle.

	Dance	Science
Learning target	Students create short choreographic sequences.	Students identify and describe the stages of the butterfly life cycle.
Evidence of student learning	The student cooperatively creates and performs a butterfly life-cycle dance that has four parts.	The student creates and performs a dance that clearly demonstrates all four stages of the butterfly life cycle: egg, caterpillar (larva), chrysalis (pupa), butterfly.
Dance elements and science vocabulary	Choreography, sequence	Butterfly, egg, caterpillar, larva, chrysalis, pupa, adult, insect
Standards	Sequencing: Demonstrate the ability to sequence a series of movements and to remember them in a short phrase (*Standards for Learning and Teaching Dance in the Arts*, p. 23).	Reproduction is essential to the continued existence of every kind of organism. Plants and animals have unique and diverse life cycles (*Next Generation Science Standards*, LS1.B: Growth and Development of Organisms).

Warm-Up

"Find your own space. Shake one hand. Shake the other hand. Shake one foot. Shake the other foot. Reach up. Reach down. Reach up. Reach down. Reach up. Turn around." Repeat this sequence five times.

Build Knowledge

"When people choreograph a dance, they choose movements and put them together in a certain order. If they repeat their dance several times, they are making a pattern. We are going to practice making small dances that have several movements. We want to remember the sequence and be able to do it together in the correct order."

EXPLORE SEQUENCING

"We are going to start with a short dance. It has two parts: skip and crawl. We are first going to skip, and then we are going to crawl. What do we do first? Then what?" Turn on the music and skip and then crawl. Freeze.

"Now we are going to start the same way. We will skip. Then we will crawl. Then we will float. What do we do first? Then what? And last?" Turn on the music and skip, crawl, and float. Freeze. "Dancers practice quite a bit. Let's practice our three moves in order again." Practice two more times.

"We are going to add one more move to our dance. First we will skip, then crawl, then float, and lastly we will bounce. Let's practice." Practice with music several times. "What is first in our dance? What comes next? Then what? And what is last in our dance? We are trying to memorize our dance. Let's practice again." Practice a few more times, encouraging memorization.

FORMATIVE ASSESSMENT

Room scan: Can the student remember the sequence?

Connect

"Butterflies have a fascinating life cycle. They begin as eggs. When they hatch they are in what is called their *larval stage*. They are caterpillars in their larval stage. A caterpillar eats and eats in order to grow rapidly. As it grows, it outgrows its skin and sheds it. The last time it sheds its skin it begins its pupal stage. Underneath the last layer of skin is the chrysalis. The chrysalis hardens and the pupa stays in the chrysalis for at least 2 weeks and sometimes for the entire winter. When it emerges out of its chrysalis, it is a butterfly. The butterfly drinks the nectar of flowers and helps to pollinate the flowers. The adult butterfly then mates and lays eggs and the cycle continues with the new eggs. The adult butterfly then dies."

BUTTERFLY LIFE-CYCLE DANCE

"There are four parts of the butterfly life cycle—egg, caterpillar, chrysalis, and butterfly. You are going to learn a butterfly dance that has four parts. Our dance is an abstract dance, meaning we are using the idea of the butterfly and creating a new work of art, a dance. We are not trying to act like the butterfly, but we are learning a dance inspired by the butterfly life cycle.

"Begin by making a circle as a class, gently holding hands. This is our egg. It is a lot bigger than a butterfly egg! Without pulling on anyone's arms, we are going to glide around the circle in a counterclockwise direction.

"Our egg is hatching—let go of hands. I am the caterpillar head, and you are the rest of the body. Follow the person beside you to form a line following me. Start very small in our caterpillar line. Because caterpillars eat so much, they grow quickly. Continue following the leader as we grow to a high level.

"The next part of our dance is the chrysalis. We are each going to make our own twisted shape and freeze.

"After the chrysalis, or pupal stage, is the butterfly. We are going to use our entire body to make large sweeping movements. Make sure you use your legs, back, and head! The butterfly life cycle starts again, and our dance is going to start again. Come back to our big circle and take hands. Our butterfly has laid an egg."

Repeat the dance four to five times, encouraging memorization. Glide around the circle as the egg. Then let go and follow the leader in the caterpillar, growing from small to big. Freeze in a twisted shape for the chrysalis. As the butterfly, encourage whole-body sweeping movements. Throughout the butterfly dance ask questions such as, "What stage of the butterfly life cycle are we now? Why are we growing from small to big in the caterpillar stage? What movements do we use to show the egg? What comes next in our dance?"

FORMATIVE ASSESSMENT

Room scan:

- Can the student remember the sequence?
- Can the student identify the stages of the butterfly life cycle?

Create and Perform

Divide the students into groups of four. In each group, assign each student one stage of the butterfly life cycle. "Each group should now include one egg, one caterpillar, one chrysalis, and one butterfly. Your first task is to create a brief movement for your part of the life cycle. If you are the egg, you will create a short egg movement; if you are the chrysalis, you will create a short chrysalis movement; and so on. After you have decided on your own movement, you will teach it to the rest of the group. The egg person will teach the egg movement, then the caterpillar person will teach the caterpillar movement, then the chrysalis person will teach the chrysalis movement, and then the butterfly person will teach the butterfly movement. Next, as a group you will all practice the egg movement, the caterpillar movement, the chrysalis movement, and the butterfly movement. Practice several times. You should all be doing the same movement at the same time. Remember that your dances are inspired by the butterfly life cycle; you are not pretending to be the butterfly. Practice several times in order to perform your dance without stopping."

As the groups are working on their dances, go to each group and encourage abstract whole-body movements and memorization of the sequence. Ask each group to perform for the class.

Students follow the leader in the butterfly dance.

SUMMATIVE ASSESSMENT

Use a checklist to assess the following:

- Can the student perform a four-part dance without stopping?
- Can the student cooperatively create and perform a dance abstractly demonstrating the four parts of the butterfly life cycle?

Review and Reflect

Reflect on dance target	Reflect on science target
"When I get up in the morning, I have a sequence of things that I do the same every morning, almost like a dance sequence. I wash my face, brush my hair, eat breakfast, and brush my teeth. Is there a certain sequence that you repeat often?" Call on several students. "When you go home today, find a sequence that you repeat often. Tomorrow you will describe a sequence that you do at home."	"What are the four stages of the butterfly life cycle (egg, caterpillar, chrysalis, butterfly)? Do other animals have life cycles?"

EXTENSIONS

- Draw or paint the butterfly life cycle.
- Write a story about a butterfly going through its life cycle.

FROG LIFE CYCLE

Frogs have a complex life cycle and undergo a big metamorphosis. Frogs are amphibians and they begin their lives in water. They lay their eggs in water but spend their adult lives on land. Frogs begin as tadpoles with gills. Throughout their cycle they grow legs and lungs to help them breathe and move both on land and underwater.

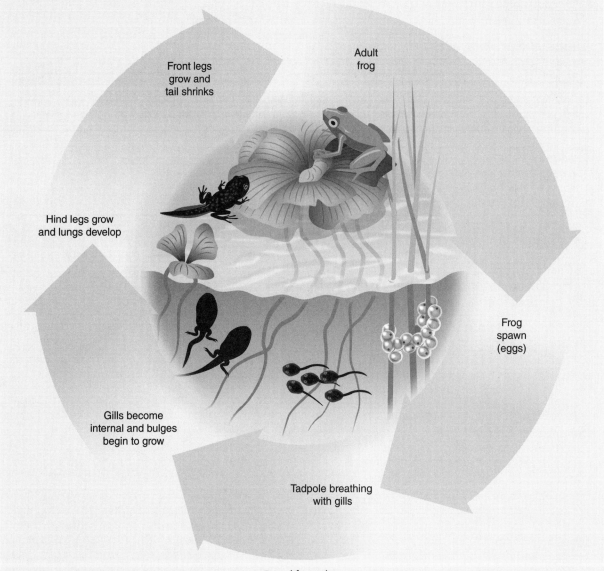

Frog life cycle.

From K. Kaufmann and J. Dehline, 2014, *Dance integration: 36 dance lesson plans for science and mathematics* (Champaign, IL: Human Kinetics).

AGES
6-8

LEVEL
Intermediate

MATERIALS NEEDED
Frog life-cycle poster (included in this lesson; before class, draw on whiteboard or easel)

MUSIC
Driving selections with a clear and steady 8-count percussive beat (see appendix B)

ESSENTIAL QUESTION
How do living things change as they grow?

ENDURING UNDERSTANDING
All living things have a life cycle.

	Dance	Science
Learning target	Students learn to move to a steady beat and count these beats musically. They memorize movements that are performed in rhythmic patterns of 4 or 8 counts.	Students identify the stages of a frog's life cycle.
Evidence of student learning	The student performs a dance using 48 counts (for younger students, 16 counts).	The student performs a dance portraying the stages of the life cycle of a frog.
Dance elements and science vocabulary	Beat, rhythmic pattern	Life cycle, frog, spawn, tadpole, gills, lungs, adult
Standards	• Dance with a steady beat in a variety of tempos. • Demonstrate the ability to dance in relation to a musical phrase (*Standards for Learning and Teaching Dance in the Arts*, p. 24).	Reproduction is essential to the continued existence of every kind of organism. Plants and animals have unique and diverse life cycles (*Next Generation Science Standards*, LS1.B: Growth and Development of Organisms).

Warm-Up
"Find your own space where you are only touching the floor and the air. I am going to count to 8. Then I will start over at 1 and count to 8 again. I will keep repeating counting 1 to 8. The first time I count to 8, we are all going to jump on the number 1 and freeze in a shape for 2 through 8. The second time, we will all jump on 1 and 2 and freeze in a shape for 3 through 8. The third time, we will jump on 1, 2, and 3 and freeze for 4 through 8. Understand the pattern? We are going to keep jumping and freezing until we are jumping on all of the numbers. Here we go!" Begin counting from 1 to 8 with the jumping and freezing pattern. After jumping on every number, tell the students to sit down.

Build Knowledge
"Dancers count the beats of the music so they know when to do certain movements. Dancers most commonly count music in sets of 4 or 8 as musical phrases."

EXPLORE BEATS AND RHYTHMIC PATTERNS
"Remain seated. Do you hear the beat? Tap your finger to the beat. Now tap your foot to the beat.
"Please stand up. Now we'll walk on the beat. Take one step for every beat. Count aloud as we step: 1-2-3-4-5-6-7-8." After several phrases of 8, freeze. "As dancers, we need to count in our heads

so that the audience does not see or hear us counting. Step on each beat and count quietly to yourself." Freeze. "Now walk for 8 counts and freeze for 8 counts." Practice for several phrases of 8. "Skip for 8 counts and freeze for 8 counts. Gallop for 8 counts and freeze for 8 counts." Continue the rhythmic phrasing (move for 8, freeze for 8) with other locomotor movements. Repeat with phrases of 4 (move for 4, freeze for 4).

FORMATIVE ASSESSMENT

Room scan: Can the student move and freeze on the correct beat?

Connect

"Today we will learn a dance with counts that portrays the life cycle of a frog. Let's look at our poster of the life cycle of a frog. We will start the dance without music so you can learn the order of the movements. Then we will add music and counts and perform the dance." (See table 10.3.)

Table 10.3 **Frog Life-Cycle Dance**

Number of counts	Stage of frog life cycle	Movements
8	Frog spawn	Wiggle at a low level.
8	Tadpole with gills	Make narrow shapes with hands behind back.
4	Gills become internal	Move hands from behind back to sides.
4	Bulges begin to grow	Turn feet out slightly.
4	Hind legs grow	Reach one leg out to side then put it down; repeat with other leg.
4	Lungs develop	Take a large breath, allowing body to respond.
4	Front legs grow	Reach both arms out to make an X with body.
4	Tail shrinks	Move whole body to a low level.
8	Adult frog	Jump from high to low levels.

FROG LIFE-CYCLE DANCE

"Frogs lay their eggs in water. Begin very close together with your classmates without touching. Start in a tiny shape at a low level, wiggling and jiggling slowly. Frogs spawn in a jellylike substance, close together in clumps. This helps to protect the eggs from predators. This floating clump of eggs is called the *frog spawn*. Wiggle and jiggle slowly for 8 counts.

"The tadpole hatches out of the egg and is breathing through external gills. Come to standing and make a narrow shape with your hands behind your back, like gills. Take 8 counts to tiptoe through the room with your gills.

"The tadpole's gills then become internal. Standing in one place, take 4 counts to move your hands from behind your back and put them by your sides.

"The tadpole develops bulges where its hind legs will develop. Take 4 counts to turn your feet out slightly. Now take 4 counts to reach one leg out to the side and put it down. Repeat with the other leg into a wide stance. The frog then develops lungs; take 4 counts to take a big full breath and exhale. Now the front legs grow, so take 4 counts to reach both arms; now you're in a big X. The frog's tail shrinks, so we'll take 4 counts to shrink our whole body to a low level, ending in a squat.

"We are fully grown frogs! Jump from low to high throughout the room for 8 counts. Adult frogs lay eggs and the whole cycle starts again. Shrink to your low-level frog spawn and let's start again."

Students form gills behind their backs.

Review the stages of the frog life-cycle dance without music, reinforcing the movements and counts. Then add music, reinforcing the counts out loud. Ask the students if they can perform the dance counting quietly to themselves.

FORMATIVE ASSESSMENT

Room scan:

- Can the student recall the movements that represent each phase of the frog life cycle?
- Can the student clearly count rhythmic phrases for each part of the cycle?

Create and Perform

Divide the class into groups of three or four. Give 2 to 5 minutes to rehearse the dance. Clarify any questions about the counts or movements for each section of the dance. Each group performs the dance for the rest of the class (to simplify, ask younger students to select one or two stages of the frog life cycle to perform).

SUMMATIVE ASSESSMENT

Use a checklist to assess the following:

- Can the student perform a dance using 48 counts (16 counts for younger students)?
- Can the student perform a dance portraying the stages of the frog life cycle?

Review and Reflect

Reflect on dance target	Reflect on science target
Ask the students, "Why do dancers use counts? How does counting the music benefit them? Why do dancers memorize sequences of movements that relate to a musical phrase?"	Discuss the frog life cycle. "Where does the frog spawn (water)? What kind of substance are the eggs in (jellied substance)? What hatches from the egg (tadpole)? What does it have on its back (external gills)? What happens to these gills (become internal and develop into lungs)? How does the tadpole develop into a frog (hind legs grow, lungs develop, front legs grow, tail shrinks)? What other living things have a life cycle?"

EXTENSIONS

- Write a short story about the life of a single frog as it moves through the life cycle.
- Draw the stages of the frog life cycle.

PLANT LIFE CYCLE

Every living thing has a life cycle. Plants begin as seeds. With sunlight, water, and nutrients from the soil, a seed germinates and begins to grow. The roots grow downward while the seedling grows upward toward the sun. The plant continues to grow a stem to support the plant and leaves to collect sunlight in order to make food. Plants then grow flowers in order to attract insects and birds to aid in pollination. During pollination, the pollen of a male flower is transferred to a female flower. Fruit is then produced. The fruit protects seeds for a new plant. The fruit may be harvested and the seeds planted, or the fruit may rot and fall to the ground where it decomposes and the seeds are planted in the earth. The cycle then continues.

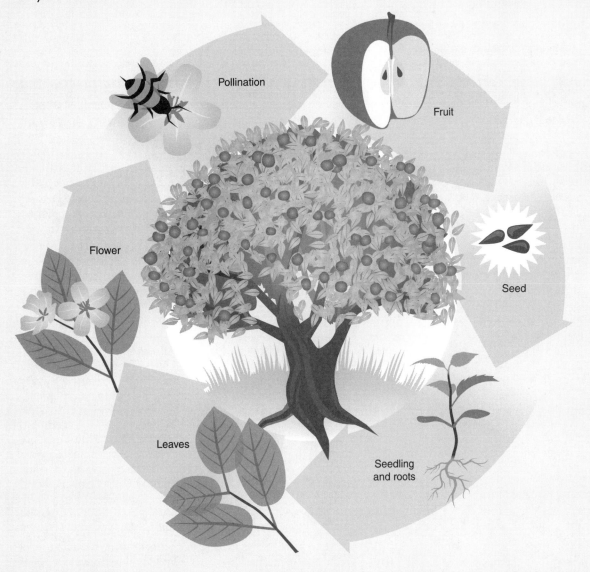

Plant life cycle.

From K. Kaufmann and J. Dehline, 2014, *Dance integration: 36 dance lesson plans for science and mathematics* (Champaign, IL: Human Kinetics).

AGES
5-8

LEVEL
Intermediate

MATERIALS
Plant life-cycle poster (included in this lesson; before class, draw on whiteboard or easel)

MUSIC
Pleasant selection (see appendix B)

ESSENTIAL QUESTION
How do living things change as they grow?

ENDURING UNDERSTANDING
All living things have a life cycle.

	Dance	Science
Learning target	Students understand the difference between size and levels and are able to combine size and levels in many ways.	Students understand the life cycle of a plant.
Evidence of student learning	Size (small, medium, large), levels (high, middle, low)	The student performs a dance displaying the life cycle of a plant (or one part of the cycle for younger students).
Dance elements and science vocabulary	Beat, rhythmic pattern	Plant, germinate, sunlight, water, soil, nutrients, seed, seedling, sprout, stem, roots, leaves, flower, pollination, fruit, cycle
Standards	• Form shapes and create designs with the body. • Dance on high, middle, and low levels with clear focus and transitions (*Standards for Learning and Teaching Dance in the Arts*, pp. 23-24).	• All organisms have external parts. Different animals use their body parts in different ways to see, hear, grasp objects, protect themselves, move from place to place, and seek, find, and take in food, water, and air. Plants also have different parts (roots, stems, leaves, flowers, fruits) that help them survive and grow (*Next Generation Science Standards*, LS1.A: Structure and Function). • Reproduction is essential to the continued existence of every kind of organism. Plants and animals have unique and diverse life cycles (*Next Generation Science Standards*, LS1.B: Growth and Development of Organisms).

Warm-Up

"When the music starts, we're going to gallop at a high level through the room. When the music stops, immediately freeze in your own high-level shape." Give students a new locomotor movement each time (e.g., walk, hop, gallop, jump, skip, prance, crawl, slither), reviewing levels by asking the students to use a high, middle, or low level each time the music starts.

Build Knowledge

Ideally, the students will have already been introduced to high, middle, and low levels; if not, please use the lesson that introduces levels in chapter 4 (Comparing Whole Numbers). "What levels do we use? We use high, middle, and low levels. Levels are different than size. Levels are how far from the floor you are. Size is how big or small your body is and can be at any level. Size describes how far or near the arms and legs are to the center of the body and how much space a dancer is taking up."

EXPLORE SIZE

"Make a small shape. Create a new small shape. Now make a large shape. Find a new large shape. Make a medium shape. Create a new medium shape. Make a small shape at a high level. Now create a large shape at a low level. You can make shapes in all sizes at all levels.

"Float throughout the room with a big size. Tiptoe with a small size. Crawl with a medium size. Reach through the room with your arms and legs in a big size. Gallop with a small size. Skip with a medium size. Choose your own way to move through the room with a big size. Now move with a small size. Dance with a medium size. Continuing to think about your size, we are going to add levels. At a low level, move with a big size. At a high level, move with a medium size. With a small size, move at a middle level. Using a big size, move at a high level. At a low level, use a small size." Continue practicing several more combinations of levels and sizes.

FORMATIVE ASSESSMENT

Room scan:

- Can the student demonstrate small, medium, and large sizes?
- Can the student clearly combine size with levels?

Connect

"We are going to dance using size and levels to show the life cycle of a plant. Let's look at our poster. What will happen if you plant a seed? The seed will germinate and sprout if it has the correct amount of water, soil, sunlight, and nutrients from the soil. The plant grows a root downward into the soil, and a seedling appears above the soil. Through the roots, the plant is able to get water and nutrients, which, when combined with light from the sun, help the plant to grow into an adult plant. Leaves grow on the stem to help collect the sunlight. Some adult plants produce flowers, and when insects and birds pollinate the flowers, the plant can grow fruit that contains new seeds. When the fruit ripens, it can fall to the ground and the seeds inside the fruit can grow into new plants, starting the cycle over again."

PLANT LIFE-CYCLE DANCE

"Start with a low-level, small shape. This is the seed. Your seed has enough water, sunlight, and nutrients from the soil to germinate. Begin growing to a middle-level, medium shape. This is the seedling. Your roots are also growing downward. Feel your body reaching down into the floor. Continue growing to a high-level, big shape. Your stem is growing strong to support the plant and you are growing your big leaves to collect sunlight. Some plants produce flowers to attract insects and birds. Keep your feet firmly rooted to the ground and use your upper body to gracefully sway and reach with your big, high-level flowers.

"When bees, butterflies, and birds are attracted to the nectar of the bright flowers, they may get pollen on them. When the insect goes to another flower, the pollen may be transferred to the other flower. This is pollination. In the plant dance, you will use touch to show the pollen moving from one flower to another via the insects. Gently touch elbows with other dancers, moving the pollen from one flower dancer to another. Imagine that you are bees or birds moving the pollen from one flower to another." This can also be done with high fives or by touching other body parts such as toes or backs. It can be the same every time you go through the cycle, or it can change every time you do the plant life-cycle dance.

"When the flowers are pollinated, the plant produces fruit. Fruit protects the new seed. Make a middle-level, medium fruit shape, protecting the seeds. Gently fall to the ground and plant your seed again."

Repeat the plant life-cycle dance several times, asking increasingly more questions to the students about what is happening, such as, "What happens when the flowers are pollinated?" or "What size and level is your fruit shape?"

FORMATIVE ASSESSMENT

Room scan:

- Can the student demonstrate the correct levels and sizes in the plant life-cycle dance?
- Can the student answer questions about the plant life-cycle dance?

Create and Perform

Divide the class into groups of three to five. With younger students, assign one part of the plant life cycle to each group (seed, seedling and roots, leaves, flowers, pollination, fruit). "Create a dance that shows your part of the plant life cycle. Choose one level and one size for your dance. Practice your dance several times, clearly demonstrating your level and size." Students perform the dances for the class in the correct order. Start with the seed group. When the seed group is finished, ask the class to identify what group goes next: "What happens to the seed next in the plant life cycle?"

Older groups can create a dance showing the entire plant life cycle. "Use a variety of levels and sizes to create a dance showing the entire plant life cycle. Practice your dance several times so that you can perform it without stopping." Groups perform the dances for the other students.

SUMMATIVE ASSESSMENT

For younger students, ask the audience, "Did we see a high level? Did we see a big size? Did we see the leaves dancing?" Use a checklist to assess the following:

- Can the student perform a dance displaying one part of the plant life cycle?
- Can the student perform a dance with a clear size and level?

For older students, use a checklist to assess the following:

- Can the student perform a dance displaying the plant life cycle?
- Can the student perform a dance with clear sizes and levels?

Review and Reflect

Reflect on dance target	Reflect on science target
Ask the students, "When do we use different sizes with our bodies? I use a small size when I am moving through a crowd, and I use a big size when I am stretching in the morning." Call on several students, encouraging them to use full sentences: "I use a _____ size when I _____." "When you go home today, find a time when you use a specific size with your body. Tomorrow, you can tell me that you use a _____ size when you _____."	Review the plant life cycle. Guide the students to describe the life cycle of a plant by calling on individual students to describe one stage each. Ask, "What other living things have life cycles?"

EXTENSION

Plant a seed together as a class and observe how it grows.

FIVE SENSES

Observing with the five senses is an important skill for scientific inquiry and investigation. Humans have specific body parts to capture information and learn about the world around them. The eyes are used for sight and the ears for hearing. Skin is used to feel, the tongue is needed to taste, and the nose is needed to smell. Information is collected through the senses and stored as memories.

Note to teachers: If you have students with food allergies or if school policy prohibits the use of fresh food in your classroom, this lesson can be done without the sense of taste. Instead of using fruit, you may use cotton balls, paper clips, marbles, tissue paper, or other objects and focus on the four senses of smell, touch, sight, and hearing.

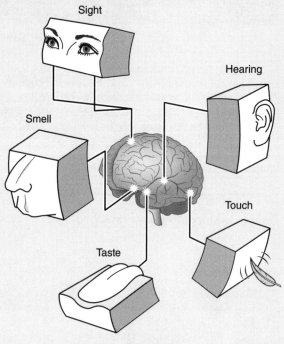

The five senses.

AGES

5-11

LEVEL

Basic-intermediate (this lesson can be done with little dance experience; however, students who have had more dance lessons will have more tools to create choreography)

MATERIALS

Before class, slice fruit into enough pieces for each student and place on individual napkins or in small paper cups (one for each student). Teachers may choose one type of fruit for the entire class or a mixture distributed among students as desired. Possible fruits include kiwi, apples, oranges, bananas, or what is available locally. Be aware if students have food allergies.

MUSIC

Contemplative selection (see appendix B)

ESSENTIAL QUESTION

How do you learn about the world around you?

ENDURING UNDERSTANDING

People observe the world through their senses.

	Dance	Science
Learning target	Students explore abstraction through choreography.	Students make observations with the five senses.
Evidence of student learning	The student creates an abstract dance sequence.	The student performs an abstract dance inspired by observations with the senses and states at least one observation.
Dance elements and science vocabulary	Sequence, abstraction, choreography	Sense, sight, see, sound, hear, smell, taste, touch, feel
Standards	Communication through dance: Improvise, choreograph, and perform dance movement based on ideas, experiences, feelings, concepts, or images (*Standards for Learning and Teaching Dance in the Arts*, p. 25).	Different sense receptors are specialized for particular kinds of information, which may be then processed by the animal's brain. Animals are able to use their perceptions and memories to guide their actions (*Next Generation Science Standards*, LS1.D: Information Processing).

Warm-Up

"Find your own space where you are only touching the floor and the air. We are going to do a milkshake dance. Make a big, round shape with your whole body. Make a new big, round shape with your whole body. These are the scoops of ice cream. Jump to make your ice cream scoops go into the blender. Jump again! Jump one more time! Now use a flowing energy quality as if your whole body is made of chocolate syrup. Don't forget to add the milk! Imagine your body is making a big splash into the blender. Without any sound, we are turning on our blender and turning or shaking. Freeze! Use a flowing, smooth energy quality for the milkshake."

Build Knowledge

"When we were doing our milkshake dance, were we acting it out as if we were actually making a milkshake? No, we used the idea of making a milkshake and turned it into a dance. We call this *abstraction*. Abstraction is when we use an idea, feeling, story, or object and change it into a dance. We use the original idea as our inspiration, but our ending dance is not always recognizable as the original idea."

EXPLORE ABSTRACTION

"I am going to say a word or phrase, and your task is to show that idea abstractly using movement. Think about how the word makes you feel or what it reminds you of. Try not to act out something as if you were that object or doing a real-world action. *Rock.*" Comment on dancers who are moving abstractly, using dance vocabulary to promote positive reinforcement, such as "I see some dancers moving strongly." Continue with the following words, pausing between each idea to give the students a chance to think of movements: *sun, lake, pinecone, happiness, anger,* and *confusion.*

FORMATIVE ASSESSMENT

Room scan: Can the student create abstract movement ideas?

Connect

"Humans use their five senses to observe and learn about the world. We use our eyes to see, our ears to hear sounds, our noses to smell, our tongues to taste, and our skin to feel and touch."

OBSERVE WITH THE FIVE SENSES

"In a moment you are going to receive a piece of fruit. Your task is to observe the fruit with your five senses. What does it look like? Does it have a sound? What does it smell like? What does it feel like? What does it taste like? Only take a small taste at first so that you may continue to observe using the other senses. At the end of the lesson you will be able to eat the rest of your piece. When you receive your fruit, you are the scientist. You will investigate the fruit with all of your senses." Distribute the fruit. Allow the students to observe for a minute. "Raise your hand if you can tell us something that you have observed with one of your senses." Call on several students, asking them which sense they used to obtain the given observation.

FORMATIVE ASSESSMENT

Room scan: Can the student state an observation using one of the five senses?

Create and Perform

"You are going to choreograph an abstract solo dance inspired by your observations." Younger students or students with less dance experience will work with one sense: "Choose one of the five senses. Choose one observation that you had with that sense. Create a movement inspired by that observation. For example, you may notice that the skin of your fruit is bumpy. You can create a movement that is bumpy. Practice your movement."

For older students or students with more dance experience, students may create more parts of the dance using more senses. "Choose one observation for each sense. Create one abstract movement for each observation. Practice your dance with all five movements in sequence without stopping." Students perform the dances for the class, with three to four students performing their solos at the same time.

SUMMATIVE ASSESSMENT

Use a checklist to assess the following:

- Can the student create an abstract dance sequence?
- Can the student perform an abstract dance inspired by observations with the senses?
- Can the student state at least one observation (or more with older students) made with the senses?

Students dance with a bumpy energy quality.

Review and Reflect

Reflect on dance target	Reflect on science target
"What is the difference between acting and dancing? How can a choreographer turn an idea into something abstract? This week, your assignment is to find a short task that you do every day, such as brushing your teeth, and create an abstract movement inspired by the task."	"What body part do we use for each of the senses? At home, find an object that you can observe with your senses. Remember to only taste things that are safe to eat. Observe the object with all of your senses."

EXTENSIONS

- Students choose one place to sit in the classroom and observe as many things with each of their senses as they can.

- Students choose a color and write a poem about it using the following structure:

Red looks like . . . _____

Red sounds like . . . _____

Red smells like . . . _____

Red tastes like . . . _____

Red feels like . . . _____

BONES

Every human has a skeleton. The bones of the body protect the internal organs, give the body support and structure, and aid in movement.

AGES
5-11

LEVEL
Basic-intermediate

MATERIALS
- Model skeleton or poster of human skeleton
- Index cards with bone names

MUSIC
Driving selection (see appendix B)

ESSENTIAL QUESTION
How is the human skeleton constructed?

ENDURING UNDERSTANDING
The body is made of interrelated parts that work together to perform a function.

	Dance	Science
Learning target	Students choreograph a sequence using a set of body parts.	Students identify various major bones.
Evidence of student learning	The student performs a dance sequence demonstrating the use of individual body parts.	The student performs a dance demonstrating the movement of specific bones.
Dance elements and science vocabulary	Body parts, choreographic sequence	Bone, skeleton, support, protect, skull, spine, ribs, pelvis Extension for intermediate level: femur, tibia, humerus, scapula, phalanges
Standards	Identify, demonstrate, and perform isolated dance movement for body parts of the head, torso, and limbs (*Standards for Learning and Teaching Dance in the Arts*, p. 23).	Plants and animals have both internal and external structures that serve various functions in growth, survival, behavior, and reproduction (*Next Generation Science Standards*, LS1.A: Structure and Function).

Warm-Up

"Move the head in many ways: up and down, side to side, in circles. Move the shoulders in every way that you can. Move the elbows, circle the wrists, and wiggle the fingers. Try to move only the ribs side to side. Move the hips in circles. Bend the spine gently to each side, front, and back. Twist the spine. March with the legs, circle the ankles, shake the feet, and wiggle the toes." Spend about 15 seconds on each body part that you introduce.

Build Knowledge

"Dancers use many parts of their bodies when they are dancing. This allows them to do a variety of movements and makes their dance more interesting to watch. When you use a variety of body parts when you are dancing, you are able to be more creative, strengthen many parts of your body, and make your dance more imaginative."

EXPLORE BODY PARTS

"Raise your hand if you can tell me a body part that we can move." Choose a student to decide the body part and then have everyone move using that body part. "How many different ways can you move this body part?" Choose five or six students to decide the body parts that are moved.

FORMATIVE ASSESSMENT

Room scan: Can the student demonstrate isolated dance movements with each body part?

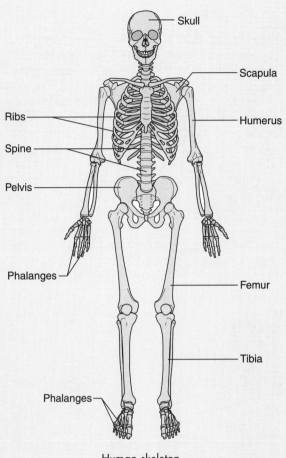

Human skeleton.

Connect

"Why do humans have skeletons? The skeleton is the body's support structure. It supports the other systems of the body and allows us to move. Some bones protect vital organs such as the brain, heart, and lungs. Bones cannot move themselves; the brain must send a message through the spinal cord and the nerves to the muscles, and the muscles move the bones.

Teacher Tip

If you are using real human remains as a visual aid, it is recommended that you teach students ahead of time about people donating their bodies to science, what to expect from the skeleton, and how to be respectful of the remains.

BONE DANCE

Identify the name and location of each bone. Point to the bone on the model or poster and point to the bone on your body. Have the students point to the bone on their bodies. Some bones can be felt with the fingertips. Describe the function and structure of each bone. Then have the students move the bone in various ways.

For example, point to the skull on the model and then point to your own skull. Say, "This is the skull. It protects the brain. Point to your own skull. It is made of several bones that grew together after you were born. Feel the top of your skull, the back of the skull where it meets the spine, your brow, and your cheekbones. Move your skull up and down. Move your skull side to side. Make circles with your skull. Now shake your skull."

Continue this process with the ribs, pelvis, and spine (for older students or for a second or third lesson for younger students, introduce the humerus, scapula, femur, tibia, and phalanges).

After introducing and moving each bone (or set of bones), review what bones have already been introduced by doing a bone dance. Move through each of the bones: "Move your skull. Move your ribs. Move your pelvis. Move your spine." You can also review by having the students point to the bones on their bodies.

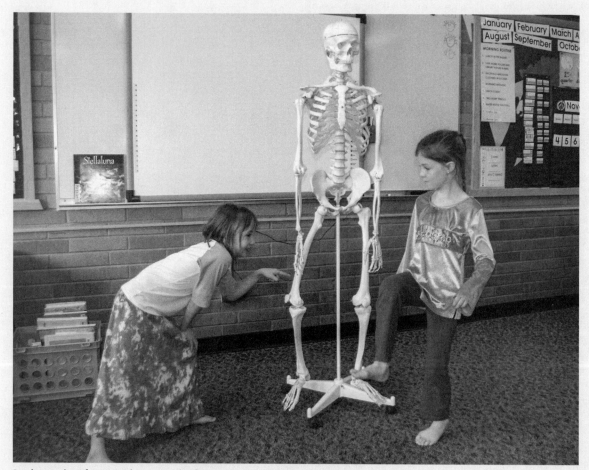

Students identifying and moving the femur.

FORMATIVE ASSESSMENT

Room scan: Can the student identify and move the various bones?

Create and Perform

Divide the students into groups of three or four. Give each group three (or fewer for younger students) bone cards. Each card has the name of one bone written on the front. Instruct the dancers to do the following:

1. Review where the bones named on their cards are located in their bodies.
2. Create a dance that clearly shows the three bones moving (e.g., dancers circle their pelvis three times, then reach their humerus bones up twice, then wiggle their phalanges).
3. Practice the dance with their group.

Students perform their dances for each other. Groups should introduce their bones and then perform their dance. Teachers should remind the groups who are not performing about proper audience etiquette.

For younger dancers who cannot read the cards, provide an image of the bone along with the word. In addition, teachers may instruct the groups verbally with one bone per group or with two bones for a second or third bones lesson. For older dancers, more bones can be used for each group, or instead of using cards, the dancers can decide together in their group which bones to use.

SUMMATIVE ASSESSMENT

Before performing, instructors may initiate a rehearsal with the entire class. Ask the students to start their dances at the same time and practice as if they are performing (i.e., not talking, doing the whole dance all the way through to the end without stopping). After the rehearsal, use a rubric to have students self-assess their dance. An example of a dance rubric for this lesson is shown in table 10.4.

Once the students have self-assessed their rehearsal, teachers may choose to do a second rehearsal for students to improve their dances. Students then perform.

After each performance, students peer assess the performers using the rubric. The audience watches the performers and claps for them when they are finished. Then, without any sounds, they hold up their fingers (4, 3, 2, or 1) to evaluate the dance. Teachers should respond to the peer assessments

Table 10.4 Bone Dance Rubric

The student's action was	
4	clear and continued through the entire dance.
3	clear but not continued through the entire dance.
2	not clear.
1	different than what was planned.

by asking questions such as, "Why are you holding up a 3?" Make sure the students can articulate why they are giving the score they are showing; for example, "The dancers were clearly showing their spine, pelvis, and ribs, but they stopped after the spine to talk about what was next so they did not dance the whole time. That is why I am showing a 3."

Review and Reflect

Reflect on dance target	Reflect on science target
"Just like dancers use many parts of their bodies when they are dancing, we use many parts of our bodies throughout our daily activities. For example, I use my shoulder to carry my book bag and I use my hip to close my car door when my hands are full. Raise your hand if you can tell me one specific thing you do with one body part. Your sentence should sound like this: 'I use my_____ when I_____.'" Call on three to five students to respond.	"What body part do we use for each of the senses? At home, find an object that you can observe with your senses. Remember to only taste things that are safe to eat. Observe the object with all of your senses."

EXTENSIONS

- Teachers copy a diagram of a skeleton without bone names. Students label the bones that they have learned. If multiple bone lessons are planned, students can fill in the names after each lesson or as a culminating activity to assess learning retention.
- Students draw (or paint or sculpt) their interpretation of a skeleton, highlighting the bones they have learned with different colors.

11

EARTH AND
SPACE SCIENCES

arth and space sciences explore the processes that occur on Earth and the place of the Earth in the universe. This chapter includes lessons on weather, constellations, moon phases, the water cycle, erosion and weathering, and the three types of rocks. The first lesson ties energy qualities to types of weather. The next lesson explores constellations using elastic loops to connect dancers into constellation shapes. Then reach and size are connected to the phases of the moon as students orbit around a prop representing Earth. The water cycle is explored with a more complex lesson using levels, qualities, relationships, and tempo. In the next lesson, erosion and weathering are connected to energy qualities to show forces acting upon rocks. In the final lesson, dance stillness is used to discover the three types of rocks: sedimentary, igneous, and metamorphic.

WEATHER

Learning to observe the weather is a skill many children acquire at a young age and is often one of the first introductions to scientific inquiry. Children learn to observe, describe, identify, and make predictions about various types of weather, such as snow, rain, wind, and sunny weather.

Snow, rain, sun, and wind.

AGES
5-7

LEVEL
Basic

MATERIALS
Whiteboard or easel

MUSIC
Pleasant selection (see appendix B)

ESSENTIAL QUESTION
What is weather?

ENDURING UNDERSTANDING
We can observe and record the weather, which changes daily.

	Dance	Science
Learning target	Students learn, identify, and practice various energy qualities.	Students identify and describe rain, snow, wind, or sunny weather.
Evidence of student learning	The student performs a dance demonstrating a specific energy quality.	The student performs a dance demonstrating an energy quality communicating a type of weather.
Dance elements and science vocabulary	Energy qualities (light, powerful, bouncy, smooth)	Weather, temperature, wind, snow, rain, sunlight, sunny
Standards	Dance qualities: Explore movement possibilities in dance using a variety of movement qualities or characteristics (*Standards for Learning and Teaching Dance in the Arts*, p. 23).	Weather is the combination of sunlight, wind, snow or rain, and temperature in a particular region at a particular time. People measure these conditions to describe and record the weather and to notice patterns over time (*Next Generation Science Standards*, ESS2.D: Weather and Climate).

Warm-Up
"Find your own place. Imagine that your body is made of jelly. Show me how your body would move. I see jiggly, wiggly, and gooey movement! Now imagine that your body is made out of taffy. It is stretchy, almost like a rubber band. Now let's imagine that all of our bodies are filled with rocks. We are so heavy, dropping our weight into the ground as we move."

Build Knowledge
"Energy qualities are movement ideas that describe how we are moving. They are not *what* we are doing but *how* we are doing it and with what sort of energy."

EXPLORE ENERGY QUALITIES
"We are going to start by walking through our dancing space. Our action is walking. Right now, we are just walking normally. In a moment, I am going to tell you *how* we are going to walk by telling you an energy quality. We are still going to walk, but we walk with a different sort of energy. Our first energy quality is light. Begin walking lightly. Imagine that you are a helium balloon floating away. Or imagine that there are marshmallows under the floor and you are trying not to squish them. Your action

is still walking, but your energy quality is light. Now try powerful energy. You are walking powerfully. Move with strength and tension. Imagine that you must push the air out of your way to move. You are still walking, just walking with a powerful energy quality. Next is bouncy. Bouncy can be very jittery. You are still walking, but maybe you are walking with a bounce or a wiggle. Bouncy is fluttering and bumpy and vibratory. Your action is still walking, but your energy quality is bouncy. The last energy quality that we are doing today is smooth. We are trying to take out all of the bumps now. We are still walking, but we are walking smoothly.

"Now that we can walk with various energy qualities, let's dance creatively with these energies. Move throughout the room using bouncy energy. You don't have to walk; you can skip, bounce, wiggle, or find your own creative bouncy movement. Now move smoothly throughout the room. What about powerful energy? Move powerfully, finding the empty spaces between dancers. And light energy— how can you move with a light energy quality?"

FORMATIVE ASSESSMENT

Room scan: Can the student identify and demonstrate the four energy qualities of bouncy, powerful, light, and smooth?

Connect

"We are going to assign energy qualities to various kinds of weather."

WEATHER DANCE

"Think about softly falling snowflakes. Are they bouncy? Not really. What about light? Yes, snowflakes are very light. We are going to dance snow using a light and soft energy quality. Practice your snow dance." Practice a light energy quality, commenting on the students' snow or snowflakes to reinforce the vocabulary.

"Snow happens when the weather is cold and moisture is falling from the clouds. In the summer when it is warm does it snow? No, when it is dry and warm in the summer it is often sunny with clear skies. We are going to think about that clear weather and move with a smooth energy quality for our sunny dance. When the sky is clear and it is sunny, there is not any snow or rain. Practice your sunny dance with smooth energy." Practice a smooth energy quality, commenting on the students' sunny and clear movement.

"Sometimes when it is not cold enough to snow but moisture is falling from the clouds, we have rain. Our dance for rain is going to be bouncy. Imagine the raindrops falling and splashing on the ground. Think about the rhythm and the sound of the rain. Practice your jittery, bumpy, bouncy rain dance."

After practicing the rain dance, introduce the wind dance: "Now we are going to do our powerful energy quality to show a strong wind blowing. Imagine that you are the wind moving the leaves and branches on the trees and pushing doors closed. Use a powerful energy quality." Practice the powerful wind dance. Review and practice all four weather dances (table 11.1).

Table 11.1 Weather and Energy Quality

Weather	Energy quality
Snow	Light
Rain	Bouncy
Wind	Powerful
Sun	Smooth

FORMATIVE ASSESSMENT

Room scan: Can the student connect the weather to an energy quality?

Create and Perform

Divide the class into groups of three or four. Assign each group one type of weather: sun, wind, rain, or snow. Instruct the students to first remember what energy quality their weather dance is and then begin practicing their weather dance using that energy quality.

After they have practiced for a few minutes, ask them to sit down for further instructions. "We are going to do a rehearsal, a practice, with all groups practicing at the same time. You will start frozen. When the music starts, you will do your weather dance. When the music stops, freeze in any fantastic shape. Please rehearse." Make sure all students are frozen, and then play the music for about 30 seconds while watching the students, checking for clear energy qualities. Stop the music and encourage the students to freeze.

"We need to evaluate how well we are dancing. We are going to rate ourselves based on what we just practiced. We will give ourselves a 4 if we danced our energy quality clearly for the entire time. We will give ourselves a 3 if we danced our energy quality clearly but not the whole time. We will give ourselves a 2 if our energy quality was not clear and a 1 if we did a different dance than our weather dance." You may need to repeat the rubric several times for younger students. For older students you could write it on the whiteboard (table 11.2). Ask the students to hold up the number that they are giving themselves.

The groups may need to practice again before performing for each other. When the students perform, ask them to tell the audience what their weather and energy quality will be before they begin dancing. Repeat the process of freezing at the start and end of the dance. After each dance has been performed and the audience has clapped, ask the audience to hold up their fingers to peer assess the performers using the rubric.

Table 11.2 **Assessment Rubric for Energy Quality**

The student's energy quality was	
4	clear and continued throughout the entire dance.
3	clear but not continued throughout the dance.
2	not clear.
1	different than what was planned.

SUMMATIVE ASSESSMENT

Use the rubric (table 11.2) to assess each student.

Review and Reflect

Reflect on dance target	Reflect on science target
"When do we use energy qualities outside of dance? I use a powerful energy when I am digging in my garden, and I sometimes use a bouncy energy when I have a mosquito following me! When do you use certain energy qualities outside of dance? When I see you again, you can describe an energy quality that you use at home."	"What is our weather like today? Does it seem to move with any of the energy qualities we were doing today? How can we describe today's weather?"

EXTENSIONS

- Draw or paint a picture of a type of weather.
- Write a poem describing the movement of the weather.
- Create sound effects for each type of weather, such as blowing for wind and tapping for rain.

CONSTELLATIONS

Students use large elastic bands to create constellations and understand how constellations are named and described.

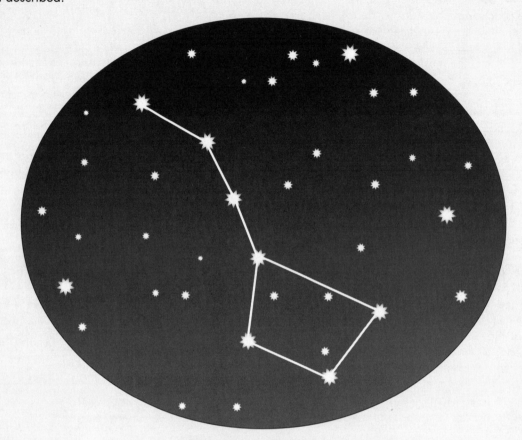

The Big Dipper constellation.

AGES
5-11

LEVEL
Basic

MATERIALS

- 2-meter strips of elastic tied or sewn together to make large elastic bands (at least one for every two students)
- Whiteboard or easel

MUSIC
Contemplative selection (see appendix B)

ESSENTIAL QUESTION
What are constellations?

ENDURING UNDERSTANDING

A constellation is a region of the sky where the stars form a pattern.

	Dance	Science
Learning target	Students use props to create shapes.	Students understand that many ancient societies associated patterns in the stars with stories from their culture.
Evidence of student learning	The student uses elastic bands to create shapes alone and with other dancers.	The student creates constellations by making and connecting shapes using the elastic bands.
Dance elements and science vocabulary	Shapes, props	Constellation, star, culture, stories, myth
Standards	Form shapes and create designs with the body (*Standards for Learning and Teaching Dance in the Arts*, p. 23).	Patterns of the motion of the sun, moon, and stars in the sky can be observed, described, and predicted (*Next Generation Science Standards*, ESS1.A: The Universe and its Stars).

Warm-Up

"Plant your feet on the floor and twist and look behind you. Twist the other way. Twist, twist, twist, twist. Reach up. Reach down. Reach up. Reach down. Turn around and jump. Turn and jump. Turn and jump." Repeat four times. "Make a twisted shape with your body. Now make a curvy shape. Make a big shape. What about a small shape? Can you make a flat shape? Make an angular shape."

Build Knowledge

Introduce the elastic bands. "Sometimes dancers use props when they are dancing. Props are objects that dancers use in their dance. You will be using the elastic bands to make shapes with your body. It is important to be safe when we are using the elastic bands. Please do not put the bands around your necks or twist them tightly around body parts. Hold onto the bands tightly so that they do not snap someone, because that would not be respectful or safe. When we make shapes, we freeze our bodies in a still shape, if only for a moment. "

EXPLORE ELASTIC BANDS

Begin with each student experimenting with making shapes individually. If there are enough bands for each student to have one, they can all explore immediately. However, if there are not enough bands, divide the class into pairs, giving each group one band. Tap one dancer in each group; this will be dancer 1. The student who did not get tapped is dancer 2. "Dancer 1 will experiment with the band, making many shapes for about 1 minute while dancer 2 watches. Then dancer 2 will have a turn. Try to make as many unique and creative shapes as you can. Make the shapes with your whole body! Can you make twisting, curvy, or angular shapes? Tall shapes? Low shapes? Flat shapes?" Switch roles so that dancer 1 watches as dancer 2 makes shapes. Continue switching three or four times each. Encourage the students to make shapes with their whole bodies. When students are waiting their turns, they watch their partners and observe their shapes.

"With your partner, make a shape together with your one elastic band. Once you find a creative shape, begin finding a new unique shape." Encourage them to create many unique shapes with many body parts for about 2 minutes.

FORMATIVE ASSESSMENT

Room scan: Can the student create shapes with the elastic band alone and with a partner?

Connect

"Ancient people saw many patterns in the stars. They drew imaginary lines between stars, forming pictures in their minds. They saw characters from their stories and myths or important animals or people from their culture. Many societies named the same groups of stars different things because they saw them in different ways. Even now, you can look at the stars at night and find your own patterns. The stars can be observed and patterns can be found, but some people may call the same patterns by different names. For example, the Big Dipper (draw the Big Dipper on the whiteboard or show a picture) was seen as a ladle in some cultures and as a bear, plough, or cart in others. We call the grouping of stars a *constellation*."

CONSTELLATIONS

Collect the elastic bands. "When you hear the music, you will gallop through the room. When the music stops, freeze." Turn on music and allow the students to gallop for about 30 seconds. Turn off the music and encourage the students to freeze. "Imagine yourself as a star and that you need to find the patterns that create constellations. I will give an elastic band to small groups of dancers that are near each other. Use the bands to create unique and interesting shapes with your whole bodies to create constellations. Use many body parts and shapes." Hand out elastic bands to students who are in close proximity. There may be groups of two, three, four, or five students creating one constellation. When all

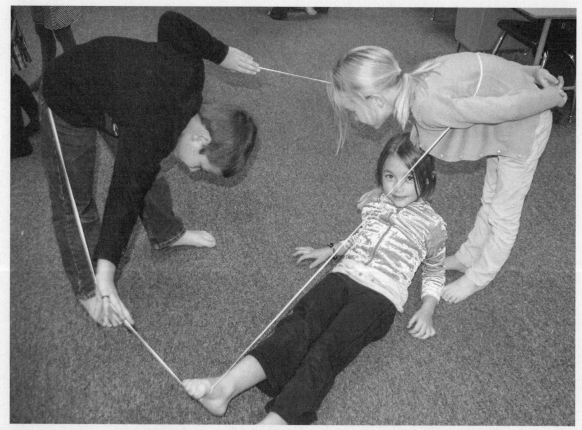

Three students use an elastic band to make a constellation.

groups have found a constellation shape or after an allotted amount of time such as 10 counts, collect the elastic bands, turn on the music, and repeat the activity.

FORMATIVE ASSESSMENT

Room scan: Can the student create shapes with the entire body and the elastic band, working together with other students?

Create and Perform

Divide the class into groups of three to five. Give each group two elastic bands. "With your group, your goal is to create your own constellation. Make sure you are working together and that not only are your elastic bands in a unique shape, but your bodies are in interesting shapes, too." When the groups appear to be almost done, direct them to name their constellation without changing the shape. "Does your constellation remind you of a dragon? The school principal? A crayon? Name your constellation." Ask each group to show and share the name of the constellation.

SUMMATIVE ASSESSMENT

Use a checklist to assess the following:

- Can the student use elastic bands to create shapes alone and with other dancers?
- Can the student create constellations by making and connecting shapes using the elastic bands?

Review and Reflect

Reflect on dance target	Reflect on science target
"We used elastic bands as props today to help us make shapes. What other props could we use to help us make shapes?"	"How were the constellations named? Your homework this week is to look at the stars, find a group of them, and decide for yourself what the pattern is. You are naming your very own constellation."

EXTENSIONS

- Students write a short story about their constellation. How did their constellation end up in the stars? Why is their creature, object, or person important? What is the legend behind their constellation?
- Students draw their constellation, displaying the stars, the lines connecting the stars, and any other details they would like to add to illustrate their constellation.
- Students research a specific constellation.

MOON PHASES

Moon phases are formed by changing angles of the moon, sun, and Earth as the moon orbits the Earth. Exactly one-half of the moon is always light and one-half is always dark. On Earth, sometimes humans see both illuminated portions and dark portions of the moon. The relative positions of the Earth, moon, and sun cause the varying amounts of the lit segment visible from Earth, thus creating the phases. The phase of the moon in which no light is visible is the new moon. As the lit portion grows, it is called *waxing*. The moon continues to the phases of waxing crescent, first quarter, and waxing gibbous. The phase in which people on Earth can see the entire illuminated side of the moon is called *full moon*. As the illuminated portion shrinks again, it is called *waning*, and the phases are waning gibbous, last quarter, and waning crescent before reaching the new moon phase.

AGES
6-9

LEVEL
Basic

MATERIALS
- Ball (or other object to designate as Earth)
- Poster or object to represent the sun
- Drawing of the moon phases on whiteboard or easel paper

MUSIC
Driving selection (see appendix B)

ESSENTIAL QUESTION
Why does the moon change its shape?

ENDURING UNDERSTANDING
The relationship of the sun, moon, and Earth causes the phases of the moon.

	Dance	Science
Learning target	Students explore far and near reach (size) and dance with their full kinesphere.	Students understand and identify the phases of the moon.
Evidence of student learning	The student demonstrates near, far, and medium reach (small, large, and medium size).	The student demonstrates near, far, or medium reach in correspondence to a moon phase based on the student's spatial position in relation to the Earth and sun props. The student verbally identifies the phases of the moon.
Dance elements and science vocabulary	Size (large, small, narrow, wide, medium), reach (near, medium, far), kinesphere	Moon, phase, pattern, orbit, waxing, waning, gibbous, crescent, quarter, full moon, new moon

(continued)

(continued)

	Dance	Science
Standards	• Shapes: Form shapes and create designs with the body. • Personal space: Define one's personal space in relation to the personal space of other dancers (*Standards for Learning and Teaching Dance in the Arts*, pp. 23-24).	Patterns of the motion of the sun, moon, and stars in the sky can be observed, described, and predicted (*Next Generation Science Standards*, ESS1.A: The Universe and its Stars).

Warm-Up

Do the BrainDance warm-up (appendix A), focusing on big and small core–distal movements.

Build Knowledge

"Dancers move within a kinesphere. A kinesphere is all of the space around our body that we can reach by extending our limbs. It's like a bubble around our body. Dancers call this *reach space*, *personal space*, and *size*. We can move with a near reach or small size, a far reach or large size, or a medium reach or size (demonstrate as you speak). Reach is the distance that the limbs are moving from the body."

EXPLORE REACH

"Make a far-reach shape. You are extending your arms and legs away from your middle. Create a new far-reach shape. Now form a near-reach shape. You are pulling your arms and legs in close to your middle. Find a new near-reach shape. Make a medium-reach shape. You are not reaching too far or too near but right in the middle. Create a new medium-reach shape.

"Find your own unique way to move through the room with a near reach. Remember that dancers are artists who go their own ways and create their own unique, interesting, and creative movements. How many different ways can you move through the room at a near reach? You are dancing with your arms and legs close to your middle.

"Now dance through the room with a far reach. You are reaching and stretching your arms and legs away from your middle. Create a new way to move with a far reach. And a new way! There are so many ways that you can move with a far reach!

"Using a medium reach, dance through the room. You are not reaching and stretching your limbs all the way to the edges of your kinesphere, but you are not holding them in tightly, either. You are moving somewhere in the middle of your kinesphere. What are other ways that you can move with a medium reach?"

Practice moving with a far-, medium-, and near-reach kinesphere four more times each.

FORMATIVE ASSESSMENT

Room scan: Can the student demonstrate a far, near, and medium reach?

Connect

"The motion of the moon has patterns that can be observed, described, and predicted. The phases of the moon are formed by the angle of the sun, Earth, and moon." Use a drawing on the whiteboard or easel paper to help illustrate these concepts. "Exactly one-half of the moon is light and one-half is dark at all times. Because the moon orbits the Earth, the angle of the sun, Earth, and moon changes. As this happens, both illuminated and shadowed portions of the moon face the Earth. The dark portion is not visible to the human eye and we therefore see the different phases of the moon.

"During the new moon phase, the sun, moon, and Earth are in approximate alignment with the moon between the sun and Earth. The lit portion is not visible on Earth and humans do not see any moon. As the moon orbits the Earth, the light part of the moon visible on Earth grows. This is called *waxing*. The moon goes through the phases of waxing crescent, first quarter, and waxing gibbous before becoming a full moon. During the full moon, the sun, Earth, and moon are aligned, with the Earth between the sun and moon. During the full moon, the entire illuminated half of the moon is visible on Earth. As the moon continues to orbit the Earth, the light portion seen on Earth shrinks. This is called *waning*. The moon goes through the phases of waning gibbous, last quarter, and waning crescent before entering the new moon phase again. The crescent phases are less than a quarter but more than the new moon and the gibbous phases are greater than a quarter but less than the full moon.

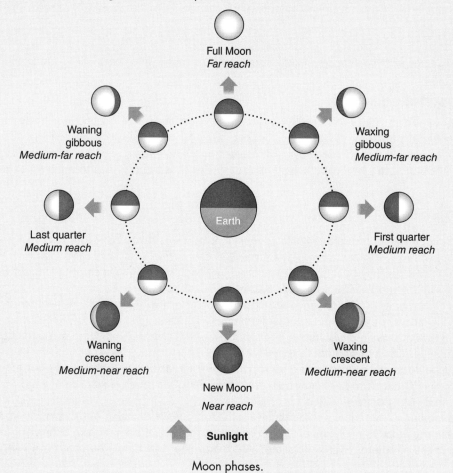

Moon phases.

From K. Kaufmann and J. Dehline, 2014, *Dance integration: 36 dance lesson plans for science and mathematics* (Champaign, IL: Human Kinetics).

"We are going to use reach to dance the phases of the moon. The more of the moon that we see, the larger our reach will be. The new moon is our nearest reach or our smallest size. The full moon is our farthest reach or our largest size. The quarter moons are our medium reaches. The crescent moons are larger than our new moon but smaller than our quarter moon. The crescent moons are a medium-near reach. The gibbous moons are larger than the quarter moons but smaller than the full moon. The gibbous moons are a medium-far reach."

MOON PHASES

"Moving through the room, use your own creative near reach to dance the new moon. We are going to wax, which means that we are growing. Grow to your medium-near reach to show your waxing crescent. Continue to use your own creative choices with your medium-near reach. Changing to our next phase, you are waxing to your first quarter moon. This is your medium reach. Growing even more, you are becoming the waxing gibbous phase. This is your medium-far reach. Make sure that it is bigger than your first quarter but not your farthest reach yet. Now we are waxing to our full moon. This is your farthest reach. The full moon is when we see the most of the moon.

"After the moon reaches its fullest, it begins to wane or shrink. Move through the room with your medium-far reach. This is your waning gibbous. I should see each dancer moving with unique medium-far movements. Wane to your last quarter. You are moving with your medium reach. Continue to shrink to your waning crescent. You are now dancing with your medium-near reach. As the moon moves back into approximate alignment between the sun and Earth, you wane to your new moon, your nearest reach." Practice the cycle three to four more times, checking for understanding.

FORMATIVE ASSESSMENT
Room scan: Can the student demonstrate reaches that correspond to the phases of the moon?

Create and Perform
Designate an object to represent Earth. An exercise ball is an exciting choice, but a playground ball, a chair, or even a piece of paper will suffice. Place Earth in the center of the room. Tape a poster representing the sun to one wall or place an object representing the sun, such as another ball, near one wall.

"Form a circle as a class around Earth. You are each going to orbit the Earth as the moon using reach to show your phase. Which side of the circle is the new moon side? It is the side between the sun and Earth. Which side is the full moon side? The side opposite from the sun. Point to where the waxing crescent will be. Point to the first quarter side. Where will the waxing gibbous be? And the waning gibbous? Last quarter? Waning crescent? As we orbit, are we all going to be the same reach at the same time? No, because we are each in our own position in relation to the sun and Earth. Let's

Students orbit an exercise ball using reach.

practice." Practice orbiting Earth with dancers using their own reaches corresponding to the moon phases. Students may whisper the name of their current phase as they orbit, which provides ease in assessing the students' understanding of the material.

Divide the students into two or more groups. One group performs its orbiting dance while the remaining students observe as an audience.

SUMMATIVE ASSESSMENT

Use a checklist to assess the following:

- Can the student demonstrate near, far, or medium reach in correspondence to a moon phase based on the student's spatial position in relation to the Earth and sun props?
- Can the student verbally identify the phases of the moon?

Review and Reflect

Reflect on dance target	Reflect on science target
"I use a near reach when I am cold. My arms and legs are moving close to my middle to try to keep me warm. When do you use a specific reach outside of dance? Raise your hand if you can describe a time when you use a far, medium, or near reach outside of dance. Your sentence should sound like this: 'I use a _____ reach when I _____.'" Call on several students. "Your homework this week is to notice when you use different reaches at home. Next dance class I will ask you to describe some of the situations when you use different reaches."	Review the moon phases. "People have been observing the moon and its phases since early times. Humans observe the moon as a way to understand the world around them. Early scientists observed patterns of the moon phases, made predictions, and used the moon phases to mark time. Your homework for the next week is to observe the current phase of the moon. Next week I will ask you to describe the phase you observed."

EXTENSIONS

- Draw an illustration or use clay to model the phases of the moon.
- Write a story that follows the phases of the moon.

WATER CYCLE

Water continuously cycles among several processes as it changes forms. Students use previously learned concepts of levels, relationships, qualities, and tempo to dance the water cycle of accumulation, evaporation, condensation, and precipitation.

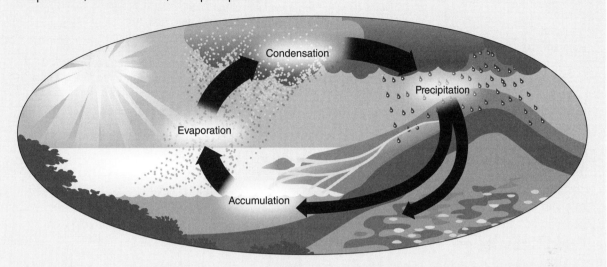

Water cycle.

From K. Kaufmann and J. Dehline, 2014, *Dance integration: 36 dance lesson plans for science and mathematics* (Champaign, IL: Human Kinetics).

AGES
6-9

LEVEL
Intermediate

MATERIALS
Poster illustrating the water cycle or whiteboard

MUSIC
Contemplative selection (see appendix B)

ESSENTIAL QUESTION
How does water change from one form to another?

ENDURING UNDERSTANDING
Water circulates through a continuous cycle.

	Dance	Science
Learning target	Students review and combine several elements of movement.	Students understand the water cycle and its four stages.
Evidence of student learning	The student creates and performs a dance demonstrating multiple movement concepts of levels, relationships, qualities, and tempos.	The student creates and performs a dance that demonstrates the water cycle.

(continued)

(continued)

	Dance	Science
Dance elements and science vocabulary	Tempo (fast, medium, slow), levels (high, middle, low), energy qualities (light, flowing, heavy), relationships (near, far, medium)	Water, cycle, accumulation, evaporation, condensation, precipitation, solid, liquid, gas, water vapor, snow, rain, hail, clouds
Standards	Create and share a short dance that demonstrates varied use of the basic elements of dance (*Standards for Learning and Teaching Dance in the Arts*, p. 25).	Global movements of water and its changes in form are propelled by sunlight and gravity (*Next Generation Science Standards*, ESS2.C: The Role of Water in Earth's Surface Processes).

Warm-Up

"Follow me and do as I do." The teacher improvises using a variety of levels, tempos, and energy qualities as students mirror the movements.

Build Knowledge

Ideally students have already been introduced to the dance concepts of relationships, levels, tempo, and energy qualities. "Dancers combine many elements of movement to make interesting dances. Today we will combine levels, tempos, energy qualities, and relationships to create interesting dances and explore the water cycle."

REVIEW AND EXPLORE COMBINED ELEMENTS

"Remember that levels are how high or low your body is to the floor. Crawl at a low level. Gallop at a high level. Dart at a middle level. Tempo is the pace your body is moving at. March with a medium tempo. Bounce with a fast tempo. Sway with a slow tempo. Energy qualities are how you are doing particular actions and with what energy. Skip with a light energy quality. Stomp with a heavy energy quality. Float with a flowing energy quality. Relationships are how you relate to other dancers. You can be near, medium, and far from other dancers. Tiptoe with a near relationship. You should be as close to the other dancers as you can without touching. Slide using a medium relationship. Swing using a far relationship.

"Now move high and light . . . fast and with a far relationship . . . heavy and slow . . . low and with a near relationship . . . flowing energy quality and middle level . . . heavy energy quality, middle level, and medium relationship . . . fast, high, and light . . . flowing, high level, and medium tempo." Continue combining three elements. Perhaps even try four dance concepts!

FORMATIVE ASSESSMENT

Room scan: Can the student combine multiple dance concepts?

Connect

Direct the students' attention to the water cycle poster or drawing on the whiteboard. "Water evaporates from oceans and lakes when it is heated by the sun, changing it into water vapor moving throughout the atmosphere as a gas (evaporation). When the water is cooled by air in the atmosphere, it is condensed back into liquid water and forms clouds (condensation). These clouds become heavy with so much water, and the water is pulled to the ground by gravity in the form of rain, snow, or hail (precipitation). The water then accumulates into rivers, lakes, oceans, and groundwater (accumulation), where it can start the cycle again. We will use several elements of dance to demonstrate the water cycle." (See table 11.3.)

Table 11.3　Water Cycle Movement Chart

Water cycle stage	Movement concepts
Accumulation	Low level, locomotor (moving throughout space)
Evaporation	High level, light energy quality, fast tempo
Condensation	Near relationship, flowing energy quality, medium tempo
Precipitation	Medium relationship, heavy energy quality, fast tempo

WATER CYCLE DANCE

"Start by moving at a low level throughout the dancing space. This is locomotor movement, which means we are moving from one place to another throughout the space. This is accumulation. You are showing the water moving on the Earth as rivers, lakes, and oceans.

"When the sun heats the water, the liquid water evaporates into a gas called water vapor. Rise to a high level and move high, light, and fast to show the energy of the water vapor in the atmosphere. This is evaporation.

"When the air in the atmosphere cools the water vapor, it condenses into liquid water, forming clouds. Begin moving at a near relationship to each other at a medium tempo and a flowing energy quality. This is condensation.

"Because the clouds have become heavy with so much water, you are becoming heavier with your body until precipitation begins to occur. You are moving heavy, fast, and at a medium relationship to each other to show precipitation. Gently sink to the ground and begin the cycle again." Repeat the cycle three to four times.

FORMATIVE ASSESSMENT

Room scan: Can the student combine the movement elements with the vocabulary of the water cycle?

Create and Perform

Divide the students into groups of four. In each group, assign each student one part of the water cycle (accumulation, evaporation, condensation, precipitation). "You will each create a movement for your own part of the water cycle (the accumulation person creates movement for accumulation, evaporation person creates movement for evaporation, and so on). You must use at least two movement concepts at the same time; for example, you must include a level and an energy quality or a tempo and a relationship. Once each person in the group has created a movement that includes at least two concepts, you will teach your movement to the rest of your group. The group will then practice all four parts of the water cycle in succession—accumulation, evaporation, condensation, and precipitation. Continue to practice until it is time to perform." Students practice their dance several times, and then each group performs the dance for the class.

SUMMATIVE ASSESSMENT

Use a checklist to assess the following:

- Can the student create and perform a dance demonstrating multiple movement concepts of levels, relationships, qualities, and tempo?
- Can the student create and perform a dance that demonstrates the water cycle?

Review and Reflect

Reflect on dance target	Reflect on science target
"Raise your hand if you can describe a time outside of dance when you use multiple movement concepts. For example, you could say, 'I use a strong energy quality and low level when I am pulling weeds in my garden.'" Call on several students. "Tonight, your homework is to find an example of when you use more than one element of movement at home. Next time we meet you can tell me what you were doing when you used more than one movement element."	Review the water cycle. "What part of the water cycle is a river (or other local body of water) (accumulation)? What part of the water cycle is the puddle that is drying up outside (evaporation)? What part of the water cycle are the clouds we can see in the sky (condensation)? What part of the water cycle is rain or snow (precipitation)?"

EXTENSION

Students draw, paint, or use construction paper to create an illustration of the water cycle.

EROSION AND WEATHERING

The surface of the Earth changes over time due to the natural processes of weathering and erosion. Weathering is the breaking down of rocks into progressively smaller pieces due to the effects of weather. Erosion is when these sediments are carried to a new location by water and wind.

Photo courtesy of Steven Dehline.

The Grand Canyon is an excellent example of weathering and erosion over time.

AGES
8-11

LEVEL
Basic

MATERIALS
None

MUSIC
Pleasant selection (see appendix B)

ESSENTIAL QUESTION
Why do rocks change?

ENDURING UNDERSTANDING
The rock cycle has an impact on the physical characteristics of the Earth.

	Dance	Science
Learning target	Students explore the energy qualities of flowing, strong, light, and melting.	Students understand the processes of weathering and erosion.
Evidence of student learning	The student correctly demonstrates flowing, strong, light, and melting energy qualities.	The student creates and performs a dance that demonstrates the water cycle.
Dance elements and science vocabulary	Energy qualities (flowing, light, strong, melting)	Weathering, erosion, rock, sediments
Standards	Dance qualities: Explore movement possibilities in dance using a variety of movement qualities or characteristics (*Standards for Learning and Teaching Dance in the Arts*, p. 24).	Rainfall helps to shape the land and affects the types of living things found in a region. Water, ice, wind, living organisms, and gravity break rocks, soils, and sediments into smaller particles and move them around (*Next Generation Science Standards*, ESS2.A: Earth Materials and Systems).

Warm-Up

"Imagine that your body is full of rocks. Show me how you would move. Now imagine that your body is filled with jelly. Do you move the same way? No! Now your body is made of cotton balls. How do you move? And lastly, imagine that you are made out of bouncy balls!"

Build Knowledge

"Dancers move with many qualities of energy. A dancer can move with energies that are flowing, light, strong, or melting. These are called *energy qualities*, and they are how actions can be danced."

EXPLORE ENERGY QUALITIES

"Moving through the empty spaces between other dancers, tiptoe lightly. Continue to move with a light and airy energy quality and skip through the room. Imagine that you are floating away because there is little gravity. Explore other ways to move with a light energy quality. You can float, bounce, twirl, and leap with a light energy quality. Choose your own creative way to dance lightly.

"Sway with a flowing and smooth energy quality. Now float smoothly. A flowing energy quality has no bumps or sharpness. Imagine that your body is silk floating in water. Choose your own way to move with a flowing and smooth energy quality. You can twirl, twist, rise, and bend with a smooth energy quality.

"Now sink to the floor slowly with a melting energy quality. Rise smoothly up to a high level. Twist and turn slowly with a melting energy quality. Slowly reach a low level and then return to your high level and start again. Try a new way to use a melting energy quality as you sink to the floor. How many different ways can you melt?

"March strongly through the room. Use a powerful energy quality to jump. A strong energy quality uses your muscles forcefully with tension and weight. Use a new action to move with a strong energy quality. Choose your own unique way to move strongly." Practice dancing with the four energy qualities of strong, light, flowing, and melting three more times each.

"Dancers are artists who make choices using all energy qualities. Using the energy qualities of strong, light, flowing, and melting, dance through the room in your own way, switching among the qualities."

Room scan: Can the student demonstrate strong, light, flowing, and melting energy qualities?

Connect

"Weathering is a process in which rock is broken down into smaller and smaller pieces. This occurs due to weather such as wind and rain, temperature, gasses in the air, and some plants and animals. Erosion is the process in which sediments, such as the pieces of broken rock that have been weathered, are carried to new locations. Erosion usually occurs when water, such as in streams and rivers, carries the sediments downstream, but it can also occur with wind.

"In our dance today, we are going to use a strong energy quality to abstractly represent rock. The light energy quality will represent wind and the flowing energy quality will represent water. We will use the melting energy quality to represent weathering."

WEATHERING AND EROSION

"Use a strong energy quality throughout the room. This represents rock. Find your own space and freeze in a strong shape. When water gets into the small spaces between rocks or in tiny holes in the rock, it can cause weathering. Use your flowing energy quality through the room. Water can freeze and expand in the tiny holes, which breaks down the rock. It can then thaw and freeze again, continuing the process slowly. Continue moving with your flowing energy quality. Gasses can also cause weathering. Use your light energy quality through the room. Find your own space and freeze in a new strong shape. You have made a rock shape. You have been weathered by water, gasses, and maybe plant roots and microscopic animals. Begin sinking and melting very, very slowly. Weathering happens gradually over a long time. As the rock is broken into progressively smaller pieces, or sediments, gravity pulls the pieces to a lower surface.

"Return to standing and move with a flowing energy quality through the room. Surface water from rain, springs, or melting snow flows to lower elevations, eventually reaching streams and rivers that carry it to the ocean. You are using your smooth energy quality as the water in these streams. Along the way, the water picks up sediments and carries them to new locations downstream. This is erosion. Sometimes the sediments reach the ocean, and sometimes they collect along riverbanks or in lakes. Sometimes the wind carries sediments to new locations as well. Use your light energy quality to represent the wind causing erosion.

"Choose a partner who is near you. Decide which one of you will be dancer 1 and which one of you will be dancer 2. If you are dancer 1, use a strong energy quality to move to the side of the room. If you are dancer 2, use a strong energy quality to move to your own space in the dancing area. Dancer 2 freezes in a strong and high shape. When I say 'Go,' those of you who are dancer 1 use a light energy quality as if you are gasses that cause weathering to move through the strong rock shapes that the dancer 2s are making. Dancer 1s will gently and respectfully tap any of the frozen rock dancers. The rock dancers then begin melting, or weathering, at the place where they were tapped. The gas dancers will continue moving lightly, tapping each dancer once and then coming back to the sides of the room. Rock dancers, you will slowly melt beginning at the site where you were tapped. You may be tapped on the head, shoulder, back, knee, elbow, and so on. You should not be all the way to the floor after the gas dancers have all tapped you, so be sure to weather very slowly. Go!" Observe the dancers. The rock dancers should be melting very slowly where they are tapped, while the gas dancers should be moving lightly from rock to rock.

"Now dancer 1 is going to use a flowing energy quality as water weathering the rocks. The water dancers are moving from rock to rock with a flowing energy quality and the rocks are continuing to melt slowly." Continue until the rocks have been weathered by gas and water.

"This time when dancer 1 taps a rock, the rock is going to use a strong energy quality and follow dancer 1 to the side of the room. This is erosion. Water and wind are carrying the weathered sediments from one place to another. Those of you who are dancer 1 now can choose between wind and water.

You will move with a flowing energy quality or a light energy quality. Go!" Observe the dancers. Dancer 1s should be moving with either a light energy quality as wind or a flowing energy quality as water. Once they tap a rock (dancer 2), the rock will move with a strong energy quality and follow the water or wind dancer to the side of the room.

Repeat the activity, switching roles. Dancer 1 now begins as the rock, and dancer 2 goes through the process of weathering the rocks with gas and water and then eroding them with wind or water.

One dancer taps another dancer.

FORMATIVE ASSESSMENT

Room scan: Can the student demonstrate an energy quality that correlates to her part in the weathering and erosion dance?

Create and Perform

Review weathering and erosion. "Weathering occurs when rocks are broken down into smaller and smaller pieces by gasses, water, temperature changes, plant roots, microscopic animals, and digging animals. Erosion happens when sediments, such as the weathered bits of rock, are carried from one location to another by wind or water."

Divide the students into groups of three or four. "In your group, your task is to choreograph a dance that clearly shows your understanding of both erosion and weathering. You must include at least two of the energy qualities that we practiced today. We explored strong, light, flowing, and melting energy qualities today. All dancers in your group must help to create your dance and must perform in the dance. You must work cooperatively." Allow the students 3 to 7 minutes to work together and then have them perform the dances for the class. After each performance, ask the students to describe the weathering and erosion processes in their dance.

SUMMATIVE ASSESSMENT

Use a checklist to assess the following:

- Can the student correctly demonstrate flowing, strong, light, and melting energy qualities?
- Can the student create and perform a dance using energy qualities that clearly illustrates weathering and erosion?

Review and Reflect

Reflect on dance target	Reflect on science target
"I use a light energy quality when I am trying not to wake up my family early in the morning. Can you think of a time when you use a light, strong, flowing, or melting energy quality at home? Raise your hand if you can describe an example. Your sentence should sound like this: 'I use a _____ energy quality when I _____.'" Call on several students. "Your task this week is to notice when you use any of these four energy qualities at home. Next week, I will ask you to describe an example."	"Erosion and weathering happen all over the world. Can you think of an example around your home or our community where we can see that weathering and erosion have occurred?" Call on several students.

EXTENSION

Research the Grand Canyon and the ways erosion and weathering have influenced it.

IGNEOUS, SEDIMENTARY, AND METAMORPHIC ROCKS

On Earth, there are three ways that rocks can be formed; therefore, there are three main types of rocks. Igneous rocks form when magma or lava cools and hardens. Sedimentary rocks form when sediments from erosion (pieces of other rocks) are deposited and then consolidated by pressure and other minerals. Metamorphic rocks are igneous and sedimentary rocks that have been transformed by great heat or pressure.

AGES
8-11

LEVEL
Basic

MATERIALS
Poster (table 11.4) or whiteboard

MUSIC
Contemplative, pleasant, and driving selections with varying tempos (see appendix B; may also use a hand drum to prompt the changing tempos)

ESSENTIAL QUESTION
How do we classify rocks?

ENDURING UNDERSTANDING
Rocks originate in very different ways.

	Dance	Science
Learning target	Students explore stillness of individuals and groups.	Students understand how igneous, metamorphic, and sedimentary rocks are formed.
Evidence of student learning	The student collaboratively creates a dance that contains moments of stillness.	The student creates an abstract dance that clearly shows an assigned (igneous, metamorphic, or sedimentary) type of rock being formed.
Dance elements and science vocabulary	Stillness vs. movement, energy qualities (flowing, stiff), tempo (fast, medium, slow)	Igneous, sedimentary, metamorphic, magma, lava, erosion, deposit, pressure, heat, transformation
Standards	Stillness: Hold still in a position or body shape while others are moving (*Standards for Learning and Teaching Dance in the Arts*, p. 23).	Local, regional, and global patterns of rock formations reveal changes over time due to earth forces, such as earthquakes. The presence and location of certain fossil types indicate the order in which rock layers were formed (*Next Generation Science Standards*, ESS1.C: The History of Planet Earth).

Warm-Up

"Listen closely. When the music is on, dance using your own creative locomotor movement such as skipping, galloping, slithering, or floating. When the music stops, freeze in your own unique frozen shape and stay absolutely still." Play and pause the music for 10 to 15 seconds each. Encourage absolute stillness when the music is off.

Build Knowledge

"Movement and stillness go hand in hand. Choreographers often use stillness in their dances because it shows relationships between dancers and makes the dance more interesting to watch."

EXPLORE STILLNESS

"Find your own space where you are not touching anyone or anything. Make a frozen shape with your whole body. When I say your name, begin galloping through the room. If you are moving and I say your name again, freeze in a shape and hold it until you hear your name again." Say one child's name and about 5 seconds later, say another name. Continue saying the students' names so that there is a mix of students moving and freezing. After 2 to 3 minutes, freeze all of the students.

Divide the students into pairs and choose one partner to be first. "When we begin, partner 1 will bounce and partner 2 will freeze. When partner 1 freezes, partner 2 will bounce. When partner 2 freezes, partner 1 will begin to bounce again. Continue to go back and forth. Only one partner should be moving at any time. Be sure to make it fair and allow your partner to have equal time to dance and freeze."

FORMATIVE ASSESSMENT

Room scan: Can the student freeze and move opposite to a partner?

Connect

"There are three types of rocks: igneous, sedimentary, and metamorphic. Rocks are categorized by how they are formed. Igneous rocks form when magma or lava from the Earth's core cools and hardens into solid rock. Sedimentary rocks form when water, wind, or the temperature erodes pieces of other rocks, breaking off small bits. Sometimes the pieces are swept away by a stream or river. Over time these pieces of rocks can collect and then be cemented together by pressure or other minerals. Metamorphic rocks are igneous or sedimentary rocks that have been changed due to extreme heat or pressure." Attach the poster (table 11.4) to a place where the students can reference it, or write the definitions on the whiteboard.

IGNEOUS, SEDIMENTARY, AND METAMORPHIC DANCES

"We are going to start dancing as if we are forming igneous rocks. Begin moving through the room fluidly and quickly. You are using a flowing energy quality. Imagine magma inside the Earth's core. Now imagine lava on the Earth's surface. The lava is being cooled by the air. Gradually, you are going to slow your flowing movement. Bring your tempo from fast to medium. Steadily slow your tempo and begin to move more stiffly. Gradually bring your dance all the way to stillness. You have formed an igneous rock! Let's try again. We will start with a fast tempo and flowing energy quality and gradually slow down and become stiffer until we harden into our solid igneous rock." Practice the igneous rock dance several times.

Table 11.4   Rock Poster

	Igneous rocks form when magma or lava cools.
	Sedimentary rocks form when pieces of other rocks collect and are cemented together by pressure and other minerals.
	Metamorphic rocks are igneous or sedimentary rocks that have been changed by great heat or pressure.

Photographs taken by Mark A. Wilson (Department of Geology, The College of Wooster).

From K. Kaufmann and J. Dehline, 2014, *Dance integration: 36 dance lesson plans for science and mathematics* (Champaign, IL: Human Kinetics).

"Now we are going to form a sedimentary rock. We are going to make one large frozen shape as a class. We will gently touch so that we are all connected. Once everyone is frozen, I will say each student's name. When I say your name, you will erode from the group shape and move flowingly to collect and form a new sedimentary rock. The first person to go will get to choose where in our dancing space our new rock will form. Once you erode and flow to the new rock, you will gently connect and freeze to wait for the rest of your rock to form." Practice several times, reminding the students to be clear whether they are in stillness or moving.

"Find your own space. Metamorphic rocks are igneous or sedimentary rocks that are transformed by great heat or pressure. Find stillness in any shape. On your own timing, begin to morph and transform slowly into a new shape. Hold your stillness in your new shape for a few seconds. Then morph into a new shape. Imagine heat and pressure changing your shape. You are using your own timing to find stillness and then move into a new stillness." Allow students to explore for 2 to 3 minutes.

FORMATIVE ASSESSMENT

Room scan:

- Can the student clearly show movement and stillness?
- Can the student connect the rock types with moving and stillness?

Groups of students form a connected shape.

Create and Perform

Divide the class into groups of three to five students. Assign each group a type of rock. "Create an abstract dance that demonstrates how your rock type is formed. Use stillness several times throughout your dance, either as individuals or as a group." After the students create and practice, they perform the dances for the class.

SUMMATIVE ASSESSMENT

Use a checklist to assess the following:

- Can the student collaboratively create a dance that contains moments of stillness?
- Can the student create an abstract dance that clearly shows an assigned (igneous, metamorphic, or sedimentary) type of rock being formed?

Review and Reflect

Reflect on dance target	Reflect on science target
"Why is it important for choreographers to use stillness in their dances? Outside of dance, when is it important for you to use stillness? Your task tonight is to find a time when you are using stillness and describe your example in our next class."	"Name the three types of rocks (igneous, sedimentary, metamorphic). How are igneous rocks formed (magma or lava cooling)? How are sedimentary rocks formed (pieces of other rocks collect and are cemented together)? How are metamorphic rocks formed (igneous or sedimentary rocks transformed by heat or pressure)? Where do you think we can find the types of rocks?"

EXTENSIONS

- Use modeling clay to make a three-dimensional model demonstrating one type of rock formation.
- Research the three rock types and find photographs of each type.

12

INVESTIGATION, EXPERIMENTATION, AND TECHNOLOGY

ance and science both require investigation and experimentation. In science, this exploration often leads to designing solutions to engineering problems and understanding the natural world. In dance, exploration is used to find solutions to movement problems and create choreography. Problem solving is the link between dance and science explorations. The first lesson of this chapter uses problem solving and investigation to find solutions to a movement problem that includes constraints and criteria.

Technology is a branch of science that is defined by *A Framework for K-12 Science Education* (2012; see chapter 2) as any modification of the natural world made to fulfill human needs or desires (p. 202). This includes modern technologies often used in classrooms and society at large, such as cameras, computers, and televisions. The second and third lessons of this chapter involve uses of technology in the art of dance.

INVESTIGATION, EXPERIMENTATION, AND PROBLEM SOLVING

Science and dance use problem solving by experimenting and brainstorming possible solutions. In science and in dance, available resources and materials can limit possible solutions. These are called *constraints*. Sometimes there are required or preferred features of a solution. These are called *criteria*. The success of a solution to a problem is based on how well the solution takes into account the constraints and criteria.

AGES
5-11

LEVEL
Basic-intermediate

MATERIALS
- 2-meter strips of elastic tied or sewn together to make large elastic bands (one for every two students)
- Whiteboard or easel

MUSIC
Driving selection (see appendix B)

ESSENTIAL QUESTION
Why is brainstorming important?

ENDURING UNDERSTANDING
We can identify new solutions to problems we encounter.

	Dance	Science
Learning target	Students cooperatively use problem solving to choreograph a dance with specified limitations.	Students experiment, explore, and brainstorm solutions to a problem and design a solution that meets the criteria and takes into account the constraints of possible solutions.

(continued)

	Dance	Science
Evidence of student learning	The student cooperatively creates and performs a dance that meets the given criteria.	The student cooperatively creates and performs a dance that meets the given criteria.
Dance elements and science vocabulary	Problem solve, choreograph, collaborate	Brainstorm, problem solve, experiment, criteria, constraints, solutions
Standards	Problem solving: Discover and explore movement solutions to technical or structural movement problems (*Standards for Learning and Teaching Dance in the Arts*, p. 25).	Possible solutions to a problem are limited by available materials and resources (constraints). The success of a designed solution is determined by considering the desired features of a solution (criteria). Proposals for solutions can be compared on the basis of how well each one meets the specified criteria for success or how well each takes the constraints into account (*Next Generation Science Standards, ETS1.A: Defining and Delimiting Engineering Problems*).

Warm-Up

Do the BrainDance (appendix A) to focus on the mind–body connection.

Build Knowledge

"Dancers are artists who make creative choices. Sometimes dancers and artists are given problems to solve or must create a dance that explores a certain idea. Dancers often experiment and explore many solutions or ways to move before choreographing or settling on one solution."

EXPLORE

"I am going to tell you an idea or a movement problem. Your task is to experiment with many different ways to solve the movement problem or show the idea. Right now you are not going to decide on a final solution but explore as many options as you can think of. You are brainstorming movement ideas! You are working individually, finding your own solutions. You can ignore your classmates and stay in your own space. All dancers are brainstorming their own movement ideas."

Give the students 1 to 2 minutes to explore the options for each of the following prompts.

- "In your own space, find as many ways to move your spine, or back, as you can."
- "How many different ways can you dance through the space with only your hands and feet touching the floor?"
- "What are the movement possibilities if one foot is glued to the floor?"
- "How can you dance if neither of your feet can touch the floor?"
- "How many different ways can you jump or hop?"

Room scan: Can the student explore multiple solutions to each prompt?

Connect

"Scientists also solve problems by experimenting and brainstorming possible solutions. In science and in dance, available resources and materials can limit possible solutions. These are called *constraints*. Sometimes there are required or preferred features of a solution. These are called *criteria*. The success of a solution to a problem is based on how well the solution takes into account the constraints and criteria."

INVESTIGATION

"In a moment, you will be divided into groups. Your task is to explore the many movement possibilities of using an elastic band. The constraints are that you only have one elastic band per group, and you must stay in the dancing space. The criteria are that everyone in your group must be touching the elastic band at all times and you must use your entire body in this investigation."

Divide the students into groups. Younger students should have two dancers in each group, and older students can have three to four dancers depending on their maturity level. Give each group an elastic band and allow the students 2 to 5 minutes to explore the movement possibilities with the constraints and criteria.

FORMATIVE ASSESSMENT

Room scan: Can the students explore multiple solutions within the constraints and criteria?

Create and Perform

"Remain in your group. Your new task is to create a dance that you can perform for the rest of the class. Your dance must move from one side of the room to the other and has constraints and criteria that I will write on the board in a moment. Artists and scientists must cooperate with other artists and scientists in order to design the best possible solutions. This dance has many possible solutions. Each group will design a unique dance. Artists and scientists must brainstorm, experiment, and explore many options before choosing their favorite solution. In your group, make sure to brainstorm and explore many options before choosing your favorite solution. Be sure to experiment and discuss, and of course, make it a dance!"

Write the following constraints on the board or easel:

- One elastic band per group
- Must stay in the dancing space

Write the following criteria on the board or easel:

- No hands can touch the elastic bands.
- All dancers must be touching the elastic band at all times.
- You cannot touch another dancer.
- The dance must travel from one side of the room to the other.

For more advanced dancers, you can add criteria such as the dance must use a variety of levels or tempos or must use a specified number of counts.

Give the students approximately 10 minutes to work, reminding them to dance with their entire bodies. Then the groups perform the dances for the rest of the class. After each group performs, ask the audience to describe whether the dance met the criteria and constraints.

SUMMATIVE ASSESSMENT

Use a checklist to assess the following: Can the student cooperatively create and perform a dance that meets the given criteria?

Review and Reflect

Reflect on dance target	Reflect on science target
"Choreographers often create dance phrases beginning with a movement problem that has many possible solutions. For example, the choreographer wants the dancers to use 32 counts to move from a low level to a high level and move to the corner of the dancing space. There are many options to fulfill this problem and a choreographer can experiment with several ways before settling on one possibility. Can you think of a movement problem that could be the starting point for a dance?" Call on several students to describe movement problems, or ask the students to journal their responses.	"In your group, you were asked to brainstorm and experiment with ideas to solve the movement problem. Describe how your group explored and worked together in order to investigate possible solutions." Call on several students or ask the students to journal their responses.

EXTENSIONS

- Students create their own movement problems for themselves or for partners and then create one or more solutions.
- Students define a movement problem (including constraints and criteria) for another group to brainstorm.

DANCE VIEWING THROUGH TECHNOLOGY

Technology influences society exponentially. Dancers learn to use technology in many ways. Choreographers film their dances to maintain records, sound designers create soundscapes to be played during dances, and film editors and choreographers create and edit dances to be viewed on film. Some pioneers of dance technology have even created computer programs to model dancers' bodies on the screen. Not only does technology help to create dance, but dances that have been recorded can also be shared with audiences all over the world. This lesson includes a dance-viewing and responding experience only made possible with modern technology.

AGES
5-11

LEVEL
Basic-intermediate

MATERIALS
- Computer or video-viewing technology (such as TV and DVD player)
- Dance video (see notes in this lesson under Build Knowledge)

MUSIC
Pleasant selection (see appendix A)

ESSENTIAL QUESTION
How does technology change our thinking?

ENDURING UNDERSTANDING
Technology generates creativity.

	Dance	Science
Learning target	Students observe dance on film and respond using movement.	Students use technology in order to observe and respond to others' work.
Evidence of student learning	The student choreographs a brief dance inspired by movements in the observed dance.	The student choreographs a brief dance inspired by movements in the dance observed through technology.
Dance elements and science vocabulary	Observation, response, choreography	Technology, observation, response
Standards	Respond to an observed dance through movement (*Standards for Learning and Teaching Dance in the Arts*, p. 26).	Over time, people's needs and wants change, as do their demands for new and improved technologies. Engineers improve existing technologies or develop new ones to increase their benefits, to decrease known risks, and to meet societal demands (*Next Generation Science Standards*, 3-5-ETS1-1 and 3-5-ETS1-2).

Warm-Up

Start with teacher-led mirroring (see appendix A) with the students trying to match your actions. Then ask the students to observe what you do and choose a new way to do the movement they are seeing. For example, if you reach your arms up, a student could reach his arms down, reach up three times, or jump and reach.

Build Knowledge

Before beginning this lesson, choose a dance video for your students to watch. YouTube can be a great resource, but links often change or disappear. Local libraries can also be a good resource. Dance created specifically for the camera are especially recommended for this lesson because they demonstrate yet another use of technology. These films can be found on YouTube or through your local library. Videos from current and past choreographic works can be found at libraries, on choreographers' websites, and on YouTube. Choose a clip that is approximately 2 to 5 minutes and is appropriate for your students, potentially showcasing some of the dance elements previously learned.

> One YouTube video suggestion for this lesson is a dance performed and choreographed by Suzanne Cleary and Peter Harding (http://youtu.be/iANRO3I30nM). In this short video, the two dancers, who are seated at a table, move their arms and heads in intricate rhythmic patterns while maintaining deadpan expressions. This video selection offers manageable opportunities in a classroom to replicate the choreography using borrowed movements while seated at desks.

"Today we are going to watch a dance through the use of technology. As you are watching, take note of the movements you are seeing." You may also ask your students to observe specific movement elements that you have been working on, such as energy qualities, tempo, use of space, or body parts. Teachers may give students a checklist of dance elements to complete as they watch the video.

OBSERVE AND DISCUSS

Play the dance video for the students. When finished, ask the students, "What movement elements did you notice? How were the dancers using their bodies? What actions were the dancers doing? How were the dancers using their space? How were the dancers using time? How were the dancers using energy and force?" Discuss the dance using movement vocabulary.

FORMATIVE ASSESSMENT

Room scan: Can the students describe the movement elements seen in the video?

Connect

Discuss the technology the students are using in order to view the dance. Is the dance being viewed on the Internet? Is the dance being played with a VHS tape, VCR, and television? Is the dance on DVD? Is the DVD playing through your computer and projected onto a screen? Describe to the students how they are viewing the dance through the use of technology.

TECHNOLOGY

"Did you notice any technology being used in the video?" This can include camera angles, sound scores, special lighting, and so on. Discuss all of the technology related to the dance and viewing the dance.

Room scan: Can the students identify the technologies being used?

Create and Perform

Divide the students into pairs. "With your partner, discuss the movement elements seen in the video. We are going to borrow movements from the video and change them for our new dance. Create three movements (more or less, depending on the students' maturity level) inspired by the dance you saw in the video. You are not re-creating the dance exactly or mimicking it. Instead, you are creating new movements inspired by the essence of what you observed in the video. For example, if you noticed that they were doing many low-level rolling movements, you should not do the exact same rolls, but create your own way of rolling at a low level. Once you have created your three movements, put them into a sequence of first movement, second movement, and third movement so that they can be repeated as a choreographed dance. Continue practicing your dance once you have choreographed your sequence."

Give the students approximately 10 minutes to work with their partners. Then have the pairs perform for the class. After each performance, ask the performers to describe how their dance was inspired by the video.

SUMMATIVE ASSESSMENT

Use a checklist to assess the following: Can the student choreograph a brief dance inspired by movements seen in the dance viewed through technology?

Review and Reflect

Reflect on dance target	Reflect on science target
Ask the students to journal or speak about how the observed dance inspired their choreography.	"In what ways can technology be used to create dances? How has technology changed the art form of dance?"

EXTENSION

Video record the dances created in this lesson and allow the students to watch their creations.

DANCE AND PHOTOGRAPHY

Classroom teachers use technology in a myriad of ways in their classrooms, and students are brought up understanding and using new technology. Digital cameras have become more affordable and ubiquitous, and photography can be used to understand and create movement inspired by still images. In this lesson, dancers create body shapes, are photographed, and then create dances inspired by other dancers' photographed shapes. This lesson can be done in two sessions.

AGES
5-11

LEVEL
Basic

MATERIALS
Digital camera and computer

MUSIC
Contemplative selection (see appendix A)

ESSENTIAL QUESTION
How does technology change our thinking?

ENDURING UNDERSTANDING
Technology generates creativity.

	Dance	Science
Learning target	Students create unique shapes. Students choreograph a movement sequence.	Students use technology to create dances.
Evidence of student learning	The student choreographs a short movement sequence inspired by photographs of still shapes.	The student choreographs a short movement sequence inspired by photographs of still shapes.
Dance elements and science vocabulary	Body shapes, choreography	Technology, observation, response
Standards	• Sequencing: Demonstrate the ability to sequence a series of movements and to remember them in a short phrase (*Standards for Learning and Teaching Dance in the Arts*, p. 23). • Shapes: Form shapes and create designs with the body (*Standards for Learning and Teaching Dance in the Arts*, p. 24).	People's needs and wants change over time, as do their demands for new and improved technologies. Engineers improve existing technologies or develop new ones to increase their benefits, decrease known risks, and meet societal demands (*Next Generation Science Standards*, 3-5-ETS1-1 and 3-5-ETS1-2).

Warm-Up

"I will make a frozen shape with my body, and you will observe my shape and move in a way that is inspired by my frozen shape. For example, I may make a straight, narrow shape, and you may walk in a straight pathway, jump with a narrow shape, or logroll in a long shape." As you make five or six shapes, the students move in response to the shapes.

Build Knowledge

"Dancers can create many shapes with their bodies. As you are making shapes with your body, you will be creating statuelike positions that you can hold very still without falling over. Your shapes should be absolutely still, as if you are frozen in a photograph. Each of you will be making your own unique shapes that are not like any of the others in the class."

EXPLORE SHAPES

"Create a curvy shape with your entire body. Find a new curvy shape. And another curvy shape. Freeze in an angular or jagged shape. Explore another option of a jagged shape. Create a big shape and now a small shape. Form a twisting shape. Make a flat shape. Create a round shape. Find a narrow shape and now a wide shape. Create your own unique shape with your entire body. Choose a new shape." Practice many shapes, reminding the students to create their own unique shapes (not copying others' shapes).

FORMATIVE ASSESSMENT

Room scan: Can the students form unique still shapes?

Connect

"I am going to photograph some of your shapes."

PHOTOGRAPH SHAPES

"Choose three of your favorite shapes. Keep practicing your shapes and making them better and better as you wait your turn." Photograph each child individually in all three shapes.

FORMATIVE ASSESSMENT

Room scan: Can the student hold three unique shapes while photographs are taken?

Create and Perform

Load the photographs onto the computer. Animoto (www.animoto.com) is a simple program for arranging and sharing photos with a high-quality appearance. This lesson can be split into two sessions to allow time for this process. If the photographs are loaded during the lesson, you can talk to the students about what is happening as you are uploading the digital images from the camera onto the computer.

Divide the students into pairs. (This activity can also be done individually.) "Each group is going to see three photographs at random. The photographs may not be of you but of other students. You will have a few seconds to look at the photographs and observe. Then with your partner, you will move into the dancing space and create a short movement phrase inspired by the shapes you observed. You will be creating a moving dance inspired by the shapes, not creating more shapes. You will only see the photographs one time and will choreograph a dance that is a response to your observations." Show three photographs chosen randomly to each group for approximately 10 seconds. Give the students 5 to 10 minutes to choreograph their sequences. Then have them perform the dance for the class or for another group.

Students create movement inspired by photos on a computer.

SUMMATIVE ASSESSMENT

Use a checklist to assess the following: Can the student choreograph a short movement sequence inspired by photographs of still shapes?

Review and Reflect

Reflect on dance target	Reflect on science target
"Describe how your dance was inspired by the still photographs." Call on several students, or ask the students to respond through journaling.	"In what other ways can photography and technology inspire dance?" Ask the students to respond either verbally or through journaling.

EXTENSION

Create a dance as a class that links all of the shapes into one dance. Start with one shape and then find a transition into the next shape. Continue until you have linked all of the shape photographs.

APPENDIX A

Additional Warm-Up and Relaxation Activities for Brain and Body

Warm-up activities begin each class and signify a change from seated learning to active, whole-body learning. Before the warm-up, students remove their shoes, move the desks aside, and prepare the classroom for movement. The purposes of the warm-up are to create a transition into the dance class and to prepare students' minds and bodies for kinesthetic learning. It enables students to mentally focus on their bodies, get the kinks out, and use control and intentionality in their movements. Warm-ups can be repeated each class period to provide a sense of familiarity for students and to help them quickly shift into the state of mind and body necessary for the dance class.

Whereas the warm-up begins every class, the relaxation activities at the end of class are optional. Centering and grounding students is most useful for those who are overly energized by the dance class. The relaxation activities help them settle down and get ready for the next school activity. Teachers can develop their own warm-up and cool-down activities that serve as daily classroom rituals.

Sample Warm-Up Activities

Following are some warm-up activities often practiced by dance teachers. They are intended as a starting point for teachers who are new to dance. With practice, the teacher can develop original warm-ups to accomplish the goal of preparing students to be alert, in control of their bodies, and ready to learn.

Mirroring the Teacher (Ages 5-11)

This mirroring activity encourages students to focus on the teacher and brings them into a deeper awareness of their bodies.

"Please find your own spot in the room, touching only the air and the floor. Make sure you can see me. I am going to turn on music and begin moving very slowly. You get to be my mirror and do everything that I do. Be sure you watch carefully so you can reflect even the smallest of my movements." This activity requires the teacher to be comfortable leading an improvised movement warm-up. All movements should be slow and deliberate, such as stretching, bending, twisting, and so on. When students are following, try changing levels and leading easy, balancing activities, always maintaining the slow tempo. (Music suggestion: contemplative selection)

Mirroring in Partners (Ages 7-11)

This warm-up is performed with a peer. The two students face one another, about 3 feet (1 m) apart. Students create a movement for a partner to follow and develop concentration while following a partner.

"Please find a partner. One of you is the leader and the other is the follower. The leader is going to slowly move one body part at a time. The follower will mirror everything the leader does. You should both be moving at the same time without touching. In a successful mirroring activity, I can't tell by watching you who's leading and who's following!" After about 60 seconds, instruct the pairs to switch leaders. (Music suggestion: contemplative selection)

Dancer's Stand (Ages 5-11)

This simple stand provides an intentional body position for students to assume while listening to directions. Students learn to remain engaged in between class activities, and the position communicates that the students are ready.

"Dancers show that they are alert and ready by the way they stand. Today we're going to learn the dancer's stand. Start with your feet pointing straight ahead and your knees straight but not locked. Your back is straight and your neck is held tall and long. Let your arms relax by your sides with just a little bit of energy (not too much!) in your hands and fingers. Feel the energy streaming up through your whole body and out the top of your head, just like water in a fountain. You should be feeling energized, alive, and alert. Keep this stand and take three deep breaths." (Music suggestion: contemplative selection)

Simple Stretches, Twists, and Bends (Ages 7-11)

Focused movement activities get the kinks out and the body ready for more full-body activity. Modify the warm-up appropriately based on the students' ages.

"Find your own personal space in our dancing area and make sure you have lots of space around you." Relocate students who are too close together into an open spot. Repeat each of these activities two to four times. (Music suggestion: pleasant selection)

- *Waking up.* Students lie down. "Just as we do in the morning when we first wake up, yawn and begin to stretch. Use your whole body, stretching your arms, shoulders, head, back, legs, and fingers. Now relax everything and slowly and gently come to standing."

- *Shoulder rolls.* "Lift each shoulder separately and drop it. Shrug both shoulders together. Drop them. Press your shoulders forward and back. Circle your shoulders. Circle your shoulders in the opposite direction."

- *Reaches.* "Reach one arm up into the air. Reach the other arm up. Open both arms and let them drop."

- *Plié.* "Stand with your feet facing straight ahead with a little space in between. Slowly bend your knees and straighten your knees. In dance this is called a *plié*. Be sure your knees are lined up right over your toes."

- *Relevé.* "Begin in the dancer's stand with your feet facing straight ahead. Without falling, rise up on your toes and then roll gently back down onto your heels. Be sure not to thump down hard; your heels come down softly and in control. The rise

is called a *relevé* in dance. *Relevé* means 'to rise.'"

- *Roll-down.* "Begin in the dancer's stand. Bend your knees and beginning at the top of your head, roll forward until your whole body is gently folded in half, feet flat on the floor; only go as far as you can without hurting your body. Take one or two deep breaths while hanging forward, letting everything relax. On the inhale, bend your knees again and roll up, starting at the base of the spine with the head coming up last."

- *Twists.* "Begin in the dancer's stand. Turn your head to the right and twist your arms and back in the same direction. Look all the way behind you. Stay there for a moment and then untwist and twist in the other direction. Now let's do our twisting dance a little quicker. Smoothly twist to the right, then to the left." Encourage students to twist with the head and spine. The feet can either stay on the floor or one foot can come off the floor in the twist.

- *Shake it out.* "Shake your two hands. Now add your elbows and your arms. Begin shaking your head, hips, and back. Now stand on one leg and shake out the other leg. Switch legs. Can you shake every part of your body? Make sure you are shaking your body but not your voice. Now stop and return to standing still. Notice how awake your body feels."

Deep Breaths for Energizing and Focusing (Ages 5-11)

Deep breathing can have a powerful influence on health and well-being. It increases vitality and promotes focus and relaxation. The value of a slow, deep breath is experienced immediately.

1. "Take a deep breath and fill your tummy with air. Now exhale and let all the air out. Let's do that again. Deep breath in . . . and let the air out."

2. "This time open your arms wide and then stretch them to the sky as you inhale. When you exhale, lower your arms to the sides and then down. Let's take three breaths and see if you can connect the lift of your arms with the inhalation and the release of your arms with the exhalation."

3. "This time as you take a deep breath, bring your palms together in front of your chest and lift up the center line of the body. Then as you exhale, open to the sides and lower."

4. Repeat the previous exercise and during the exhalation, twist the upper body to the right and open the arms wide and down. Return to center for the inhalation and lift. Repeat on the left.

(Music suggestion: silence or contemplative selection)

Freeze Dance (Ages 5-11)

The word *freeze* can be used to quickly bring all movement to a standstill. The freeze allows the teacher to give a new instruction or clarify how the movement should be done. "Friends, we're going to listen carefully. When the music starts, we're going to tiptoe through the room. When the music stops, immediately freeze in your very own shape."

Give students a new locomotor movement each time (e.g., walk, hop, gallop, jump, skip, prance, crab walk, crawl, slither). Students can create their own shapes or the teacher may ask them to find a specific shape (e.g., curving, stretching, twisting, balancing, small, large, wide, narrow). Play the music for 10 to 15 seconds and then pause it. Acknowledge those students who freeze quickly and are very still. (Music suggestion: driving selection)

BrainDance (Ages 5-11)

Developed by Anne Green Gilbert, the Brain-Dance comprises a series of eight developmental patterns that healthy humans move through in the first year of life. Repeating these patterns as a warm-up helps to increase energy and reduce stress. It also serves as a centering activity for brain reorganization, oxygenation, and recuperation. The BrainDance is a useful warm-up to the integrated dance class because it unites the body and mind and promotes learning. For more information about the BrainDance and teacher training workshops, visit www.creativedance.org/about/braindance.

- *Breath.* Take four to five deep breaths through the nose, filling the belly, diaphragm, and lungs, and exhale out the mouth.

- *Tactile.* With your hands, squeeze strongly each arm, each leg, and the torso, back, and head (whole body). Then tap lightly your whole body. Slap sharply but gently. Brush smoothly. Explore a variety of other tactile movements such as scratching, rubbing, soft pinching, and so on.

- *Core–distal.* Move from the center out, through and beyond the fingers, toes, head, and tail. Then curl back into the torso while engaging the core muscles. Find movements that grow and shrink, stretching into big *X*s and curling into little *O*s.

- *Head–tail.* Move the head and tail (lower part of the spine or coccyx) in a variety of directions and pathways. Play with movement that brings the head and tail curving forward and backward and side to side. Keep the knees bent to release the pelvis. Wiggle the spine like a snake.

- *Upper–lower.* Ground the lower half of the body by pressing into the floor with a slight knee bend. Swing your arms in various directions and stretch and dance the upper body (arms, head, spine) in a variety of ways. Now ground the upper half by reaching your arms into space with energy as though you were hugging the earth. Dance with the lower half (marching in place, simple knee bends, jumps, leg brushes).

- *Body side.* Make a big *X* with your body. Dance with the left side of your body while keeping the right side stable. Then keep the left side stable and dance with the right side. With the knees and elbows slightly bent like a *W*, bring the left half of the body over to meet the right half and reverse, like a book opening and closing. Follow your thumb with your eyes as it moves from right to left and left to right. Next, do the lizard crawl with arms and legs open to the sides. Reach your left arm and knee up and then right arm and knee up, like a lizard crawling up a wall. Move your eyes right to left and left to right, looking at the thumb near your mouth. This develops horizontal eye tracking.

- *Cross-lateral.* Do a parallel standing crawl with knees and hands in front of you. Let your eyes travel up and down, looking at one thumb as it reaches high and low for vertical eye tracking. Do a cross-lateral boogie dance, finding as many ways of moving cross laterally as possible.

- *Vestibular.* Choose a movement that takes you off balance and makes you dizzy. Stand with your legs in a wide stance and drop and lift your upper body from side to side. Then stop and slowly let your equilibrium return. This may also be done by spinning in a circle for 15 seconds or any other movement that makes you dizzy.

Anne Green Gilbert, creativedance.org.

Relaxation and Centering Cool-Down (Ages 5-11)

At the end of class, it's important to cool down and relax students in order to help them transition into the next subject or activity. Sometimes the cool-down is directly connected to the integrated theme; other times it is independent and used solely for the purpose of relaxing and centering. The movement ritual for the end of class helps signify that the class is over and acknowledges the important work being done with the body. Following are five examples for ending the class. Modify them appropriately based on the students' ages. (Music suggestion: contemplative selection)

1. *Quick transition.* "Please select one movement we did today and perform that movement as you travel over to put your shoes and socks on."

2. *Cooling down with the class theme.* Select one movement or prompt from the integrated dance activity. Ask students to do that movement and tell them to "gradually begin to slow it down, slower and slower and slower until you're barely moving at all. The movement is so small that I can hardly see it, but you can still feel it inside. Now, bring the movement to a complete rest and breathe quietly."

3. *Floor relaxation.* "Roll over onto your back. Relax completely and let all your weight drop easily into the floor. Breathe deeply and on each exhale, relax your body even more. We're going to lie here

for 1 full minute. As you're lying still on the floor, think of one thing you did especially well today. Give yourself a big hug, and then slowly come to sitting."

4. *Palming.* "Lie down on your back and cover your eyes with cupped hands, blocking out all the light. Lie quietly and enjoy the darkness and stillness. Let your mind and body relax. When it is time to release the fingers, do so very slowly and gently."

5. *Group sway.* "Come sit cross-legged in a circle. We're going to begin a group sway, first to one side and then to the other. Keep both hips on the floor and don't let your sway get too big, or you'll rock off your seat. It's a medium-sized sway that keeps you on your seat. Let's see if the whole class can rock together, right, left, right, left, feeling the motion together as a group." Once the sway is established, ask the class to let the motion slowly and gradually subside until the sway is tiny and then still.

Yoga Breathing and Postures (Ages 5-11)

Yoga promotes physical health and vitality and allows students to reconnect with themselves. Yoga is an ancient art originating in India. The word *yoga* means "binding," "joining," or "uniting." Several yoga postures are provided here to help students center themselves and relax. The duration or length of time a child holds a yoga posture will vary, but it should be long enough to provide some recuperation. (Music suggestions: silence or contemplative selection)

- *Seated meditation.* "Find a comfortable seated position with your legs crossed and your back straight, hands in your lap. Close your eyes and slowly breath in . . . and out . . . five times."

- *Diamond pose.* "Sit with the soles of your feet touching so your legs make a diamond shape. Take a deep breath. Exhale forward so your head drops toward your feet. Relax and breathe."

- *Twist and breathe.* "Sit with your legs crossed. Twist your upper body so your chest is over your knee and fold forward, bringing your heart to your thigh. Close your eyes and breathe." Lift and repeat on the other side.

- *Cat and cow.* "Begin on your hands and knees in the table position. Inhale and look up to the ceiling, arching your back. Exhale and look to your naval, curling your back." Repeat four times.

- *Table balance.* "Begin on your hands and knees in the table position. Stretch your right arm forward and left leg back, balance, and breathe. Slowly return to the table." Repeat with the left arm forward and right leg back.

- *Child's pose.* "From the table position, sit back on your heels and lay your chest on your thighs. Relax and breathe."

- *Sphinx pose.* "Lie flat on your belly with your elbows under your shoulders and hands pointing forward on the floor. Keeping your lower arms on the floor, push your head and shoulders up gently so you're looking forward. Look right slowly and then left. Relax your shoulders and let your belly drop into the floor."

- *Downward-facing dog.* "Begin on your hands and knees. Spread your fingers and bend your toes into the ground. Inhale and lift your hips in the air, stretch your legs, and look at your naval. Your hands and feet are flat on the floor. Breathe gently in and out. Return to the original position." Repeat.

- *Tree.* "Stand up tall and still. Bend your right knee slightly and grab your left ankle with your left hand. Place your left foot against the inside of your right knee and straighten your right leg. Put your hands together in front of your chest and balance. Take two deep breaths." Repeat on the other side. If students have trouble balancing, this can be done near a wall to help them get into the posture.

APPENDIX B

Music Resources

Many musical selections are used in school dance classes. Most dance educators have a working playlist of 8 to 25 songs from which they select the music for class. Music is highly individual, and teachers are encouraged to create their own library that resonates with their preferences. Teachers should also consider their group of students when selecting music. In some cases they may wish to choose calming music to settle students down; other times, pleasant or upbeat music may be desired to motivate the students and help support the movement experience.

Following is a list of music resources useful for K-5 school dance classes. We provide this list as a starting point; these selections are by no means exhaustive and are only a tiny sample of what is available.

The music selections are divided into three broad qualitative categories:

1. Contemplative
2. Pleasant
3. Driving

These are not meant to be exclusive categories, and one selection may exist in more than one category. The tracks span a variety of musical genres (classical, new age, jazz, world rhythms, and so on) and include music for creative dance, film scores, and other musical ideas. These selections are easy to search for, and teachers can create their own playlists using them as a starting point. When in doubt, choose music you like and become familiar with it. As you encounter new selections, you can add them to your music library.

Contemplative

These selections feature slow to medium tempos and music that is calming and thoughtful. Contemplative selections are often selected for the warm-up and for relaxation at the end of the lesson.

Song	Album	Artist
"Touching Calm"	Relax—A Liquid Mind Experience	Liquid Mind
"Waves of Light"	Reiki—Hands of Light	Deuter
"Quietly Floating Home"	Healing Sanctuary	Dean Evensen
"Sacred Splendor"	Spa Dreams	Dean Evensen and d'Rachael
Nocturne No. 2 in E-Flat Major, op. 9, no. 2	Chopin: The Complete Waltzes	Peter Hough
"Inward Journey"	Canyon Trilogy	R. Carlos Nakai
"A Fresh Wind"	The Dance of Innocents	Nawang Khechog and Peter Kater
Pachelbel's Canon in D Major	Pachelbel's Canon in D Major	Pachelbel Orchestra
"Tales From the Far Side"	Bill Frisell Quartet	Bill Frisell

(continued)

(continued)

Song	Album	Artist
Piano Sonata, Sonata No. 14 in C-Sharp Minor, op. 27:2 ("Moonlight Sonata")	The 50 Greatest Pieces of Classical Music	Finghin Collins
"Adagio Sostenuto"	Hotel Costes 12	Orsten
Serenade No. 13 in G Major, K. 525 ("Eine Kleine Nachtmusik")	100 Classical Essentials	Radio Symphony Orchestra

Pleasant

These selections feature slow, medium, and fast tempos that are motivating and pleasing.

Song	Album	Artist
"Triciclo"	Acalanto	Tuti Fornari
"Between Friends"	Ukelele Classics and Originals	Daniel Ho
"Caliban's Dream"	Isles of Wonder: Music for the Opening Ceremony of the London 2012 Olympic Games	Underworld
"Journey"	The Meeting Pool	Baka Beyond
"Night Over Manaus"	Satta	Boozoo Bajou
"Trilogy (at the White Magic Gardens)"	The White Winds	Andreas Vollenweider
"Rain on Me"	Zen Pause	Thierry David
"Here to Stay"	We Live Here	Pat Metheny Group
"Are You Going With Me?"	Offramp	Pat Metheny Group
The Four Seasons	Vivaldi: The Four Seasons	Antonio Vivaldi
Brandenburg Concerto No. 3 in G	Bach: Brandenburg Concertos	Academy of St. Martin in the Fields and Sir Neville Marriner
"Stay"	Rare Requests Smooth Jazz, Vol. 5	Club 1600

Driving

These selections feature medium to fast tempos that are percussive or rhythmic and easy to count.

Song	Album	Artist
"Requiem"	*Rebirth of Detroit*	J Dilla
"A Thousand Years (Sunrise Vocal Mix)"	*Abstract Latin Journey*	Julius Papp
"Another Country"	*Pure Shadowfax*	Michael Spiro, Shadowfax, and Stuart Nevitt
"The Boogie Bumper"	*Big Bad Voodoo Daddy*	Big Bad Voodoo Daddy

(continued)

(continued)

Song	Album	Artist
"Amber"	*Karaoke—Rock 2002*	Pro Tracks Karaoke
"B for My Name"	*The Mix-Up*	Beastie Boys
"14th St. Break"	*The Mix-Up*	Beastie Boys
"Me Gustas Tú"	*Proxima Estacion: Esperanza*	Manu Chao
"Shining Pains"	*Momento*	Soel
"Flight of the Bumblebee"	*Classical Drumming*	Vadrum
"Stompin' at the Savoy"	*Swingsation: Benny Goodman*	Benny Goodman
"Le Vicomte"	*Momento*	Soel
"I've Just Seen a Face"	Karaoke Hits in the Style of the Beatles, Vol. II	Stingray Music

Additional Suggestions

Film scores often feature familiar melodies that children enjoy. The following selections provide a wide range of qualities and tempos.

Song	Album	Artist
"Harry Potter"	The Greatest Instrumentals of All Time	The Session
"Titanic"	The Greatest Instrumentals of All Time	The Session
"Tubular Bells (Exorcist Theme)"	The Greatest Instrumentals of All Time	The Session
"Now We Are Free (Gladiator)"	The Greatest Instrumentals of All Time	The Session
"Mission Impossible"	The Greatest Instrumentals of All Time	The Session
"Chariots of Fire"	The Greatest Instrumentals of All Time	The Session
"War of the Worlds"	The Greatest Instrumentals of All Time	The Session
"The Sting"	Greatest Movie Hits of All Time	Countdown Studio
"Axel F"	The Greatest Instrumental Tracks of All Time	Studio Players

Music for Dance

The following albums provide music developed for creative dance, modern dance, or disco.

Album	Artist
Music for Creative Dance (Vol. I and II)	Eric Chappelle
Move—Music for Creative Movement + Modern Dance	Chris Cawthray
Disco Dance Ottanta	Various artists

APPENDIX C

Additional Assessment Ideas for Dance

As described in chapter 2, dance assessments are generally accomplished using a simple checklist, a reverse checklist (also called a *room scan*), or a scoring rubric. Individual lesson plans throughout this book features numerous sample assessment checklists and scales for assessing student learning in dance.

Though used less frequently, written tests and quizzes, reflective journal assignments, and short-answer response sheets may also be used for assessment purposes. Following are some examples designed to help teachers assess students' understanding of the dance material.

Sample Quiz and Test Questions

The sample test questions that follow are drawn from the elements of dance and are designed to test knowledge. Quizzes should be designed around specific focus areas explored in class.

- Name three body parts:

  _____ _____ _____

- Name three levels in space:

  _____ _____ _____

- Name three directions we can travel in space:

  _____ _____ _____

- Define an *axial movement:*

  _____ _____ _____

- Name three axial movements:

  _____ _____ _____

- Define *locomotor movement:*

  _____ _____ _____

- Name three locomotor movements:

  _____ _____ _____

- Name three body shapes:

  _____ _____ _____

- What three tempos are found in music and dance?

  _____ _____ _____

- Name three energy qualities:

  _____ _____ _____

Reflective Journals and Short-Answer Response Sheets

Journals and response sheets provide learners with opportunities to reflect on their experiences. Through regular practice, reflection becomes a significant part of the learners' experience, reinforcing the importance of their individual perceptions in the learning process. Journals may be collected by the teacher or may remain the dancers' private reflections. They are useful for footprinting (i.e., gathering information about) learning over a length of time. Short-answer response sheets consist of two to four open-ended questions and are collected by the teacher afterward. Examples of reflection prompts suitable for children aged 7 to 11 are listed next.

Reflections on My Dancing

- Describe how you felt dancing today. What did you think about? How did it feel in your body?
- What were your favorite movements today? Why?
- What were your least favorite movements today? Why?
- What kind of music do you most enjoy while dancing?

- What was your favorite part of performing dance today? What was your least favorite thing about performing?
- What challenges did you face in class today?
- What three things would you like to improve upon as a dancer or performer? What will you do to work on this?

Reflections After Watching a Dance

- Without naming the person, describe something you appreciate while watching another mover.
- Describe the choreography you just watched. How many dancers were there?

What did they do? What movements stood out? What was the strength of the piece?

- What suggestions would you give these dancers to revise and improve their dance?

Remembering a Dance

- Draw each of the movements in the dance you just performed (using stick figures, a pathways map, or any other designs).
- Your job is to remember the dance you did today. Using your own shorthand, record the movements in the dance you just performed and the order in which they were performed. Be specific so you can refer to your notes when we do this again next week.

APPENDIX D

Additional Resources

Research, Schools, and Organizations

Alabama Institute for Education in the Arts: www.artseducation.org/integratedartscurr.html

Arts Education Partnership: www.aep-arts.org

Arts Every Day: www.artseveryday.org

Arts Integration: www.neiu.edu/~middle/Modules/science%20mods/amazon%20components/AmazonComponents3.html

Arts Integration in the DC Area: http://dc.gov/DCPS/In + the + Classroom/Academic + Offerings/Catalyst + Project/Arts + Integration

Arts Integration Solutions (formerly the Opening Minds Through the Arts Foundation): artsintegration.com

Arts and Science Council: www.artsandscience.org

The Chicago Guide for Teaching and Learning in the Arts Online: http://chicagoguide.cpsarts.org/instructional-support/integration-case-5

The Inspired Classroom: http://theinspiredclassroom.com/2012/02/4-steps-to-creating-an-arts-integrated-lesson/

The Kennedy Center ArtsEdge:

artsedge.kennedy-center.org/content/arts-integration.aspx

Partnership for 21st Century Skills: www.p21.org

Perpich Center for Arts Education: www.mcae.k12.mn.us

Project Zero: www.pz.harvard.edu

A Research-Based Approach to Arts Education: www.edutopia.org/stw-arts-integration-research

Scaffolding Learning: www.myread.org/scaffolding.htm

The Silk Road Project: www.silkroadproject.org/Education/EducationOverview/tabid/170/Default.aspx

Southeast Center for Arts Integration: centerforartsintegration.org

Strategies for Arts Integration: www.scholastic.com/teachers/collection/strategies-arts-integration

Articles and Books

Barrett, J. (2001). Interdisciplinary work and musical integrity. *Music Educators Journal, 87*(5), 27-31.

Botstein, L. (1998). What role for the arts? In W.C. Ayers & I.L. Miller (Eds.), *A light in dark times: Maxine Greene and the unfinished conversation* (pp. 62-70). New York: Teachers College Press.

Bransford, J.D., & Schwartz, D.L. (1999). Rethinking transfer: A simple proposal with multiple implications. In A. Iran-Nejad & P.D. Pearson (Eds.), *Review of research in education* (Vol. 24, pp. 61-100). Washington, DC: American Educational Research Association.

Bresler, L. (1995). The subservient, co-equal, affective, and social integration styles and their implications for the arts. *Arts Education Policy Review, 96*(5), 31-37.

Brewster, G. (1985). *The creative process.* Berkeley and Los Angeles: University of California Press.

Brown, S.L. (2007). An arts-integrated approach for elementary-level students. *Childhood Education, 83*(3), 172-173.

Bruer, J.T. (1991) The brain and child development: Time for some critical thinking. *Public Health Reports, 113*(5), 388-397.

Bruner, J. (1960). *The process of education.* Cambridge, MA: Harvard University Press.

Bruner, J. (1979). *On knowing: Essays for the left hand.* Cambridge, MA: Belknap Press.

Burnaford, G., Arnold, A., & Weiss, C. (Eds.). (2001). *Renaissance in the classroom: Arts integration and meaningful learning.* Chicago Arts Partnerships in Education. Hillsdale, NJ: Erlbaum.

Burnaford, G., Brown, S., Doherty J., & McLaughlin, H.J. (2007). Arts integration frameworks, research and practice: A literature review. Arts Education Partnership. www.eugenefieldaplus.com/academics/A + %20research/artsintegration.pdf.

Catterall, J.S. (2009). *Doing well and doing good by doing art: The effects of education in the visual and performing arts on the achievements and values of young adults.* Los Angeles/London: Imagination Group/I-Group Books.

Clancy, M.E. (2006). *Active bodies, active brains: Building thinking skills through physical activity.* Champaign, IL: Human Kinetics.

Consortium of National Arts Education Associations. (2002). Authentic connections: Interdisciplinary work in the arts. www.arteducators.org/research/InterArt.pdf.

Csíkszentmihályi, M. (1990). *Flow: The psychology of optimal experience.* New York: Harper and Row.

Deasy, R.J. (Ed.). (2003). *Creating quality integrated and interdisciplinary arts programs: A report of the Arts Education National Forum.* Washington, DC: Arts Education Partnership.

Dewey, J. (1934). *Art as experience.* New York: Penguin.

Eisner, E. W. (2004, October 14). What can education learn from the arts about the practice of education? *International Journal of Education & the Arts, 5*(4). Retrieved [10/20/13] from http://ijea.asu.edu/v5n4/.

Fiske, E.B. (1999). *Champions of change—The impact of the arts on learning.* Washington, DC: Arts Education Partnership and President's Committee on the Arts and the Humanities.

Gardner, H. (1983). *Frames of mind: A theory of multiple intelligences.* New York: Basic Books.

Gelineau, R.P. (2012). *Integrating the arts across the elementary curriculum.* Belmont, CA: Wadsworth.

Gilbert, A.G. (1992). *Creative dance for all ages.* Reston, VA: AAHPERD.

Ginot, H. (1969). *Between teacher and child.* New York: Avon.

Goldberg, M. (2012) *Arts integration: Teaching subject matter through the arts in multicultural settings.* Boston: Pearson.

Grumet, M. (2004). No one learns alone. In N. Rabkin & R. Redmond (Eds.), *Putting the arts in the picture: Reframing education in the 21st century* (pp. 49-80). Chicago: Center for Arts Policy at Columbia College.

Grumet, M. (2007). Third things: The wondrous progeny of arts integration. *Journal of Artistic and Creative Education, 1*(1).

Hanna, J.L. (2001). Beyond the soundbite: What the research actually shows about arts education and academic outcome. *Journal of Dance Education, 1*(2), 81-85.

Hanna, J.L. (2008). A nonverbal language for imagining and learning: Dance education in K-12 curriculum. *Educational Researcher, 37*(8), 491-506.

Jensen, E. (2000). *Learning with the body in mind.* San Diego: Brain Store.

Johnson, E. (2003). Sharing your art form. Unpublished workshop materials.

Kaufmann, K.A. (2006). *Inclusive creative movement and dance.* Champaign, IL: Human Kinetics.

King, A. (1993). From sage on the stage to guide on the side. *College Teaching, 41*(1), 30-35.

Kinoshito, H. (1997). Run for your brain's life. *Brainwork, 7*(1), 8.

Marshall, J. (2006). Substantive art integration = exemplary art education. *Art Education, 59*(6), 17-24.

McCutchen, B. (2006). *Teaching dance as art in education.* Champaign, IL: Human Kinetics.

Miller, R. (2005). Integrative learning and assessment. *Peer Review, 7*(4), 3-11.

Nash, M.J. (1997). Fertile minds. *Time, 149*(5), 48-56.

Piaget, J. (1952). *The origins of intelligence in children.* New York: International University Press.

Pogrebin, R. (2007, November 7). Book tackles old debate: Role of art in schools. *New York Times.* www.nytimes.com/2007/08/04/arts/design/04stud.html.

Pomeroy, S.R. (2012). From STEM to STEAM: Science and art go hand-in-hand.

Scientific American, guest blog, August 22, 2012. http://blogs.scientificamerican.com/guest-blog/2012/08/22/from-stem-to-steam-science-and-the-arts-go-hand-in-hand/.

Popovitch, K. (2006). Designing and implementing exemplary content, curriculum, and assessment in arts education. *Art Education, 59*(6), 33-39.

President's Committee on the Arts and the Humanities. (2011). *Reinvesting in arts education: Winning America's future through creative schools.* www.pcah.gov/sites/default/files/PCAH_Reinvesting_4web_0.pdf.

Robelen, E. (2010, November 16). Schools integrate dance into core academics. *Education Week.* www.edweek.org/ew/articles/2010/11/17/12dance_ep.h30.html.

Robelen, E. (2011). White House panel calls for 'reinvesting' in arts education. *Education Week.* http://blogs.edweek.org/edweek/curriculum/2011/05/white_house_advisory_panel_hig.html?qs=white+House+panel+calls+for+Reinvesting+in+Arts+Education.

Seidel, S., Tishman, S., Winner, E., Hetland, L., & Palmer, P. (n.d.). *The qualities of quality: Understanding excellence in arts education.* www.wallace-foundation.org/knowledge-center/arts-education/arts-classroom-instruction/Documents/Understanding-Excellence-in-Arts-Education.pdf.

Sousa, D.A. (2006). *How the brain learns.* Thousand Oaks, CA: Corwin.

Stevenson, L.M., Deasy, R., & Arts Education Partnership. (2005). *Third space: When learning matters.* Washington, DC: Arts Education Partnership.

Vygotsky, L.S. 1962. *Thought and language.* Cambridge, MA: MIT Press.

Wiggins, G. (2010). Authentic education: What is transfer? *Big Ideas.* www.authenticeducation.org/ae_big-ideas/article.lasso?artid=60.

Wiggins, G., & McTighe, J. (2005). *Understanding by design.* Alexandria, VA: ASCD.

Wiggins, R.A. (2001). Interdisciplinary curriculum: Music educators' concerns. *Music Educators Journal, 87*(5), 40-45.

Wilhelm, J., Baker, T., & Dube, J. (2001). *Strategic reading: Guiding students to lifelong literacy.* New Hampshire: Heinemann.

ABOUT THE AUTHORS

Karen Kaufmann (left) and Jordan Dehline (right).

Karen Kaufmann, MA, is a professor of dance and the head of the dance program at the University of Montana. With more than 35 years in dance education, she has published journal articles and a text for classroom teachers; spearheaded a model program that laid the groundwork for this book; and prepared dance teachers, classroom teachers, and future teachers to use dance and creative movement in their classrooms.

Kaufmann directs the CoMotion Dance Project, which promotes dance in K-12 classrooms, tours school performances, offers professional development for classroom teachers, and establishes service learning opportunities. She is also director of the Creative Pulse, a summer graduate program for teachers in the arts and education.

Kaufmann has received numerous awards over the years, including the Artist Innovation Award from the Montana Arts Council, the Distinguished Faculty Award from the University of Montana, and the Artist/Scholar Award from the National

Dance Association. Kaufmann serves as a fire lookout in the mountains of Idaho. She also enjoys whitewater canoeing and backcountry skiing.

Jordan Dehline, BFA, is a dance teaching artist for the CoMotion Dance Project and an adjunct instructor at the School of Theatre and Dance at the University of Montana. She has been teaching dance integrated into elementary school curriculums since 2008. Dehline has taught numerous current and future classroom and dance teachers and collaborated with dozens of classroom teachers to identify learning targets in mathematics and science. She has also created hundreds of dance integration lessons connecting to mathematics, science, social studies, and language arts. Dehline is a professional dancer with Bare Bait Dance and is a member of the National Dance Education Organization. In addition to dance integration, Dehline teaches ballet and modern dance.

You'll find othe
dance resour
www.Huma

HUMAN KINETICS
The Information Leader in Physical Activity & Health
P.O. Box 5076 • Champaign, IL 61825-5076

.747.4457
3372 0999
.465.7301
Europe . . . . . +44 (0) 113 255 5665
New Zealand 0800 222 062